GW00392786

THE BERNESE MOUNTAIN DOG

THE BERNESE MOUNTAIN DOG

Paddy Petch

DICKSON PRICE

Dickson Price Publishers Ltd.
Hawthorn House
Bowdell Lane
Brookland
Romney Marsh
Kent TN29 9RW

First published 1992
© Paddy Petch

British Library Cataloguing in Publication Data

Petch, Paddy
  The Bernese mountain dog.
  1. Dogs
  I. Title
  636.73

ISBN 0 85380 152 5

*All rights reserved. No part of this publication may be
reproduced, stored in a retrieval system or transmitted in any
form or by any means electronic, mechanical, photocopy, recording
or otherwise, without the prior permission of the publishers.*

Set by R. H. Services, Welwyn, Hertfordshire
Printed and bound by Biddles Ltd, Guildford and King's Lynn.

Contents

Introduction

I saw my first Bernese Mountain Dog at the City of Birmingham Show in 1971, when I was lucky enough to win Best in Show Brace with two Flat Coat Retriever littermates under Judge A. B. Nicholson. Runners up were these two large tri-coloured, and to me totally unknown, Bernese Mountain Dogs belonging to Irene Creigh of the Kisumu prefix. I found out later that they were Oro de Coin Barre of Kisumu and Carin von Hinterfield, two of the first three Swiss imports in England since the Second World War. I decided then that when I had the opportunity and the money to run to a second breed, Bernese Mountain Dogs were going to be it.

Nine years later I started my two year search for the right brood bitch to begin the Rase Bernese kennel. This I found in Champion Dagill Solitair of Rase, my special dog Tara, and due to her and her off-spring, plus other examples of the breed, I became completely smitten. Not to the extent of erasing my first love, Flat Coats, but certainly they now run neck and neck in my affections.

Bernese Mountain Dogs are like no other dogs I know, and I have had a few different breeds in my time and trained many more. They seem sometimes to be a law unto themselves and I have written this book in the hope that it will help others to understand the Bernese Mountain Dog – its temperament, beauty and character.

Paddy Petch 1992

— 1 —
Origins of the Breed

'What kind of dog is that?' 'It's a Bernese Mountain Dog.' 'Oh, a Burmese.' 'No, a Burmese is a cat, a Bernese, from Berne in Switzerland.' How many times I wonder has a Bernese Mountain Dog owner carried on the above conversation with an interested by-stander. Almost as often as they have had hot dinners if my experience is anything to go by. The Bernese Mountain Dog is still rare enough in this country to occasion quite a deal of interest from the man or woman in the street, and with his striking good looks, tri-colouring and presence he certainly fills the eye of the beholder.

Switzerland conjures up thoughts of cuckoo clocks, chocolate, dairy produce and practical Swiss citizens in their mountainous country working hard. Not for them a dog that doesn't stand the test of time or hard work. The St Bernard, surely the best known of the Swiss canine exports, has long been famous by reputation. His work as a rescuer in the mountains and bearer of liquid sustenance to the traveller in the form of a brandy barrel round his neck, has bought him recognition in many countries. The less well known but just as useful Schweizer Laufhundes helped the Swiss hunt their daily ration of meat through the centuries and the four Sennen (herding) breeds helped the farmer with his work.

THE SENNENHUNDE BREEDS

As our interest is with the breed the Swiss call the Berner Sennenhunde I shall not spend a great deal of time speaking about the other three except to explain a little of their origins and type so that people can recognise the similarities and differences.

They are believed by many to have Molossian or Assyrian Mastiff ancestry from the dog of classical antiquity, however I am told by the Swiss authority on the breed, Margaret Bartchi that this is not so. She believes the mountain dogs originated in Switzerland and Northern Germany and were produced from a cross-breeding of native breeds who bred on until they reached the form we know today.

1

THE BERNESE MOUNTAIN DOG

The three other mountain breeds differ from the Berner Sennenhunde in that they are short coated. All four are named after the regions, or cantons, in which they were to be found and have similar markings.

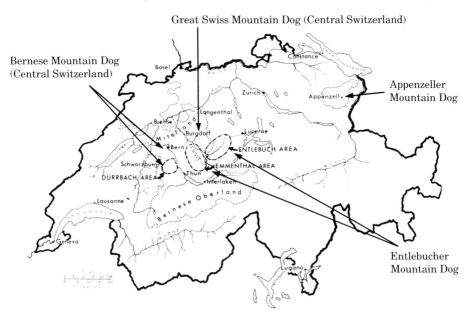

A map of Switzerland showing the areas from which the four breeds came.

The Great Swiss.

The Great Swiss

The tallest of the Sennenhundes is the Great Swiss who stands up to 28 inches (71cm) tall, although there is a great variety in height.

The Appenzeller

A medium sized dog is the Appenzeller who was used mainly as a cattle dog and grows to 23 inches (58.5cm). He is distinctive in that he has a curled tail.

The Appenzeller.

The Entlebucher

The smallest of the group is the Entlebucher at 20 inches (56cm), looking somewhat similar in build to a Rottweiler with the same stump of tail, except that he is born with his. I believe that there are one or two imported Appenzellers in this country but to my knowledge neither of the other two breeds are yet in Britain at the time of writing.

The Bernese/Dürrbächler

That now leaves the Bernese, which is the second biggest of the four Sennenhundes, nicknamed the Bear Cub, long coated and to my mind much the handsomest dog in the group. He is sometimes called the Dürrbächler from the canton in Berne where the first seven dogs were exhibited in 1904. *Hutchinson's Encyclopaedia* of 1935 records the Bernese Mountain Dog under the Berghunde group.

The Entlebucher.

The Bernese or Dürrbächler.

EARLY HISTORY

If one looks at the history of Switzerland it is very much governed by its position on the map of Europe bordering on a number of cultures. At the beginning of the First Century AD the northern borders of the then Roman Empire skirted Lake Geneva and the garrisons guarding the Alpine passes kept large dogs of the Mastiff type as watchdogs. Many believe that the Romans brought these dogs with them, but according to information gained from Mrs Bartschi this is incorrect, the conclusion being based on the discovery of one skull which was later found to be of Medieval ancestry and not Roman.

When the Roman Empire fell to the Vandals of the North a number of these dogs came into the possession of the local population, who almost certainly did cross breed them with their own shepherd dogs. As the invading tribes also brought with them Mastiff type dogs the general stamp of the Swiss dog became established. By the Middle Ages there were various varieties used in all sorts of agricultural work and these were the forerunners of the present breeds found in Switzerland.

They were first and foremost farm dogs who had quite a lot in common with their farmer owners who had to work hard throughout the centuries to build up the prosperity their country now enjoys. The dogs had to live on left overs from the farmers table which was likely to have been milk, cheese and cereals with very little meat, for indeed this was a delicacy for the humans let alone the dogs. Even on this meagre diet they had to be strong and able to work hard.

From the litters born the farmers selected the strongest and sturdiest of the animals; speed did not matter for it was forbidden for dogs to chase hares or pheasants (they were the prerogative of the land owners) and the farmers could be heavily fined for such transgressions. Indeed, an edict that would have meant the destruction of all farm dogs was issued on these grounds by the then Burgermeister of Zurich in 1489. Fortunately for us the ruling caused such an outcry that the Mayor not only lost his job but his head as well, and the dogs were saved according to the old story teller.

These farm dogs were trained to stay with the cattle and to guard the farm, and were used regularly to pull the milk cart and also, according to Clifford Hubbard in his book *Working Dogs of the World*, to fetch rushes for baskets and meat for the butcher. The farmers lived lonely lives and strangers were noticed from afar by the dogs and a warning given by their loud barking. A type, therefore, developed that had a strong territorial bent with no wish to go off hunting and was without doubt the forerunner of the present breed as we know it.

NINETEENTH CENTURY

Switzerland entered a new era after the French Revolution and the Napoleonic Wars and by about 1830 many of the old traditions had died out and with them the interest in the native farm dog, leaving the St Bernard to become the favourite canine representative of the country.

F. V. Tschudy in his book *Animals That Live In The Alps*, published in 1853 mentions the Sennenhunde in connection with guarding cattle and the herdsmen's huts on the mountains. When the Swiss Kennel Club was founded in 1883 Tschudy became one of those responsible for keeping the stud book. One or two names of people appearing in the stud book from around 1892 are repeated as certain men brought up and bred from the best Sennenhunde mountain stock.

Among these were an inn keeper of a pub called the Red Hill named Franz Schertenleib from Burgdof, a factory owner in the same town Max Schafroth and a vet from Langenthal, a Dr Scheidigger. These three men collaborated on breeding policy producing for sale dogs uniformly sound, sturdy and possessing the correct colouring, that of the 'blassi' or white blaze markings. Those named 'ringi' had a white collar which was not allowable, nor was a very narrow white stripe on the face or just black and tan face markings, which was called a 'bari'. So it was that a breed type began to be formulated.

At the founding of the Swiss Kynological Society (for movement) in 1883 no one spoke of the Sennenhunde and at the first dog shows held in Zurich and Aarburg no Sennenhundes were shown at all. In fact the first mention of the Sennenhunde as a breed in public was by a man called Fritz Probst in the newspaper *Central Platt* in 1889.

The name of the breed is, therefore, relatively young and according to records it was not known to Jeremias Gotthelf, a one time priest in the Emmental village of Lutzelfluh. He was famous for his nineteenth century portrayal of Bernese farming life and folk customs. In Emmental the dog was also called a Gelbackler or 'yellow cheeks' because of its tan markings, while the term 'four eyes' or Vieräugler was also used referring to the tan markings above each eye, which are also to be found in other breeds such as the Dobermann and the Rottweiler.

Four Sennenhundes were registered in Stud Book No.9 and these were Phylax (Blass x Nettie); Prince (Bäri x Belline); Ringi (Blass x Belline) and Berline a bitch whose breeding is not known.

One gets an idea of the versatility of the breed when one reads in the nineteenth century of the farmers dog, the drovers dog, the butchers dog etc, and it was about this time that dogs were beginning to be kept as pets. Also according to Raber, at the turn of the century there were such things as organised dog fights taking place for which people wanted fierce looking dogs. Some Sennenhundes were bred with cloven noses showing their teeth which made them look very vicious, this defect could be fatal and was often combined with other deformities. Fortunately common sense prevailed and this fault was bred out.

The black pigment found inside the mouth and the double dew claws (which must now be removed soon after birth) are indicative of this breed and the people of the last century believed these factors, along with the dense black coat, kept the devil at bay, a sentiment with which Professor Heim agreed. He also stated that the occasional wall eye (blue eye) and curled tail would have come from the crossing of the dogs with a Nordic strain, for example the Siberian Husky.

TWENTIETH CENTURY

The first dogs known to be referred to as Bernese were those exhibited by Schertenleib under his prefix Rothohe at the dog show in Berne in 1904 and judged by Probst. There were six dogs and one bitch exhibited. Three years later the Swiss Dürbach Club was formed, growing to such an extent that only one year after that in 1908 it changed its name to the Bernese Sennenhunde Club. At the Langenthal Dog Show in 1908, 21 Dürrbächlers were brought before the judge, a Professor Albert Heim (1849–1937).

Professor Albert Heim.

Professor Heim was in charge of geology at Zurich University and was one of the first members of the Swiss Kennel Club. Commencing as a breeder of Newfoundlands, which he trained to sleigh work, he then became more interested in the Sennen breeds and researched their background collecting a vast number of skulls of the breeds in the process. It was in recognition of this labour of love that the Swiss Kennel Club, in conjunction with the Director of the Swiss National History Museum, founded the Albert Heim Stiftung which primarily helps research into the developnment and history of the Swiss canine scene.

The first Bernese dogs to gain entry into the Swiss stud books were in 1908, all were born in 1907 and they were Bello (von Bäri x Belline), Nero (von Turk x Belline), Prinz von Burgdorf (Bäri x Priska) and Sultan. The bitches were Belline von Burgdof (von Bäri x Priska), Miss von Burgdof, Hettie von Burgdof (von Bäri x Priska) and Priska von Burgdof. One or two of these names, as can be seen, are of unknown parentage. Belline was adjudged the foundation brood bitch of the breed. Many dogs continued to be shown without being registered and a case in point was that of Champion Leo Grainer whose dam was covered at least twice while she

Netty von Burgdof.

was in season. Owned by Doctor Sheidigger Champion Leo Grainer was a strong sire after the First World War.

It is to Albert Heim to whom the name Berner Sennenhunde is credited, a fine sounding title for the old farm dog, and by 1910 107 dogs appeared at a breed show in Burgdof, of which the professor in his judges report stated 'it was as if a lost son had been found in Oberaargau and Emmental'. After the 1913 Langenthal show he was able to write 'that among the Bernese there was not a poor specimen for all were good'.

The Bernese began to gain popularity in the central area of Switzerland in Emmental and in the Voralp region in the late nineteenth and early twentieth centuries. They were not so uniform in appearance as present day examples of the breed but there was a similarity with regard to their temperament, size and markings, which increased as the dogs gained popularity over the Apellzellers, Entlebuchers and Great Swiss. In 1917 the registrations were higher than those of the Appellzellers, and by 1939 the breed was more popular than the St Bernard, and that position is the same in the 1990s.

The dominant black colouring of the coat might formerly have been rare, for even today in Bernese Oberaufen when they wish to illustrate a frequent occurence they say 'there are more of them than red dogs' although there are scarcely any red dogs seen on the farms today.

INTRODUCTION OF NEWFOUNDLAND BLOOD

During the years of the Second World War breeding was very much restricted in Switzerland, for although the country was neutral it was surrounded by other powers that were not, and farmers were encouraged to cull mis-marked pups usually putting down about half the litter. This period had a bad effect on the breed as many of those bred from were shy and retiring.

As a result during the late 1940's thoughts were given to the problem of how to improve the breed. This was solved for the Swiss when in 1948 a Newfoundland dog, Pluto von Erlengut, mated the Bernese Mountain bitch Christine von Lux belonging to an architect named Bosiger. The bitch eventually produced a litter of four dogs and three bitches, all resembling the father, with white paw and chin markings. Three dogs were reared none of whom were used at stud and one bitch, eventually called Babette, was given to a Doctor Hauser. He mated her two years later to a Bernese Mountain Dog Algo von Tieffart and in March 1951 she produced eight puppies, one of each sex being Bernese. Three were born dead, and the rest were culled except the Bernese bitch Christine von Scharzwasserbachti who went to the president of the Berner Sennen-hunde Club Herr Mischler, who mated her at the very early age of 10 months to the Bernese dog Osi von Allenuften. On March 15, just one week before her first birthday, Christine had five puppies with Bernese markings, of which three died at birth and only a bitch Bella, and a dog Alex von Angstorf were reared. Bella herself was mated to Dana von Enggistern producing eight Bernese Mountain Dog puppies, but she unfortunately had to be put down at the early age of four.

Alex von Angstorf however went on to become an International Champion and in 1956 was World Champion at the Dortmund Show. He was much used at stud by Herr Mischler and had 51 litters to his credit at the time of his death. This Newfoundland/Bernese Mountain Dog cross had some very good effects on the Bernese breeding, the Newfoundland type being bred out completely by about the third generation, but traits of increased substance, improved temperament, better stance and good shining straight black coats were retained, improving the Bernese breed beyond measure.

THE BREEDS POPULARITY SPREADS

Today in Switzerland there are about 200 breeding kennels, but they only have, or at least only register, an average of two litters per kennel per year and many breeders are still farmers to whom dog breeding comes a poor second to their job of running the farm. Interest in the breed spread and now there are breeders of Bernese Mountain Dogs in nearly every European country and others like the USA and Australia.

— 2 —

The Breed in Great Britain

Introduced into Great Britain by Mrs Egg-Leach of Switzerland (an Englishwoman living over there) the first Bernese Mountain Dog to be imported into this country was bought in by two ladies, Mesdames Patterson and Perry in 1936 when their three year old bitch Sente von Sumiswald was sent over by Herr Iseli. His kennel is the oldest in Switzerland having been founded in 1923 and is still functioning today in the 1990's. Mrs Perry, already a well known Samoyed breeder (whose affix was 'Kobe') imported a further five bitches in 1937, one of which whelped in quarantine. Mrs Perry was followed in her interest in the breed by her daughter Irene, who later became Mrs Ashfield, and who did in fact become the first president of the British Bernese Mountain Dog Club on its foundation in 1971.

Three further litters were bred by Mrs Perry but no records of owners were kept except that a dog and a bitch were sold to a Major Stacey who himself bred one litter. But with the onset of the Second World War breeding became too much of a problem for the Perrys who gave three dogs to the army as mascots and sent others to various pet homes in different parts of the country. Eventually these dogs died and consequently the breed too died out over here until 1969.

RE-ESTABLISHMENT OF THE BREED SINCE 1969

On July 12, 1969, the first dog was imported into Great Britain from Switzerland since the war by Jackie Sherwin from Staffordshire who is herself Swiss. This was Hasso von Goetschiacker born in April 1969 and bred by Alf Geotschi, although he was actually exported by Fritz Mischler, one-time patron of the Bernese Mountain Dog Club. Unfortunately as the breed was not recognised in this country at that time the Kennel Club refused to register him. As Jackie was busy having a family she did not have the time to pursue the matter, and so the chance of a new blood line for use with later imports was lost. Hasso was run over on the road on June

6, 1979. It is interesting to note that Jackie actually still has in her possession a copy of the bill of sale for Dora von Bretenhof dated 30.4.70. The cost was 600 francs or £200, which is considerably cheaper than it would be today.

So it is to Mrs Irene Creigh, a breeder of the well known Kisumu Mastiffs that the credit goes for re-introducing the breed into this country. This came about in a rather round about way for a Swiss owner of one of her exported Mastiff puppies sent her back a photograph in 1969 in the background of which were two Bernese Mountain Dogs. These really interested Mrs Creigh and jointly with her friend Mabel Coates of the 'Nappa' prefix, she began proceedings to import two of these dogs. A three month old dog Oro de Coin Barre for herself from Herr Mathes, and a year old bitch Dora von Bretenhof from Herr Kobel who eventually went to Mrs Coates, who was at that time very well known for her English Setters. The following year Mrs Creigh imported Dora's half sister Carin von Hinterfield and it was then she sold Dora to Mrs Coates who mated her to Oro, which is why the resulting puppies bore the 'Nappa' prefix. It was Oro and Carin that I first saw at Birmingham, as I said in the introduction, that inspired my own interest in the breed.

This first litter though had to be born in quarantine for a rabies scare had increased the statutory six month quarantine period by a further three. Mrs Creigh also had trouble registering her imports but persevered and eventually they were accepted by the Kennel Club. Dora produced a further litter to Oro and was then given to the Guide Dogs for the Blind as a brood bitch and subsequently had two or three more litters. From one of these came the first working Bernese guide dog, but she was rather shy, a

Oro de Coin Barre of Kisumu.

trait she passed on to some of her off-spring. These puppies were not able to be bred from as they were neutered which is part of the guide dog policy. Oro was unfortunately lost to the breed when he was given to a friend of Irene Creigh's when she became ill and he was not used further for stud work.

An Army couple called Gray returned from service in Germany in 1971 importing a young dog called Groll von der Leckenbecke. He sired two well known sons, Lena Robbin's Tarncred Drummer and the Mackays' Champion Meiklestane Black Benjamin. Unfortunately Groll died young so his influence on the breed was curtailed.

But another dog with a longer lasting stud life was Fox von Grunenmatt imported from his Swiss breeder Herr Stadman (who at one time had been a patron of the Swiss Bernese Mountain Dog Club) by Heather Curtis (daughter of the Orrs of Valgarv fame), who had already made her name with the Takawalk Old English Sheepdogs. She exhibited Fox at many shows in the Any Variety classes, which were all that were available at that time and even many of the judges under whom he was shown were ignorant of the breed. He won a number of classes and his biggest success was winning the large class of Any Variety Not Separately Classified Working at Crufts in 1975. Fox was a great success with his handsome

Fox von Grunenmatt.

Duntiblae Nalle.

appearance and typical outgoing temperament and made many friends for the breed.

When Certificates were awarded for the first time to the breed in 1977 he obtained two but unfortunately did not obtain his third before his death in 1978. His was a great influence for good on the breed and he left many award winning children and grandchildren, two of the latter in particular became foundation brood bitches for two well known kennels. These puppies were out of Kisumu Aphrodite who was an Oro x Carin daughter. Champion Kisumu Bonne Esperance started off Carol Lilliman's Millwire strain and Champion Kisumu Belle Fleur did the same for Don and Brenda Griffiths' Forgeman Kennels.

About this time Diana and Graham Cochrane, who were breeding Duntiblae Rough Collies became interested in the Bernese and Diana herself imported from Eva Berndt, who was later given the Sennengarden prefix in Sweden, a dog called Nalle and a bitch called Eva after her breeder, both of whom were registered over here and carried the Cochrane's prefix. There is not much information on the latter but the dog had a good influence on the stock he produced, particularly in regard to hips and correct dentition before being run over and killed. He was the sire of the first three Champions to be made up in Great Britain, namely Forgeman Folksong of Tarncred, Forgeman Fusilier and Tarncred Puffin. Later three more of Nalle's children Tarncred Tarquin of Temeraire (Puffin's litter brother), Meiklestane Dark Ace and Duntiblae Dark

Avenger all received their titles. He was also the sire of the first two dogs to be tested under the hip dysplasia scheme to gain clear certificates, these were Diana's Duntiblae Dark and Endearing and Dark Fortune. Most kennels find they have Nalle somewhere in their pedigree for he was an outstanding influence for good in the breed. It is most unfortunate, therefore, that genetic tests have proved that Nalle was a carrier for the 'Trembler' disease syndrome manifesting itself at the present time.

Of other imports into Great Britain at this time three are listed, Faro von Hurstfield (Mr and Mrs Horrex's) dog Erika von Schnetzenchacher of Majanco (Mrs Lendon's bitch) and John and Sonia Gorboulds' dog Mustang von Nesselacker of Glanzberg who proved a potent sire. Others have been imported over the last decade and information on these will be found later in this chapter.

Of particular note is Jude and Brian Simonds' Ch Jumbo von Waldacker at Coliburn who was the first of 10 Swiss imports brought in by these breeders.

The early dogs of necessity were very closely bred for Dora and Carin were half sisters, both being mated to Oro. Daughters of that mating were put to Fox and yet other bitches from that second mating were covered by Nalle, so the original pedigrees read like one extended family. However, despite this closeness of breeding, the Bernese in this country have thrived and produced a large number of Champions whilst maintaining the breed attributes.

Franz Raber in his book *Die Schweizer Hunderasen* gives the following attributes of the Bernese which are valued very highly by the Swiss farmers – 'A dog is good when it is watchful and lively, does not run into the crops, protects its master when in difficulty and does not poach or wander.'

These characteristics are to be admired in the breed even in this day and age.

START OF THE BREED CLUB

The history of the breed club seems to have become somewhat distorted even in so short a time as 19 years. The breed was established in this country after the Second World War at the end of the 1960's by Irene Creigh, who, with her friend Mabel Coates, imported Oro and Dora and a little later Carin. Being such striking dogs they had many admirers and people began to get interested in the breed and were interested in acquiring a pup for themselves.

Eventually Irene Creigh started writing notes in the dog papers under the general heading 'Rare Breeds'. The first column in *Dog World* was dated May 29th 1970 and told of her joint purchase with Mabel Coates of Oro and Dora and their incarceration in Hackbridge quarantine kennels from where, because of the extra three months kennelling imposed on imports due to a rabies scare, Mrs Creigh said that they would not be able to get them out until March 1971 but that they were visiting them once a fortnight. She asked for interested people to get in touch with her.

The notes appeared roughly once a month for the rest of that year. In the August 28th issue Irene Creigh reported that Oro and Dora had appeared on TV's *News at Ten* on the Monday of that week to reinforce the pressure that was building up to reduce the length of quarantine time. Apparently they were fed in front of the cameras to keep them still but Dora was rather unco-operative!

The first mention of the formation of a club comes on September 18th when Irene Creigh reported that she had had a letter from Margaret Crawshaw with this suggestion. Margaret Crawshaw bred and showed Beagles and Border Terriers and had hopefully booked a puppy when Dora and Oro could be mated. I have a copy of the letter Mrs Creigh consequently sent to the Kennel Club dated 7th September 1970 suggesting names

> The Bernese Mountain Dog Club of England
> The English Bernese Mountain Dog Society
> The Bernese Mountain Dog Club

along with the guinea (£1.05) fee. These suggestions were printed in the November Kennel Gazette and the first name was eventually approved by the appropriate Kennel Club Committee in a letter dated 29th September 1971, the whole procedure having taken just over a year. A few years later in the summer of 1976 the 'of England' in the title was changed to 'of Great Britain' as it was felt the former was too restrictive.

Mrs Crawshaw was so full of ideas for the club that she was asked to be Secretary by Irene Creigh who had received a form from the Kennel Club which required the names of 25 founder members each willing to pay £2 in order to get the proposed club off the ground. Mrs Coates was by now the Treasurer.

The collection of the 25 names took about six months but eventually the form, dated 1st May 1971 and signed by Bill Creigh, the then Secretary, went up to the Kennel Club bearing the following signatures:–

1	Chairman	Mrs Irene Creigh (Kisumu)
2	Secretary	Mr Bill Creigh (Kisumu)
3	Treasurer	Mrs Mabel Coates (Nappa)
4	Peter Oriani (Stormsail Newfoundlands)	
5	Mrs K Crawshaw	
6	Irene Ashfield (Kobe) (Miss Perry prior to her marriage)	
7	Gladys Clayton (Barvae Beagles)	
8	Joyce Collis (Beagold Beardies and Border Collies)	
9	Heather Curtis (Takawalk)	
10	I Dolan	
11	Mrs Alison R Gray (Importer of Groll)	
12	D Holt	
13	Mrs D Irvine	
14	J Lloyd	
15	C O H Marsh	
16	C Neilson	

17	G O'Brien	22	Brenda Stamper
18	Judy Oriani (Stormsail)	23	Justin Warren
19	Mrs R P Harris	24	M F Brown
20	C W Pearce	25	D Murdoch
21	Lena Robbins (Tarncred)		

Margaret Crawshaw was not actually on the list as Secretary as although she had already signed it in this office, Bill Creigh took over this job temporarily at the end of March when, owing to pressure of work, she resigned, and she did not go further with her purchase of a puppy either. The signatures were finally gathered together at the very first meeting of interested people, which took place at WELKS show on May 1st 1971 at 12 noon when the last four vacant spaces were filled. The first meeting of the newly formed club took place at 12 noon on June 6th at Guilden Morden Village Hall near Royston in Herts when 25 people, including two judges, attended and a good time was had by all.

The following year, in July, a second meeting was held at Guilden Morden when Mrs Tittel a Dutch judge came over with the Secretary of the Dutch Bernese Club to talk to members. It had been planned to also hold the first AGM early in 1972, but there were insufficient of the members present so the AGM was postponed till 12th November 1972 at the home of the Cochranes in Alderminster when the rules drawn up in the summer of 1971 were ratified and the constitution of the club passed. Bill Creigh had by now resigned as Secretary and, after a temporary holding by Judy Oriani, Diana Cochrane was voted in at the November meeting with her husband Grahame as Treasurer.

The Committee consisted of Mrs Alison Gray, Mrs Heather Curtis, Mrs Mabel Coates, Miss Carol Lilliman and one sole male, Mr Brian Pitty. The Chairman and President was Mrs Irene Creigh (who brought out the first newsletter in July 1972) and continued in this office until May 1974 when she was replaced by Mrs Irene Ashfield. In August 1975 both the Cochranes resigned owing to pressure of work and the Burbank Griffiths took over these offices, Dennis as Secretary and Margaret as Treasurer, until the November when Brenda Griffiths (Forgeman) was elected Secretary, a position she held until the AGM in November 1977 when Fiona Karolus took over the hot seat for the next five years to be succeeded by her immediate predecessor Brenda, for the next two years. Bernice Mair followed her in the office for five years until the March 1989 AGM when Angela Hadon took over as the present incumbent.

At the time of writing the Patron is Mr M Johnson, President Diana Cochrane, Vice President Bill Creigh, Treasurer John James and Committee Mr Steve Green, Mr Frank Whitbread, Mesdames Gatwood, Robbins, Sharman, Thorman and Davenport under the Chairmanship of Marie Steele. Angela Hadon also deals with rescue, a job so ably coped with for so long by Don and Brenda Griffiths, and Helen Davenport edits the magazine succeeding Diana Cochrane's seven year stint.

Each year the Club runs a Championship Show, two Open Shows, one in Kent and the other in Yorkshire and a fun day known as the 'Garden

Party' so called because the first one was held in the Cochrane's garden in June 1973. That day Margaret Osbourne judged a match consisting of 12 dogs with around 40 people present, nowadays somewhere like Stoneleigh is needed to host the same annual event!

The breed had to be shown in AVNSC (or Any Variety Not Separately Classified) classes at first but in the summer of 1973 the National Working Breeds Championship Show scheduled Bernese Mountain Dog classes for the first time, judged by Irene Ashfield, daughter of Mrs Perry who had imported the first Bernese in 1936. By 1977 Bernese had six sets of tickets at Championship shows and had moved out of Rare Breed status. The six shows and judges were **Crufts** – Mr A J Chandler; – **Birmingham National** – Diana Cochrane; **Scottish Kennel Club** – Bill Foster; **National Working Breeds** – Lionel Hamilton-Renwick; **Richmond** – Ulla Segerstrom (Sweden); **LKA** – Irene Ashfield. The total rose to 11 in 1980. The first Breed Championship Show was held on June 21st 1981 when Tom Horner officiated. To date CCs are on offer at 27 Championship shows, three Breed shows and the judges 'A' list spans about 50 names.

Every four years or so the club runs an assessment which is, as its title implies, an examination of each exhibit to decide on its closeness to the standard. Each animal is graded either **Excellent**, **Very Good**, **Good** or **Acceptable** (except for puppies whose top grading is **Very Good**) by the judges who give an individual written critique on each dog, rather in the same way as shows are judged on the continent under the CICIB system (International). The first assessment took place in 1975 when 40 dogs were examined by two judges from Switzerland, Herr Krauchi and Herr Schluchter, (the breeder of Heather Curtis's import, Fox von Grunenmatt).

The second assessment was run in conjunction with the club's first Open show at Redditch in 1979 when again Herr Krauchi came over, accompanied this time by Herr Iseli, the owner of the oldest kennel breeding Bernese in Switzerland dating from 1932, and 49 dogs were assessed. There were 100 dogs entered in the show which was judged by Harry Glover. The BIS winner was Carol Lilliman's Ch Kisumu Bonne Esperance of Millwire, Best Dog was Mustang von Nesselacker of Glansberg owned by the Gorboulds and bred by Herr Krauchi.

The next assessment took place in 1983 with two Norwegian judges, Rigmar Ulstad for the dogs and Tore Fossum for the bitches, and the winner was Ch Temeraire Penny Black of Crensa. The last one was in 1987 with 190 dogs for Herr Krauchi once again to go over in company with Herr Imhof and best in assessment was Diana Cochrane's Duntiblae Protector. The next assessment is being planned for September 1991 at Coventry.

A character assessment is also run regularly when one judge sets up a series of contrived situations to test the dogs as to temperament, guarding, aggression, fear etc.

Each dog is graded **Excellent**, **Very Good**, **Good** or **Unsatisfactory** and given a certificate at the end if in the first three categories.

Membership of the Bernese Mountain Dog Club at the present time stands at approximately 1000, a far cry from the original 25 only 19 years ago. In 1985 the Northern Club was recognised by the Kennel Club followed a year later by the Southern Club and in 1987 by the Scottish Club. Both the Northern and Southern clubs gained Championship status in 1991.

BERNESE MOUNTAIN DOG CLUB OF GREAT BRITAIN POINTS SYSTEM FOR CLUB TROPHIES

Championship Shows Offering CCs

Best in Show – 100   Reserve B.I.S. – 50
Best Puppy in Show – 50   Reserve – 25
Best in Group – 50   Reserve – 25
Best of Breed – 10
C.C. Dog or Bitch – 20   Reserve C.C. – 10
Best Puppy in Breed – 10
1st in Class – 10
2nd in Class – 5
3rd in Class – 1

Club Championship Show

Best in Show – 30
Best Puppy – 15
C.C. Dog or Bitch – 20   Reserve C.C. – 10
1st in Class – 10
2nd in Class – 5
3rd in Class – 1

Trophies On Offer For Championship Show Wins Are

Caprima Trophy for Dogs
Timberlog Trophy for Bitches
The Kobe Trophy for Puppy
The Choristma Plate for Best Opposite Sex Puppy

Championship Shows Without C.C.s and Open Shows Scheduling three or More Breed Classes

Best in Show – 50   Reserve B.I.S. – 25
Best Puppy in Show – 25   Reserve Puppy – 12
Best in Group – 12   Reserve in Group – 6
Best of Breed – 10
1st in Class – 5
2nd in Class – 3
3rd in Class – 1

Variety and Not Separately Classified Classes at Championship and Open Shows

Best in Show – 50	Reserve B.I.S. – 25
Best Puppy in Show – 25	Reserve Puppy – 12

Best Any Variety Not Separately Classified – 10
1st in Class – 10
2nd in Class – 5
3rd in Class – 2

Shows With Fewer Than three Breed Classes

1st in Class – 3
2nd in Class – 2
3rd in Class – 1
NOTE no points for Best of Breed

Breed Club Open Shows

Best in Show – 15	Best of Sex – 7
Best Puppy in Show – 7	

Other placings as for Open Shows

Trophies On Offer For Open Show Wins Are

The Kisumu Dog Cup
The Nappa Bitch Cup
The Gillro Puppy Trophy

Points for Open and Championship show wins must be listed separately and members must say for which category they are competing.

Only points gained from 6 – 12 months may be used towards Puppy Trophies but they may be carried forward to add to adult points won.

Points to be counted from Jan 1st to Dec 31st in any one year.

As will be gathered from the foregoing information there are only two founder members still actually concerned with the breed, the first is Lena Robbins of Tarncred fame who is still on the Committee and the second Heather Curtis who does not show or breed now although she is still judging Bernese. Other very early members were Carol Lilliman who joined in June 1971, the Burbank Griffiths and Brenda and Don Griffiths whose son Alan was the first junior member. Towards the end of that first year Grahame and Diana Cochrane came on the scene.

Lena Robbins and Heather Curtis both had puppies from the first Oro and Dora litter born December 1st 1970 and registered under Mrs Coates' Nappa prefix. Lena (Tarncred) had Black Velvet of Nappa and Heather

19

(Takawalk) Black Chiffon of Nappa, while out of the second mating of these two dogs Carol Lilliman (Millwire) had Nappa Cherion, the Horrexs' (Sinova) Nappa Capercaillie and Diana Cochrane (Duntiblae) Nappa Confucius and Cassiopeia, their date of birth being 2nd July 1971.

The *Dog World* breed notes for 1970/71 also gave an indication of the growing interest in the new imports as the story of Oro and Dora continued. In response to Irene Creigh's request for those interested to contact her on May 29th by the next entry (June 12th) she had had 10 letters and a phone call, most of them requests for bitch puppies when they mated Oro and Dora, and in the notes of November 6th, Mrs Creigh was able to report this had been successfully accomplished. In the December 18th issue she told readers that Dora had produced three bitches and four dogs on December 1st, was a wonderful mother with plenty of milk and that puppies would be allocated in date order of letters.

She also reported that her bitch puppy Carin von Hinterfield had arrived on November 27th and was better marked than Oro or Dora, having less white on her, and in the issue of June 18th 1971 she was reported as being out of quarantine.

The January 15th column contained news of Oro who was by now at home with the Creighs but he was very quiet and sad. Apparently of the seven puppies born to Oro and Dora three were perfectly marked, two had white patches on the neck and two with white collars went to obedience and pet homes. All but one dog pup had gone off to their new owners by February 12th. These were Mr Coates, Mrs Curtis, Mrs Robbins, Mrs Pearce and Mrs Collis. Also in that issue Irene Creigh reported that Oro's state of depression, which had been put down to pining, was in fact due to illness and that he had a high temperature. He took many weeks to recover but by mid-March was reported to be the happiest dog one could wish to see. Apparently he nearly died but when taken to Cambridge for tests the conclusion was reached that he had had an outsize headache, accounting for his unsteadiness, and that the very high temperature was due to the three rabies jabs he had received, one in Switzerland and two over here. The dog had been suffering from inflammation of the brain lining as a result. He had now apparently so improved that he was after all the girls and had earned the nickname 'Hot Pants'. He was 24 inches in height and weighed 70 lbs, which was within both the Swiss and American height and weight limits, but had re-occurrences of the vaccine trouble from time to time.

In the issue of July 16th Irene Creigh commented on the jealous rumours that were flying around saying that the turns Oro experienced could be passed on, like the conditions that caused his illness, to his pups. But Mrs Creigh countered these silly old wives' tales by quoting Dr Hall at Cambridge University who said that his 'turns' stemmed from side effects of the rabies vaccine. The time in between the attacks lengthened and eventually he was completely cured. Meantime, public interest in the breed continued to grow and Guide Dogs for the Blind sent Derek Freeman down to see Mrs Creigh and her dogs and one went to be trained at Kenilworth. Dora, Oro and the pups of the litter also appeared on the

BBC TV programme *Blue Peter*. Black Magic of Nappa belonging to Joyce Collis also appeared on the ITV Children's programme *Magpie* after his win at Crufts under Mr Warner Hill. Much later 'Duster' appeared in *Alphabet ZOO* along with Ralph McTell and Nerys Hughes.

WELL KNOWN KENNELS

At the time of writing the breed has only been in the country for just over 20 years so there are still not a large number of breeders. However, some of the most well known of the Bernese kennels have been established for most of that time and I thought it would be interesting to look at how they became involved in Bernese Mountain Dogs. There are a number of other breeders that have come to the fore in the last decade but space forbids description of them all and those mentioned below were founded in the first 10 years of the breed's history in this country. I have taken them in alphabetical order.

Bernax

This is the affix of Fiona Karolus who in 1972 was a member of the Tyrolean Club in Austria with the prefix of Starkenbichel. She advertised for help for her kennels where she bred Long Haired Dachshunds and Leonbergers and Jean Syms came to live with them bringing her Bernese, Tarncred Mandy, who was the source of much admiration.

Returning to the U.K. in 1974 with four Dachshunds and an in-whelp Leonberger Fiona was unfortunate to lose both the Leonberger and her nine puppies whilst the dogs were in quarantine, so she went to Birmingham City Show in the September and spent two days looking for a breed to replace her. Remembering Mandy, Fiona went to look at the Bernese ring. Whilst there she spoke to the Horrex's (Sinova) who by chance had a four month old bitch in the car which they had intended to keep, but as they were importing a dog from Switzerland they agreed to sell Sinova Solo to Fiona for £75. It was love at first sight and for 12 years Solo was all that Fiona could ask of a dog. She was registered under her

A Bernax litter.

Austrian affix of Starkenbichel but later this was dropped and the more English Bernax substituted for the puppies. Interestingly, this first litter was not from Solo but from Jean Syms Tarncred Mandy's offspring Freyja. Jean had also returned to this country to a job as head kennelmaid at Haxted Quarantine Kennels but before she left Austria she mated Mandy to Pascha von Hofweisental in Bavaria and the subsequent litter was born in quarantine. A puppy from that mating called Freyja went up to Scotland but her owners split up when Freyja was in whelp. Fiona was offered her as Jean could not take her and so it was that Biggnst Freyja whelped the first Bernax litter although Fiona had had nothing to do with the mating. Solo's line however goes back now for five generations, some through Sue Hardwicks' Hashenka Kennel.

Fiona chooses names for her puppies from the North American Indian tribes and uses a different tribe to identify each litter. Most of Solo's litters names were tribes of the Sioux nation while Freyja and later bitches had names from other American tribes, the only exceptions being Diana Cochranes Duntiblae Bernax Bardot.

Caprima

Marie Steeles family of four youngsters wanted a dog in the family and although other breeds were considered when, in 1972, they saw the *Blue Peter* programme with Oro, Melody, Aphrodite and pups, a Bernese Mountain Dog was the obvious choice. Marie telephoned the Kennel Club, was given the Cochrane's number and began to get involved. In 1973 they bought their first dog the eight month old Duntiblae Draught Dog or 'Nog' (Fox x Dora), from Diana via the Guide Dogs for the Blind and they were hooked. The following year Duntiblae Dark Attraction or Nooka (Nalle x Eva) was also obtained from the Cochranes. She was joined by Cita von Holz Chilchli, bred by Monta Wütricht in Switzerland in 1978, and when Cita was mated to Mustang, Marie kept a daughter Carisma who is now 9½. Her other bitch at the present time is a granddaughter of Cita, Clover Leaf of Caprima, plus she has also the bitch imported from Canada, Bigpaws Guinevere, but the Canadian dog, Bigpaws Guy, brought in at the same time has been passed on to Maggie Davis.

Her choice of Caprima as an affix was word play with Madcap as its root, which the Kennel Club disallowed. Marie joined the Breed Club in July 1973 and is the present Chairman of the Committee and has also been a past Treasurer.

Coliburn

Jude and Brian Simonds were initially interested in working Border Collies in Obedience and Jude was Instructor and Chairman of the Sudbury (Suffolk) Dog Training Club. In the mid 1970's interest in Obedience waned when they saw the Bernese and they bought their original dog, Duntiblae Dark Frolic, from Diana Cochrane in 1976. Unfortunately this dog had to be put down early on and they turned to

Coliburn Marvin.

importing Swiss dogs and brought in Felix von Unterzelg (details p. 185) from Herr Schmid. To date they have imported 12 dogs from Switzerland, the best known being Ch Jumbo von Waldacker at Coliburn (from Vreni Gasser) who has sired several Champions – Ch Lacelaw Statesman, Ch Meadowpark Captivation and Ch Brick Kiln Matilda.

Jude was a *Dog World* Breed Columnist and has been Secretary of the Bernese Breeders Association since its inauguration in 1983. In 1989 her book the *Complete Bernese Mountain Dog* was published.

Duntiblae

Home of one of the older kennel names in the breed, Grahame and Diana Cochrane started to produce their Duntiblae Bernese Mountain Dogs in 1974. Their first interest was in Obedience followed by Rough Collies but a trip to the Amsterdam Winners Show in 1969, where Bernese were being exhibited, opened up new horizons. Eventually they were able to purchase a dog and bitch puppy from Mrs Coates' second litter in 1971. These were Nappa Confucius (who was put down at eight months with bad HD) and

Ch Duntiblae Dark Protector.

Nappa Cassiopeia from Oro x Dora. The bitch was very shy so the Cochranes decided to import a dog and a bitch from Sweden, to where they had earlier exported Rough Collies, and brought in Nalle from Eva Berndts Sennengarden kennel and Eva from the Strombergs.

Duntiblae Nalle, as he was named, was frequently used at stud and sired the first six of the early breed Champions and was still top stud dog in 1979. Three years later he was unfortunately killed on the road at a young age. Shown before the breed had CC's he played his part in getting Bernese recognised in the Any Variety classes being very sound.

Eva had four litters for Diana, who evolved a system of naming each litter in alphabetical order. The choice of the prefix Duntiblae came from the name of Graham's grandfather's Scottish farm and there have been five Duntiblae bred Champions, four English and one American. Ch Duntiblae Dark Protector having been twice Best of Breed at Crufts. The Cochranes also had a run of bad luck first importing a Danish bitch who turned out to be undershot and much too big. Then Eva was sent to be mated in Denmark and missed so all the expense and hassle was to no avail and then of course they lost Nalle. But they started again with a rescued son of Nalle, Forgeman Fusilier, who gained his title and was the sire of the present line of Duntiblaes. Author of the first book of the breed, *The Bernese Mountain Dog*, and a Championship show judge Diana, now widowed, is still very much involved with the breed having been Secretary, Magazine Editor and now President.

Forgeman

Brenda Griffith's parents bred racing Greyhounds so she was surrounded by dogs from the very early days. When she married Don they became interested in breeding and showing Dobermans registering their Prefix Forgeman at this time, the front part comes from their house name FORGEmill and the latter from the breed name DoberMAN. Besides the dogs they also reared three sons.

It was in 1970 that Brenda saw a Bernese for the first time in the shape of Oro de Coin Barre belonging to Irene Creigh from whom she later had a Bernese dog puppy which died of heart failure at 10 weeks. The Griffiths then bought Kisumu Cleopatra but she only lived till she was nine months old when she had to be put down due to illness. They then tried again and

Ch Duntiblae Forgeman Fusilier.

imported a bitch, but once more Lady Luck was against them and they lost her soon after she came out of quarantine. However, if one is persistent enough luck usually turns and in 1973 the Griffiths bought Kisumu Belle Fleur (Fox x Kisumu Aphrodite) who was to become their foundation bitch and the second of a long line of Forgeman Champions. The first Champion was actually a daughter of Belle Fleur by Nalle, Forgeman Folksong, who went to Lena Robbins and became the first English bred Bernese to gain her title. Also out of that first litter came Ch Duntiblae Forgeman Fusilier and Swedish Champion Forgeman Fellini. In total there were seven English Champions, two Swedish Champions, two Australian, one New Zealand and one Irish Champion bearing the Forgeman prefix up to 1986.

The present breed record holder with 29 C.C.'s, Ch Forgeman Footpad owned by Pam Aze was also bred by them while the Crufts Working Group winner of 1980 Ch Folkdance at Forgeman was bred by Lena Robbins but sired by their Ch Forgeman Folksong.

Brenda was involved in the Bernese Club of Great Britain in a number of ways. She was a Committee Member from 1973 and became Secretary from November 1975 to May 1981 and again from 1982 to 1984 also producing the newsletter. For many years she and Don ran the rescue service from their home near Redditch. Their son Alan was the first Junior Member of the Club. Both Brenda and Don are Championship judges in the breed and although not as active in the show world as they were, the present healthy state of Bernese Mountain Dogs owes a great deal to the thought and dedication of these clever breeders.

Gillro

The Gillro Kennel formed from the first part of the names of Gillian Sharman and her husband Roger started in 1974 when they bought the bitch Forgeman Fiesta from Don and Brenda Griffiths. Gill had grown up with Lurchers and had Labradors, mongrels and a Dachshund herself. Later, Fiesta was mated to Fox the union producing three dog puppies one of which became Gillro Gambler, Gill's special dog who although not gaining his title did win two CC's and a reserve CC at a time when there were only six CC's on offer to the breed.

In 1978 the Sharmans imported a bitch Onka Von Grunenmatt from Herr Schlucter, the breeder of Fox, and she was the first bitch to be graded HD hips normal under the KC/British Veterinary Association Scheme. Eventually she was mated to Gambler producing Gadabout who gained seven Best Puppy in Breeds at Championship shows also notching up one CC and three Reserve CC's but she did not live very long unfortunately. Gill has made up one of her homebred dogs herself and two more have gained their titles in other hands; one of which Ch Gillro Jack Flash of Manadori was still being shown by Dot Fry at the age of 10.

Glanzberg

Sonia Gorbould, herself Swiss, had German Shepherd Dogs until 1973 when she fell for a Bernese. Coming out of hospital with a new baby, she and husband John went straight off to pick up a bitch puppy from Pam Schurer (Now Clark) from a mating of Nalle x Tarncred Myra. Their first dog, however, imported from Herr Krauchi in Switzerland in 1975, Mustang von Nesselacker marked the real start to the Glanzberg Kennels. He was used at stud on a number of occasions and is of course the sire of Ch Forgeman Footpad the breed record holder owned by Pam Aze. He nearly did not live to tell the tale, however, for he had heatstroke on release from quarantine and only prompt action by a vet saved his life, for in Bernese this can be a killer, see page 104. The Gorboulds also imported a bitch Hiska from Herr Krauchi in 1979, a dog Bernerbakkens Froy from the Skaugs in Norway in 1981 and another Swiss bitch, Belinda von Lehnwaldi, from O Streit.

Sonia now has the Glanzberg Kennels on her own and in 1988 imported, once again from Herr Krauchi, a dog Amor-Grey. Her latest import in 1990 was again from Switzerland, this time bred by the Linders, named Fero Von Buetigen. Thus this Kennel has established its own line of outcrosses by the use of mostly Swiss bloodlines. There have been two Glanzberg bitches made up, but Mustang did not manage to acquire that elusive third ticket to give him Champion status.

Kisumu

This is the oldest name associated with the breed and although Irene Creigh is now unfortunately dead her husband Bill is still Vice President of the Bernese Mountain Dog Club of Great Britain, although no longer active in breeding Bernese. It is really due to Mrs Creigh that Bernese returned to this country in 1969 as it was she who saw a Bernese in the background of a photograph of a Mastiff puppy she had exported to Switzerland.

Majanco

Another Swiss national, Doris Lendon came to England in 1954. She had Bull Terriers but wanted to have Bernese again, having been brought up with them. Eventually in 1973 her brothers bought her the bitch Erica von Schnetzenschachen, from Herr Pfister in Switzerland, who lived to be over 14 years old.

Doris Ludweg married in 1956 and became Doris Lendon and their three children Mark, Jan and Corinne formed the basis for the affix she registered as Majanco. She has had eight litters, starting in 1975 when Erika was mated to Sinova Larch and from that union came Gordon Howard's Champion bitch Majanco Gallina and New Zealand Ch Majanco Ghianti owned by Doreen Murdoch. Erika was mated three times more producing American Ch Majanco Languardo from the second mating (to Faro von Hurstfield), who was still siring litters at 11 years old.

Doris had been out of breeding for the last seven years but had a new litter out of Majanco Tamara x Duntiblae Dark Viking in 1990 and hopes to pick up the threads of active showing once more.

Meadowpark

I remember standing in the ring next to Bernice Mair in my early days in this breed and her remarking to me that she wondered if they would ever aspire to a CC. Well, the Meadowpark dogs have certainly made their presence felt since that time.

Bernice was brought up in a doggy family for her father kept a boarding kennel in Rochdale in which she helped. Her first dog was a working sheepdog in 1947 whose upkeep she paid for out of her wages. She learnt grooming and hand stripping while still at school and in 1949 on leaving started work at the local Greyhound racing club as a kennelmaid. Joining the WRAF at 17½ she met husband John and they left the service when Bernice became pregnant, moving back to take over the Rochdale boarding kennels and set up a trimming parlour. The Mair's main interest at this time was in Shelties and Cavalier King Charles Spaniels so they joined the local canine society where Bernice became Secretary for 11 years.

In 1956 they were granted the affix Meadowpark taken from the names of their road Bent Meadows and the bordering Falinge Park.

Daughter Carole joined her mother in the kennel business on leaving

Meadowpark Early Exodus, Early Election, Ch Ways and Means of Meadowpark and Meadowpark Early Embargo.

school and when the land the Kennels were on was sold they moved to their present site at Lawn Cottage, from where John started his own business.

The Mairs first saw Bernese in shows in the AVNSC classes at the end of the 60's and for a 21st birthday present Carole received Duntiblae Dark and Handsome bred by Elizabeth Wrighton (then Walpole Day). He was soon followed by Duntiblae Dark and Endearing bred by Diana Cochrane who, when mated to Duntiblae Forgeman Fusilier produced the first Meadowpark Champion (owned by John) Ch Meadowpark the Brigadier made up in 1985. In all this kennel has produced a total of seven English Champions but as yet no foreign ones. Bernice and Carole are both Championship show judges for the breed and Bernice was Secretary for the Bernese Mountain Dog Club of Great Britain from 1984 to 1989 when the present incumbent Angela Hadon took over.

Meiklestane

Not very dominant at the present but Wendy Morphet (Fletcher) is still active in the breed as Vice President of the Northern Bernese Club. She has been involved with dogs all her life starting in Surrey and then moving to Birmingham where she became interested in Dobermans, Boxers and German Shepherd Dogs, but was particularly known for her mongrel terrier who was part of the Birmingham Dog Training Clubs' Obedience Team in 1951.

On leaving school in 1955 she got a job with a vet in Cumberland taking with her the terrier and two German Shepherd Dogs the latter unfortunately soon died, but they were replaced by a rescued German Shepherd Dog and Boxer who were going to be put down plus a Dobe, a gift from the veterinary surgeon.

She married in Cumberland, her husband adding Labradors to the menagerie and Wendy started Workington Dog Training Club using particularly her terrier, now up to test C obedience, Boxer and German Shepherd Dog. She also bred Irish Setters.

Her first Bernese was seen in the Observer Book of Dogs, which she bought with some obedience prize money. Wendy went to several Championship Shows and there saw Nalle and Eva shown by Diana Cochrane in the N S C Classes. The Fletchers were by then living in Sedbergh and a master at Sedbergh Schools daughter had a Bernese from Lena Robbins, and this led to Wendy acquiring Tarncred Tara from the same source. Tara was mated to Nalle and produced in 1975 Meiklestane Dark Ace owned by Cynthia Bailey. Two years later Tara was put to Groll and produced Black Benjamin who gained his title in 1982 for the McKays. Wendy has bred seven litters in all.

There were not many Bernese in Cumberland except for the Meikle-stanes so Wendy used to hire a coach in Penrith and go round picking up dogs and owners and transporting them to the shows during the late 1970's. She had five children one of which had leukaemia so dogs had to take a backseat, and then when her marriage broke up other things took

Meiklestane Dusky Fiddler.

precedence and she could not keep dogs on the same scale. However, she has now remarried and keeps her interest in the breed with her connections with the Northern Club in her new name of Morphet. The pinnacle of her ambition was achieved at Crufts in 1977 where Bernese gained tickets for the first time and the dog CC was won by her Ch Meiklestane Dark Ace, at the same time a German Shepherd Dog bred by her gained third in the Bitch Obedience Championships and an Irish Setter also bearing the Meiklestane prefix took part in the Personality Parade as the top Mountain Search and Rescue dog in the country at that time.

Millwire

Carol Lilliman saw the picture of Dora and her first litter of puppies born in quarantine in the Daily Mirror of December 19th 1970 just before they were collected to go to their new homes and her interest in the breed started from that point. She was actually showing Wire Fox Terriers at that time having bought her first as a pet and gone on from there as so many of us have done. She started to read the notes in the dog papers under Rare Breeds written by Irene Creigh and it was here she saw the notice of the first meeting, which was to be held at Guilden Morden in Herts calling to all those who were interested to attend to formulate a Club. June 6th 1971 was the date and it was here that she joined and booked her first puppy so apart from Lena Robbins, Carol is the oldest breeder still alive in Bernese.

Her first puppy was out of the Oro x Dora second litter (but the first to be born out of quarantine) she was called Nappa Cherion and was bred by Mrs Coates, but Carol's real foundation bitch was Kisumu Bonne Esperance bred by Irene Creigh and made up in 1979 at the age of six, but remember tickets were in very short supply at that time in the breed's history.

There have been three Millwire Champions, a dog and a bitch in this country, Double Blank and Forever Esperance and a dog, Clockwork Soldier that went out to Australia.

The affix Millwire was formed in the 60's from the name of their house at the time, Mill View and 'Wire' from the breed of terriers that she kept, and although Carol still maintains her terrier interest with Manchesters she also has a Bernese bitch for breeding and showing and expects to go on for a long time yet.

Tarncred

Ch Tarncred Puffin was the first Champion made up both for the kennel and for the breed. Lena Robbins left school early being only interested in animals and bought an unregistered Maremma puppy from John Holmes (Formakin) in 1960. This she showed under the Tarncred affix, which she took from Shakespeare's Italian Prince and thought was applicable for an Italian Sheep Dog.

Lena got married in 1963 but in 1969 the marriage broke up and at this time she decided to come out of Maremmas as they were too like the Pyraneans being very independent and just coexisting with their owner. It was now that she read in the dog papers about the newly imported breed in the Rare Breeds column and read the news of the first litter. Making enquiries from Irene Creigh resulted in Lena becoming a founder member of the Bernese Club and having one of that first litter born on 29th November 1970 and so it was that Black Velvet of Nappa went down to Sussex to become Lena's Tarncred foundation bitch. From her first litter Lena kept the dog Tarncred Drummer and from the second the bitch Tarncred Black Watch and these two coupled with the acquisition of the bitch, Forgeman Folksong on breeding terms from the Griffiths' formed the nucleus of the success of her breeding. The first Tarncred Champion was, as I have said, Ch Tarncred Puffin born in 1976 and made up in 1978 when there were only six sets of tickets on offer. But the Tarncreds really had come to stay in 1977 when the Tarncred Puffin x Forgeman Folksong litter produced four champions. Tearose and Folksong stayed at home while Tzarina became an American Champion and Trooper both an International and Norwegian Champion. A dog was imported from Switzerland in 1978, Ceasar von Chugerhof, but at 10 months he became

Ch Tarncred Kleine.

undershot so was found a pet home and the expensive experiment was not repeated.

Other litters followed and in fact Lena has bred a total of 17 and made up eight champions in this country, plus the two foreign ones already mentioned. Lena became a Committee Member in 1975 and is also currently the Club Stores Manager taking the stand to shows like Crufts and Club Championship events. Her list of achievements cover winning the Dog CC and BOB at Crufts with Puffin in 1979 and 80, the latter year also seeing her breeding in Folkdance win the Working Group and the bitch CC in 1982, while Ch Tarncred Tarquin took the dog ticket in 1983. It was also a Tarncred dog, Puffin again, who went BIS at the very first Breed Championship Show held in 1981 under Tom Horner even repeating the achievement a second time. Although not so active in the showing field these days Lena is still breeding for quality not quantity and Bernese owners owe her a considerable debt of gratitude.

Temeraire

It seems strange that as a small child Elizabeth Wrighton, or Walpole Day as she was then, was so terrified of dogs that her parents had to buy her a Dachshund puppy in order to conquer that fear. She worked as a medical secretary and went over to Canada for a year where she came into contact

Ch Temeraire Penny Black of Crensa.

with Rough Collies. On her return to England she started to breed and show this type of Collie and took out the affix Temeraire. She wanted Tamarisk but that was not available and on the bedroom wall was a painting by Turner of *The Fighting Temeraire* so that was her final choice.

It was through Collies she met husband Geoff and together they became interested in the Bernese. They obtained a bitch from Diana Cochrane but that had various problems and could not be bred from or shown so they then obtained the bitch Bisquet Bergitta from breeder Jill Gratledge and had her in partnership with Diana, but eventually made over full ownership to her.

In 1976 they bought Tarncred Tarquin of Temeraire (who gained his title in 1979 and won a CC at Crufts in 1983) from Lena Robbins. Meantime, they mated Bergitta to Duntiblae Forgeman Fusilier and kept the bitch Temeraire Tranquility who was the dam of the James' bitch Ch Temeraire Penny Black of Crensa who was Best Dog over all in the 1984 Breed Assessment, and also Ch Temeraire Tender Tymes who was Best in Show at both the 1986 and 1988 Bernese Mountain Dog Club of Great Britain Championship Show thus making breed history.

The Wrightons have had six litters and have made up to Champion the dog and bitch named above.

BERNESE AFFIX HOLDERS 1990

Affix	Holder

Affix	Holder	Affix	Holder
Abbeycott	Mr and Mrs Wilshaw	Caprima	Mrs M Steele
Acara	Mrs C Bodman	Cardair	Mrs A Quigley
Aceca	Mr and Mrs B Hall	Carlacot	Mrs J Vaughan
Aceworth	Mr and Mrs R	(Wales)	
	Worthington	Carnbazz	Mr and Mrs
Alfross	Mr and Mrs Lear-		Hellingsworth
	Egerton	Cassvales	Mrs J Cassidy
Altair	Mr and Mrs Maylor	Cavanero	Mr and Mrs Checketts
Alpengeist	Mr and Mrs J Garrod	Ceader	Mrs N Rich
Alyngam	Mr and Mrs Rawson	Chalindy	Mrs L Sharples
Anbrough	Mrs P Craig	Chantelle	Miss D Nichols and Mr
Anderbern	Mrs K Haddon		A Mackie
(Australia)		Chardonyx	Mrs K Oseman
Arvella	Mr and Mrs S Green	Chasecroft	Mrs J Williscroft
Attila	Mr and Mrs A Bryant	Chiskian	Mrs K Langbridge
Austlan	Mr and Mrs M Franks	Choristma	Mrs M Majerus
Aughtercony	Mr P Balderson	Cherrymount	Mrs S Varley
Ashbrook	Miss A Reeves-Smith	Clashaidy	Mrs V Stenner
(Ireland)		Clenraw	Mr and Mrs E
			Clendenning
Badgerdale	Miss H Ingram and Mrs	Clynymona	Mrs V Fick
	R Eyres	(Isle of Man)	
Balahu	Mrs Y Fison-Bates	Coliburn	Mr and Mrs B Simonds
(New Zealand)		Coligny	Mr and Mrs P Watson
Bearstakes	Mr and Mrs D Luckham	Collansues	Mr and Mrs Botting
Begaville	Mrs L Coulthard	Cotshill	Mr and Mrs J Haden
Bellasden	Mrs M Freeman	Correnie	Mrs J Weinberger
Belynken	Mr and Mrsa K Gardner	Corrlough	Mrs B Ladd
Bernalpen	Mrs and Miss Lamb	(Ireland)	
Bernax	Mrs F Karolus	Cortuber	Miss L Peacock
Bernfold	Mrs A Wells	Cottonsocks	Mrs Rix
Bernhaus	Mrs K Schwartz	Courtsherry	Miss E Sherry
Bernholm	Mrs A Hodge	(Ireland)	
Bernlaken	Mr and Mrs J Bracey-	Crensa	Mr and Mrs J James
	Davies	Crevenagh	Mrs N Murnaghan
Bernmast	Mr and Mrs A Thew		
Bigginstronn	Mrs J Sims	Dagill	Mrs J Jeffery
Birchwheel	Mrs H Cooper	Dalsetter	Mr and Mrs G Fallas
Bisquet	Mrs J Grattidge	Danstra	Mr and Mrs A Hughes
Boneidle	Mrs R Smith	Darlodge	Mrs R Cobb
Braccate	Mr and Mrs E Felows	Delhurst	Mrs Ackroyd
Bramblecroft	Mr and Mrs Smith	Denaca	Mrs J Foster
Branbern	Mrs L Brand	Dhesmar	Mr M Wheadon
(Australia)		Douneburns	Mrs E Jardine
Brickkiln	Mrs A Francis	Downlands	Mr and Mrs P Worrow
Brightcharm	Mrs M Bright	Drogos	Mrs Chapman
Brockhouse	Mr and Mrs J Morgan	Drumadraw	Mrs K Davidson
Briniago	Mrs T Allen	Drumbroneth	Mr Catliffe
(Wales)		(Ireland)	
Buganeezee	Mrs S Hogg	Drummann	Mrs R Curle-Lane
Burbank	Mrs M Griffiths	Duldan	Mrs B Warren

Dundesert	Mr and Mrs W Graham
Duntiblae	Mrs D Cochrane
Durrbach	Mrs L Stephenson
Elnside (Scotland)	Mrs H Mcaulay
Elrone	Mr and Mrs N Rigley
Estcarp (New Zealand)	Mrs B Tate
Eyros	Mrs D Soyer
Florizel	Mrs E Wardrop
Fordash	Mrs A Fuggle
Forgeman	Mr and Mrs D Griffiths
Forima	Mr and Mrs J Baird
Garacombe	Mr and Mrs P Ellis
Gillro	Mr and Mrs R Sharman
Glanzberg	Mrs S Gorbould
Gravesdale	Mr and Mrs A Graves
Haizoe	Mrs E Woodridge
Halesbern	Mr and Mrs F Page
Harjen	Mr and Mrs W Haigh
Hasenka	Mrs S Ward
Heatherapeel	Mrs S Lowes
Highflight	Mrs J Hipkiss
Hildrek	Mr and Mrs D Edmunds
Hillbank	Mrs I Malpass
Hollyanne	Mrs V Brown
Holmedale	Mr and Mrs M Taggart
Holzern	Mr and Mrs Elliot
Homaris	Mr O Madha
Husheen	Mr and Mrs D Pharo
Immense	Mr and Mrs J Coombes
Inchberry	Mrs D McVicar-Campbell
Iveshead	Mr A Cockayne
Jannavic	Mrs M Jones
Julesvick	Mr and Mrs Grayson
Karchibach	Mr and Mrs Szitkovics
Karensdale	Mrs and Miss K McLellan
Katelyn	Mr and Mrs H Frost
Kemow	Mrs S Bridges
Kirbeon	Mrs N Kirby
Kisumu	Mrs I Creigh
Knockenden	Mr and Mrs R Shaw
Korinti	Mrs P Elvidge
Kossberne	Miss C McMahon
Krisenda	Mrs L Shepherd
Kurtlees	Mrs M Lee
Kwai's	Mr J Mackie
Kyleburn	Mrs M Eaves
Kynaro (Wales)	Mr and Mrs G Wooldridge

Lacelaw	Mr and Mrs Wallace
Lancarty	Miss A Brooks
Lathbern	Mr and Mrs F Whitbread
Legecium	Miss A Longbottom
Leonfort (Ireland)	M Leonard and M Forte
Leumasleiloc	Mr and Mrs S Cooper
Leven Corroch (Scotland)	Mrs L Aird
Lirilee	Mrs L Turner
Liskarn	Mr and Mrs G Bridges
Littondale	Mr and Mrs Lock
Lordell	Mr and Mrs S Blair
Majanco	Mrs D Lendon-Ludwig
Malcesine	Mr and Mrs R Cashen
Manadori	Mr and Mrs R Fry
Margand (Scotland)	Mr and Mrs A Skedd
Mavanne	Mrs M Yates
Meadowpark	Mrs B Mair
Meiklestane	Mr and Mrs L Fletcher
Millwire	Miss C Lilliman
Millermead	Mrs H Head
Mixbury	Mrs Flynn and Mrs Lee
Mobella	Mr and Mrs G Harrison
Nappa	Mrs M Coates
Nellsbern	Mrs H Davenport
Nethercroft	Mrs M Buck
Newarp	Mrs P Lister
Norfoot (Scotland)	Mrs J Laurie
Oakben	Mr and Mrs G Benning
Oberland	Mrs K Robinson
Parracombe	Mr and Mrs H Nelson
Pendlalp	Mrs E Bailey and J Medley
Penninghame	Mr and Mrs D Graham
Philwhit	Mr and Mrs W Whitlock
Pickersditch	Mrs J Cox
Plymus	Mr and Mrs J Brown
Pownall	Mrs J Bateson
Pytaura	Mrs S Pyner
Purleypot	Mrs M Calverley
Ralymin	Mrs M Fletcher
Rase	Mrs P Petch
Ravensberg	Mr and Mrs R Stringer
Rickath	Mr and Mrs Tudor
Rottabox	Mr and Mrs J Emptage
Rowbridge	Mrs F Stembridge
Rumbernays	Mrs J Stowers
Sarraman	Mrs J Sowerby
Sadirse	Mr M Forte

Sandydown	Mr and Mrs D Slater	Timberlog	Mrs S Gatward
Saxburn	Mr and Mrs T Parker	Topspurs	Mr and Mrs K Greaves
Schonbar	Mrs N Pampling	Tourneil	Mr and Mrs C Williams
Senbreeze	Mr and Mrs K Renkin	Trenson	Mrs J Thomas
Sentaria	Miss M Newton	Trelassick	Mr and Mrs D Harrison
Seveek	Mrs M Keeves	Tricias	Miss P Burns
Severnside	Mr and Mrs D Wardle	(Ireland)	
Severon	Mr P Bridges	Turnbeck	Mrs R Suttill
Shauntrae	Mrs P Cooper	Twymuir	Mrs A Twizell
Sheltrice	Mrs A Holdsworth		
Shimisu	Mrs J Cowderoy	Uniquecottage	Mrs J Parker-Tucker
Shirdees	Mrs S King	Ursine	Mr and Mrs G Wilson
Shirldave	Mr and Mrs D Franks	(Scotland)	
Shirracorn	Mr and Mrs P Allsop		
Shorrain	Mrs P Harrison	Vaccari	Miss M Evans
Sinvoa	Mrs M Horrex	(Wales)	
Sitzendorf	Mrs S Ashford	Valgarv	Mr and Mrs G Orr
Snoanda	Mrs A Hearne	Vindissa	Mrs A Waterman
St Fillans	Mrs G Sansom	(Australia)	
Spiretown	Mrs J Cross	Vindolanda	Mrs E Coid
Spitzburn	Mrs N Headington	Vinule	Mr and Mrs E Rule
Starstreem	Mr and Mrs B Johnson		
Stirleyhill	Mrs Slater and Mrs Waring	Waddenzee	Mr E Westerhuis
		Walchwil	Mr and Mrs G Howard
Stoneswood	Mrs M Smith	Warbern	Mr D Ward
Stormbridge	Mr C Huxtable	Westhurst	Mr Dawe
(Wales)		Wendardebs	Mrs W Chalkley
Surefire	Mrs P Clark	Wiamaru	Mrs J Milliken
		Wildingwood	Mrs H Mansell
		Windlenell	Mrs L Fitch
Takawalk	Mrs H Curtis		
Tangyachates	Mrs H Turner	Yatelyn	Mr J Yates
Tarncred	Mrs A Robbins		
Temeraire	Mr and Mrs G Wrighton	Zilken	Mr and Mrs K Sayer

— 3 —
The Breed Overseas

The history of the breed in other countries makes fascinating reading and I thought it might be a good idea to outline a few of the better known names in this section.

SWITZERLAND

First of all must come the country of origin, Switzerland and the Schweizerischer Klub fur Berner Sennenhunde. Berners are still numerically very strong as might be expected with an indigenous breed. I covered the early growth of the breed in Switzerland in Chapter 1, up to the end of the Second World War, since when the club has developed along very controlled lines due to the fact that they have a very strict breeding policy. Each area has a puppy controller who must be informed when a new litter is born and the breeder must only rear six puppies from any one bitch, who may only be mated once a year. The bitch must also be approved for mating by the Club which means she has to pass a temperament test, be properly marked and have a hip score of 0 or 1 grades. All these restrictions result in a very uniform look to the breed and the Swiss think, rightly or wrongly, they have the best Bernese in the world.

I have already mentioned in Chapter 1 that Herr Iseli's von Sumiswald kennel started in 1923 the name being carried on by both father, who is now one of the elder statesmen of the breed, and his son who was President of the Swiss Berner Sennenhunde Klub for the whole of the 1970's. Another early breeder with foresight was Frau Tschanz whose Dursrutti dogs are in many of the early pedigrees as are the von Grunenmatt dogs of Ernst Schlucter from whom came the early import to Britain of Fox.

Another kennel with an international name having exported to Britain, America and other European countries is that of Herr Amadeus Krauchi's von Nesselacker dogs (the Gorboulds importing Mustang from here) which have produced many champions over the years. Frau Vreni Gasser's von Waldacker dogs have a name for dual purpose results and several have been imported by Jude Simonds, their pedigree going back in a number of cases to Herr Mosers Bernetta lines, the most famous of which was the dog Int Ch Hondo von Bernetta.

Yet others, for example Herr Streit (Lehnwaldi) Herr Zbinder (Schwarzwasserfluh) and Frau Frankhauser (Chujerhof) to mention but a few, have all contributed to the picture. The present Secretary of the Swiss Club is Mrs Eve Walliser of Rutschelen, Switzerland.

UNITED STATES OF AMERICA

It is not absolutely clear when the first dogs were imported into America as Swiss Farmers who emigrated to the New World may have brought with them their indispensable dogs. It is known, however, that in January 1926 Isaac Scheiss, a farmer of Florence, Kansas imported the bitch Donna von der Rothöhe born 27.5.25 (Max Pulfer ex Trix von der Rothöhe), from Franz Schertenleib and a dog, Poincare von Sumiswald 24.7.24 (Ch Leo Greiner ex Netti Iseli), bred by Herr Iseli. They were eventually mated resulting in the birth of five puppies on May 29th 1926. Because the American Kennel Club refused to register either of the parents, the pups were also unregistered but Schiess registered them with the Swiss Kennel Klub under the name Of the Clover Leaf.

An enthusiastic article in the *American Kennel Gazette* of June 1st 1935 written by Mrs L Egg-Leach extolling the virtues of the Bernese (the same lady was responsible for the breed coming to England) caught the eye of Glen Shadow of Rushton, Louisiana. He then wrote an article in the *Western Kennel World* in January 1938 detailing his experiences with the breed both when a child and later in France in 1918/19. As a result of Mrs Egg-Leach's article he contacted her and she bought for him the top European show bitch, Fridy von Haslenbach from Fritz Stalder and a nice dog, Quelt von Tiergarten (pet name Felix), from G Walti. These two Bernese arrived in America on the S.S. Normandie on November 10th 1936. Mr Shadow said of the dog 'He was not the best to be had as the owner of the best male refused to sell him at any price'. These two imports were the first of the breed to be recognised in America and were accepted for registration on April 13th 1937, details appearing in the June issue of the *American Kennel Club Registrations*. For the next decade Glen Shadow was the only owner-breeder of Bernese in America. The first litter in 1938 only produced one puppy but a repeat mating in 1940 was luckier, producing four dogs and four bitches, but because of the war no more dogs were registered and all importing stopped.

AMERICAN BERNESE MOUNTAIN DOG STANDARD

GENERAL APPEARANCE

The Bernese Mountain Dog is a striking, tri-coloured, large dog. He is sturdy and balanced. He is intelligent, strong and agile enough to do the draft and droving work for which he was used in the mountainous regions of his origin. Dogs appear masculine, while bitches are distinctly feminine.

SIZE, PROPORTION, SUBSTANCE

Measured at the withers, dogs are 25 to 27½ inches; bitches are 23 to 26 inches. Though appearing square, Bernese Mountain Dogs are slightly longer in body than they are tall. Sturdy bone is of great importance. The body is full.

HEAD

Expression is intelligent, animated and gentle. The **eyes** are dark brown and slightly oval in shape with close-fitting eyelids. Inverted or everted eyelids are serious faults. Blue eye colour is a disqualification. The **ears** are medium sized, set high, triangular in shape, gently rounded at the tip, and hang close to the head when in repose, When the Bernese Mountain Dog is alert, the ears are brought forward and raised at the base; the top of the ear is level with the top of the skull. The **skull** is flat on top and broad, with a slight furrow and a well-defined, but not exaggerated stop. The **muzzle** is strong and straight. The **nose** is always black. The **lips** are clean and, as the Bernese Mountain Dog is a dry- mouthed breed, the flews are only slightly developed. The **teeth** meet in a scissors bite. An overshot or undershot bite is a serious fault. Dentition is complete.

NECK, TOPLINE AND BODY

The **neck** is strong, muscular and of medium length. The **topline** is level from the withers to the croup. The **chest** is deep and capacious with well-sprung, but not barrel-shaped, ribs and brisket reaching at least to the elbows, The **back** is broad and firm. The **loin** is strong. The **croup** is broad and smoothly rounded to the tail insertion. The **tail** is bushy. It should be carried low when in repose. An upward swirl is permissible when the dog is alert, but the tail may never curl or be carried over the back. The bones in the tail should feel straight and should reach to the hock joint or below. A kink in the tail is a fault.

FOREQUARTERS

The **shoulders** are moderately laid back, flat-lying, well-muscled and never loose. The **legs** are straight and strong and the **elbows** are well under the shoulder when the dog is standing. The **pasterns** slope very slightly, but are never weak. **Dewclaws** may be removed. The **feet** are round and compact with well-arched toes.

HINDQUARTERS

The **thighs** are broad, strong and muscular. The **stifles** are moderately bent and taper smoothly into the hocks. The **hocks** are well let down and straight as viewed from the rear. **Dewclaws** should be removed. **Feet** are compact and turn neither in nor out.

THE BERNESE MOUNTAIN DOG

COAT

The **coat** is thick, moderately long and slightly wavy or straight. It has a bright natural sheen. Extremely curly or extremely dull-looking coats are undesirable. The Bernese Mountain Dog is shown in natural coat and undue trimming is to be discouraged.

COLOUR AND MARKINGS

The Bernese Mountain Dog is tri-coloured. The ground colour is jet black. The markings are rich rust and clear white. Symmetry of markings is desired. Rust appears over each eye, on the cheeks reaching to at least the corner of the mouth, on each side of the chest, on all four legs, and under the tail. There is a white blaze and muzzle band. A white marking on the chest typically forms an inverted cross. The tip of the tail is white. White on the feet is desired but must not extend higher than the pasterns. Markings other than described are to be faulted in direct relationship to the extent of the deviation. White legs or a white collar are serious faults. Any ground colour other than black is a disqualification.

GAIT

The natural working gait of the Bernese Mountain Dog is a slow trot. However, in keeping with his use in draft and droving work, he is capable of speed and agility. There is good reach in front. Powerful drive from the rear is transmitted through a level back. There is no wasted action. Front and rear legs on each side follow through in the same plane. At increased speed, legs tend to converge toward the centre line.

TEMPERAMENT

The **temperament** is self-confident, alert and good natured, never sharp or shy. The Bernese Mountain Dog should stand steady, though may remain aloof to the attentions of strangers.

DISQUALIFICATIONS

Blue eye colour. Any ground colour other than black.

The Bernese Mountain Dog was the name given to the breed in England so America followed suit, although the literal translation of Berner Sennenhunde means 'Bernese Alpine Herdsman's Dog' which is a bit of a mouthful and in fact today most Americans refer to their dogs as 'Berners'.

After the war another dog, Cedrico von Allenluften was imported by Glen Shadow and three other people also bought in Bernese from Switzerland. With matings numbers began to increase and a number of articles were written, not only in the *American Kennel Gazette* but also in such publications as the *National Geographical Magazine* and the breed began to feature in illustrations in various dog books. By 1962 there were nine BMD owners listed with the American Kennel Club but they were spread throughout the country and as America is sizeable, to put it mildly, meetings were difficult. A Swiss woman, Nelly Frey in Vermont had bred a litter in 1959 and gradually the breed numbers exhibiting at shows increased, but many judges did not know what they were looking for. In 1967 Roberta Subins' Sanctuary Woods Black Knight was made up and became the first Bernese Show Champion being bred by Mrs Beatrice Knight who was instrumental in promoting the Bernese cause. The first Bernese to gain a working award was the Horsticks' Aya of Veralp who gained a Companion Dog award in June 1962.

In the U.S.A. the total cumulative individual registrations since 1937 of Bernese Mountain Dogs is 8,220. The numbers having risen in the last decade from 238 dogs from 64 litters in 1978 to 1011 dogs from 249 litters ten years later. In 1988 there were 104 Champions and the total number of shows (at all levels) scheduling Bernese was 265. A total of 53 dogs had working trial qualifications.

The American Bernese Mountain Dog Club started in the summer of 1967 when Carol Pyle of California, who had been inspired by Bea Knight, began the job of welding together Bernese owners scattered all over America. Her first Club newsletter went out in March 1986 to 33 members (owning 50 Bernese between them). A sizeable increase on the nine founder members of six months previously and by the end of that year the number had risen to 62. The first AGM took place in April 1969 when Carol Pyle became the first official Secretary and Newsletter Editor and the Club held its 50th anniversary in 1987. The first National Speciality (like our breed Championship Show) was held in March 1976 at Harrisburg, Pennsylvania when there were 71 dogs entered but numbers now are well past double that total! Some of the best known of the present American Bernese Mountain Dog Kennels are:

BEVS	– Beverly Burney
DE LI	– Lillian Ostermillar
DEERPARK	– Denise Dean
HALIDOM	– Millicent Parliman
SHEERSOM	– Robert and Caroline Kinley
SANDUSKY	– Sandra Ongemach
BROKEN OAKS	– Gale Werth

The interest in the breed continues to grow all over the States and the number of devotees increases steadily as the Bernese become even better known.

CANADA

1988 was the 10th anniversary of the Canadian Bernese Mountain Dog Club but there is no substantiated account of the first entry of the breed into the Country. The Canadian Kennel Club publishes yearly registration numbers but because of the size of Canada, there is no way of making sure of the numbers, and of course all owners do not join the Club. Ontario has by far the highest number of shows scheduling the breed, in 1988 it was 118 out of a total of 178 countrywide, but the average entry was only 20 dogs.

The Secretary of the Club is Coral Dennis from British Columbia and it is in British Columbia that the Bernese first made its show appearance in Canada, in the unclassified breeds at the North Shore Show in Vancouver in 1968, when an American lady, Mrs Barbara Gold of Washington crossed the border to exhibit. Ron Smith from Ontario was really a Newfoundland fancier but he first saw a Bernese at the kennels of Betty Cummings in the summer of 1973 and changed his allegiance. His first dog came from another of the earlier fancier's Grace Borg when, in 1975, he bought the bitch Valleyvu's Heidi von Gartenhugl.

Another of Mrs Borg's dogs Valleyvu's Georg won the first B.O.B. at Elgin County Show in May 1977. From 1973 the breed had been gathering strength. In 1977 there was a nucleus of 12 enthusiasts and there had been several attempts at getting the breed recognised by the Canadian Kennel Club all to no avail, Georg's win at Elgin turned the tables and the necessary 25 founder members were found over the next two years helped by the arrival of two Swiss families who bought over five adult Bernese which were duly mated. Most of the early spade work was done by Ron Smith who was later joined by a St Bernard breeder from Ontario, now into Bernese, Ray Fernandez. They, and others, eventually managed to convince the Canadian Kennel Club and the Bernese Mountain Dog Club of Canada (now consisting of 50 members) was inaugurated on November 24th 1979, hence the 10th year birthday I spoke of in the first paragraph.

NORWAY

The Norwegians saw their first Bernese Mountain Dogs in 1940 when they accompanied some Italian soldiers into their country, but the first attempt to start the breed seriously came in 1956. In that year two bitches were imported from the Sennengarden kennels of Eva Brandt, Dana Deantus went to Martin and Martha Gultvedt and Dolly Dolactol to Rhona and Johan Christensen. Seven months later the Christensens also imported a dog, half brother to the bitches from the same kennel, named Egge. These three Bernese formed the nucleus of the Norwegian breeding programme in the late 50's, but further imports were brought in mainly from Switzerland to widen the gene pool.

By 1962 there was a Joint Association which covered the big breeds like Great Danes, Newfoundlands, St Bernards and the Bernese Mountain Dogs. In 1984 the breed broke away to form an unofficial club just for Bernese and this was recognised in 1987, and by the end of 1988 the Norwegian Mountain Dog Club numbered approximately 1,000 members. Today the number of Bernese in Norway is estimated to be about 2,000 and they work hard to keep the HD rate down to about 12%. The dog is used as a working animal pulling sledges in the winter and taking part in Obedience and Agility competitions all year. Some of the most important kennels for Bernese in Norway are Bjorn and Greta Skaugs' Bernerbakken dogs; (it was they who bred Froy the Gourbould's 1981 import from Norway) and Willi and Elsa Jensens' Teroheimen affix and Cere and Christophe Stgöestads Treses dogs. There are also two very well known breeders who have been in Bernese for many years but who do not have a kennel name. The best known of these is Lieb Flathauf followed by Astred Hernansen.

FINLAND

Two Swiss dogs, Alex von Oberthal and Alma von Tücleboden, were the foundation of the breed in Finland in 1950 when they were imported by Mrs Saga Lindroos-Palmgren into her Lonneboda kennel. They proved a good investment, Alex gaining his International and Nordic (Swedish, Norwegian and Finnish) titles, while Alma was a Nordic Champion. The pair were mated in 1952 and produced three puppies, the first to be born in any of the Nordic countries.

The most important of the early kennels, besides Lonneboda, were Mrs Anne-Louise Relanders' von Alpenhütte Bernese, J and M Olanders Bjorntorp dogs, Mrs Rauha Heinos's Corinheimo BMD's and the Anssilan kennels owned by Armi Havukainen. The top kennels these days are the Ablaze Bernese owned by Mrs Sirkka Lahtinen and the Alpenbach dogs of Mrs Mervi Kaskiniemi, with the Corinheimo dogs still going strong.

There is a combined club for all of the four Swiss Herding Breeds (Great Swiss, Appenzeller and Entlebucher) which was set up in 1965. The Chairman is Mr Tuomo Tulokas and the Secretary Miss Satuula Mononen, Suutarintia 1, 36200 Kangasala. Tel: 931 790060. There are at present 992 members, most of whom are Bernese Mountain Dog owners, and about 1200 Bernese. Around 300 puppies are registered each year, in 1990 there were 329 making the breed 24th in the popularity stakes. It is not classified in the Working group, as in the UK, but in the Companion group. A few are trained to draw a cart or as search and rescue dogs, while quite a few compete in obedience. Some have been trained as guide dogs for the blind but I understand that at the time of writing there are no dogs doing this work. All Bernese Mountain Dogs must be X-rayed for Hip Dysplasia before being used for breeding and if found to have a reasonable hip score they may be used.

The breed is classified at most of the general Championship shows as well as at the Sennenhunde club itself which holds three specialist Championship shows a year. There are shows every weekend somewhere in Finland, most of which schedule classes for Bernese. The Standard is the same for all the countries in the FCI group but changes are possible in the future.

There have been no imports from Finland into the UK, but going the other way there have been 11 exports between the years 1970–1990. Of these three of the early ones were Tarncred bred; Blackjack (77), Gladiator and Karla (81) who went to Mrs Retander, Diana Cochrane and Liz Walpole Day (Wrighton) sent out Duntiblae Dark Ideal in 1979. Bergpuur of Glanzberg (84) bred by R G Bacon was exported by Sonia

Gorbould to Mr Tuukaanen and features in a number of present day pedigrees. In 1985 Knockeden Colette bred by R Shaw joined them. In 1989 the Watsons exported Coligny Blue Moon. Two dogs Benjamen Voltaire and William Ampere by Froy of Glanzberg bred by Mr O'Reilly and Mrs Y S Gilbert were born in 1986 and exported four years later in 1990. In the same year Kyleburn Night Bonanza (d) and Glanzberg Jasmine (b) were sent out to Mr Tuukaanen and the dog Duntiblae Midnight Magnum to Mrs Lahtinen.

The Bernese is a popular breed in Finland and the standard of those being shown is very high.

GERMANY

The four Bernese breeds are very strong in Germany and there is one club catering for all. Membership stands at around the 3,000 mark and is divided into 11 regional groups each with a breed representative. There are a number of shows held yearly plus about four Special Conformation events, as all animals used for breeding must have permission to be bred from.

The 10th September 1989 saw the 7th Club Show take place in Paderborn, the biggest to date, organised by the Swiss Sennenhunde Club of Germany. It occurs every three years and on this occasion out of 300 or so exhibitors there were 201 Bernese, 99 dogs and 102 bitches.

The history of the breed in Germany dates back prior to the First World War when Professor Heim, at a dog show in Munich in 1911, recommended that Nancy and Frank Behrens (well known for their Rottweilers) obtain a Bernese Mountain Dog; incidentally they also imported and bred the first Appenzeller in Germany. Eventually the Behrens acquired a dog Senn von Schossgut in 1911 and six years later he was joined by a bitch, Regina von Oberaargau from Dr Scheideggar in Zvinger, Switzerland. Despite First World War restrictions the first litter was born 8th January 1919. The following year Regina was mated to Ch Leo Greiner (the parentage of whom is a matter of conjecture) and from that litter appeared Cato von Seiberhaus the so called 'Father of the Breed' in Germany.

Interest in the Bernese grew and the German Club was formed on 3rd August 1923 with six founder members including Georg Regner who became the first President. In 1925 the Bernese Club became affiliated to the International Federation and the following year the first International Dog Show was held in Munich, where a number of the breed were exhibited and shown in a large cage to the public. The first Stud Book was produced in 1933 covering the decade in which were listed 17 breeders and 182 dogs, 18 of these being Swiss imports. In the following three years registrations increased greatly and the collective Stud Book showed 114 Bernese.

The war created difficulties but Bernese continued to be bred and in the 25 years from 1923–1948, 1450 were registered with the German Kennel Club and at the AGM on the 10th April of that year the rule to cull litters of

Int Ch Berri Max von der Horlache.

more than six puppies was introduced to prevent the numbers increasing out of hand. At the big show on 11th April 1948 60 Bernese were exhibited a number not reached again until the 1960's.

One of the most successful of the modern German Bernese Mountain Dogs was the Int Ch and German Ch Berri von der Horlache, or Max for short, owned by Prof Dr Bernd Gunter and his wife from Gaggenau – Freidlsheim. Max had a very successful show career being the only non-Swiss Bernese to win at shows in Switzerland, and one of the very few Bernese to gain an International Championship, he was the first of the German BMD's to pass the Swiss breeding test for conformation and temperament and was certified 'Excellent' for his hip score. He was used at stud to some effect with a resultant improvement in German stock.

DENMARK

Bernese are a popular breed with the Danes where they are increasing in numbers. It is thought that there are now about 1,000 dogs in the country, a big rise from the original 102 registered in 1979. The Danish Bernese Mountain Dog Club was started in that year and in contrast to the procrastination of the American hierarchy the Danish Kennel Club recognised it the same year. They adopted a similar Standard to the Swiss and also passed a set of breeding rules laying down criteria like a maximum 2–2 hip dysplasia score, all bitches must be 18 months old and every dog must have been placed at least 2nd at a specialist show before being mated. Defects such as blue eyes, incorrect coat or bite and a number of other faults also debarred an animal. About five Bernese are imported a year, mostly from Switzerland although some come from Germany and Sweden. The leading kennel is the Olsens' Tertzo Affix but most people have their Bernese as pets and only keep two or three at a time.

The Club runs three specialist shows out of a total of nine annual events, the other six being organised by the Danish Kennel Club. A maximum of 50 dogs are exhibited at each of the club shows which have specialist judges. At the others when all rounders officiate the number of entries drops by half with many of the same faces attending all the events.

BELGIUM

The Belgian Bernese Club was started in October 1979, covering all four of the Sennen breeds. The membership numbered 190 of which 140 were Bernese Mountain Dog owners. The Secretary, an owner of an Appenzeller is Lilly Nilsen of Brasschaat.

Bernese came into Belgium early in the 1970's but the first really active people in the breed with regard to Shows and Assessments were Mr and Mrs Mast. In 1974 they brought in a bitch from the Von Obersfield Kennel of Herr Zumstein in Switzerland. The 'father' of the breed in Belgium, however, was Ch Mutz von Overfield who was HD free, and the only dog to whom the Swiss character judges awarded 100% marks for temperament, a trait he passed on to his puppies. One of which, a bitch from his second litter called Atara van Het Bressershof belonging to the recent Club Secretary Mariette von Assche, became European Champion, Belgium and Luxembourg Champion and was 3rd best bitch at the World show in Dortmund in Germany, she died from liver cancer at the age of nine.

Unfortunately at the height of his career Mutz was poisoned in his garden due to jealousy. A grievous loss for Belgian Bernese as he passed on so many of his good points to his offspring, a complete generation of the breed.

HOLLAND

Interest in Bernese was inspired in the mid 1920's by Professor Heim when the Lanschot Brothers imported the first dog from Switzerland in 1924, Hector von Rohr, followed the next year by the bitch, Juno von Bartschi. The first litter was born on 29th October 1926, but unfortunately they only found pet homes and for a year or two the breed died out. However, in 1935 Albert de la Rie became interested and inspired Van Hobotker in Rotterdam and importing recommenced. A Club for all four Sennen breeds was set up in the late 1930's but breeding was again disrupted this time by the Second World War.

After the war bad temperament was a problem and all breeding was forbidden. The breed restarted in the Netherlands in the 1970's when Swiss puppies were imported and a new Club was formed on 27th June

1978. Mr Haayhaert (Oud Czeer) was the first to re-import and other top kennels are the Caense dogs of Mr Borst and the Von Oud Leusen Bernese of the Vegt and Dreven partnership. Unlike their German and Swiss counterparts the Dutch breeders do not cull their litters and the breed is numerically strong in this country.

SWEDEN

Bernese Mountain Dogs came into Sweden from Finland in late 1954 when the two bitches Charlotte and Cecilia Lonnebodas were imported by Marianne Oberg in Gatsland. She kept them only a short time then sold them to the late Mr Malte of the Soderkullas Kennels. It was he who, around the same time (1955), brought into the country the first dog, Uno von Der Nau, from Germany and also a bitch, Tolr von Der Nau, from the same breeder. The first litter born in Sweden was from the mating of Uno x Charlotte on the 12th December 1955.

Other people began to import Bernese, mostly from Switzerland although some from Germany, and the breed numbers grew quite quickly. The Swedish Berner Sennen Club started in 1968 and there are strict rules laid down by the Club to the effect that all breeding stock must be HD free.

There are five or six big kennels producing Bernese Mountain Dogs in Sweden, one of which will be known to people in Great Britain that of the Soderkullas Affix. The oldest Kennel is that of Hollvekens belonging to Mrs Tekla now aged 85. She has handed over the actual breeding to someone else but still maintains an active interest in the breed.

NEW ZEALAND

The development of the breed in the Antipodes is very much interwoven but I will look at New Zealand first as that was the country that began to breed Bernese before the Australian kennels developed.

Doreen Murdock emigrated from England in the early 1970's taking with her the dog Kisumu Achillies (Oro x Carin) to start her Durbachler kennels. She then imported Kisumu Bonne Chance, who died early from a strangulated hernia and was replaced by Kisumu Desiree on 13th March 1975 and three months later she bought N.Z. Ch Majanco Ghianti, litter sister to Gordon Howard's Gallina. Mrs Murdock bred several litters and exported to Australia to start the breed over there, and later imported the only other English bred N.Z. champion – Forgeman Fancy.

Another early New Zealand kennel was that of Yvonne Fison-Bates (Balahu) who had also emigrated from England. She had been involved in St Bernards in Britain but had bought a litter brother of Tarncred Drummer from Lena Robbins and joined the Bernese Mountain Dog Club of Great Britain in 1972. When she settled in New Zealand she had Dürbächler Chiana (N.Z. Ch Majanco Ghianti x Kisumu Desiree) and used Dürbächler Merlin, but he was found to have bad hips so she imported Meiklestone Dusky Emperor from Britain. From subsequent matings she produced several New Zealand Champions adding to her stock in 1985 with Claishaidy Winged Dagger line bred to Fox, and most recently Coligny Edelweiss from the Watsons. So far there have been 10 litters bred from these lines.

An unofficial club was formed on 30th April 1988 when about 50 people supported the idea and the Secretary Barbara Tate (Escarp), plus her steering committee, have organised match days, show attendances and several Garden Parties to date. Bernese have also put in entries for both Agility and Obedience competitions scoring some successes. It is hoped to apply to the New Zealand Kennel Club for official recognition once they are on a financially sound basis.

AUSTRALIA

Pauline Leeton (Tudorhill) imported a bitch into Australia from Doreen Murdock which she eventually made up, this was Aust. Ch Dürbächler Mufti CD and Margaret Clayton brought in Aust. Ch Millwire Clockwork Soldier sent out by Carol Lilliman. This dog was running loose for six weeks and was involved in a car crash and when Margaret was murdered, being shot whilst at work, the dog eventually came into the ownership of Lyn Brand (Branbern) who had imported Aust. Ch Marking Time from Mrs J Holdsworth.

In June 1979 Malcolm Smith returned to live in Australia taking with him Aust. Ch Forgeman Figaro and Aust. Ch Attila Snow Princess both of whom later went to Lyn Brand in New South Wales as puppies. He later also imported Aust. Ch Forgeman Folkhero from the Griffiths. Another well established kennel is that of Anderbern owned by Mrs K Haddon, and a useful addition to Australian stock was that of Ann Waterman's Eng. and Aust. Ch Choristima Monch of Vindessa. At the present time the Australian breeders are having problems with Osteochondritis but it is hoped that this will sort itself out as the breed grows in numbers. The latest import is Meadowpark Beta Bravo from the Mairs to Lyn Brand in 1990.

The Bernese Mountain Dogs in Australia are mostly located around the capital cities in each state, and due to the vast distances between states, it has not been possible to get enough Bernese lovers to come together to form an active club. In 1990 the number of Bernese increased to over 200. It is hoped as the numbers increase even more, people will get interested in showing and clubs will be formed. Most puppies are sold as family pets and companions because of their undeniable beauty and ideal temperament. Several of the breeders keep in close contact with each other and most are aiming to improve the breed by encouraging breeders to x-ray stock, through the Australian BVA-HD scheme, and to keep in mind the standard, particularly with reference to bone, size, height and temperament.

Australia has a similar points system for showing as the USA. A minimum of six points are awarded for each dog challenge, with an additional point gained for each dog competing. Twenty five points are awarded for Best Exhibit in Group and 100 points are required to gain a title. This system is necessary due to the low number of entries at shows. Australia comes under the English standard for judging. Dog shows are very popular in Australia and if one is prepared to travel, you can enter a show in most states every weekend, and at least one Championship show during most months.

Most Australian breeders now feel more new blood lines are needed to improve existing stock. Thanks to the efforts of those untiring breeders who have the breed at heart this new blood from Swedish sperm should soon be available.

— 4 —
The Standard

As the breed is a relative newcomer into Great Britain we have no chance of comparing present day type with that of 100 years ago, as we can with Flat Coated Retrievers for instance. We can, however, compare our dogs with photographs of Bernese Mountain Dogs in their native areas of Switzerland and I think that the main differences one notices are that the present day dogs appear to be bigger all round and have heavier coats.

In Great Britain each breed has a Standard, or list of attributes, which is drawn up by the Breed Standards sub-committee of the Kennel Club in conjunction with each individual club. This Standard sets out the factors necessary to produce a typical specimen. The British Bernese Mountain Dog Standard was first drawn up in 1971 when it was classified as a Rare Breed, since when it has been slightly amended and copies of it can be obtained from the Kennel Club, which publishes all Standards for individual breeds in the six recognised groups. The Bernese one can now be found in the Working Group booklet as it lost its Rare Breed status on the award of Challenge Certificates in 1977. Any new breed coming into this country uses the Standard of its country of origin as the basis for the new British Standard which the Kennel Club adopts, probably with slight modifications, to produce first an interim standard and then the completed draft.

To describe the breed in layman's terms is very difficult and Professor Dr E Hauck also made this point in regard to his own research. But nevertheless the aim of a Standard is to describe a dog and provide a good guideline in particular for breeders and judges to use for reference.

We all know that a perfect specimen has yet to be born in any breed. All have faults in either type, conformation or temperament, and it is the Standard that is used by breeders as a measuring stick, for all are attempting to produce a dog as near perfect as possible. It is to the Standard of a breed that I go to refresh my mind's eye when I am to judge that breed, whether it be one that I am already familiar with or one that I have not yet had under my hands in the ring.

Breed Standards need to hit the happy medium between being too verbose so you can't see the wood for the trees or not detailed enough. For example if the dog is stated to be of medium size and build, a definite size and weight should be given, because what might be seen by some people as a medium size, will be to others too big or alternatively too small. Each Standard produced by the Kennel Club is prefaced by saying that any dog may be disqualified from any award by the General Committee of the Kennel Club if it is proved to be totally blind or deaf, or if it is unable to breed due to a surgical operation, unless special permission has been issued or it has progeny registered although this latter requirement was rescinded by the Kennel Club in 1990.

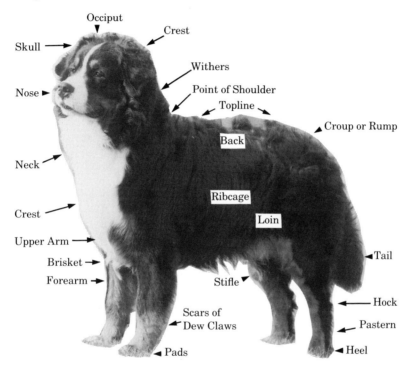

Points of the Bernese.

GENERAL APPEARANCE

Strong, sturdy working dog, active, alert, well boned, of striking colour.

CHARACTERISTICS

A multi purpose farm dog capable of draught work. A kind and devoted family dog. Slow to mature.

TEMPERAMENT

Self-confident, good natured, friendly and fearless. Aggressiveness not to be tolerated.

It should be remembered however that these dogs grow up into big strong and often boisterous animals, and one has only to look around at a show to see Bernese who are in charge of their people and not the other way round. I would not advise anyone to start off with a Bernese as a first dog as they are of a very complex make-up and there are many less difficult breeds on which to cut one's teeth.

They are very receptive to human moods and if one gets really cross and shouts at them they can snarl in return so an owner has to remember that he or she is the leader of the pack and go forward to, if necessary, shake the dog because if you back off you have lost forever your position of top dog. There is also a tendency for some young Bernese to go through a teenage stage of being rather retiring and difficult to handle in the ring and the only answer is to persevere and hopefully they will come through it in time.

As a breed these dogs are not aggressive but they can give a good account of themselves if they have to. They love people and will allow small children to ride either on their backs or in a cart, and even to lie in their baskets with them. They will warn of visitors to their properties with their deep resonant bark.

HEAD AND SKULL

Strong with flat skull, very slight furrow, well defined stop; strong, straight muzzle. Lips slightly developed.

Strength of head is typical of the breed although it does not want to be too heavy so as to be bear-like. There is a slight furrow with a well defined stop, which is the definite depression where the skull's frontal bones meet the top of the muzzle resulting in a change of level between the skull and the muzzle. The latter should be strong and straight, lips should be slightly developed and need to be well braced so as to be able to carry objects if necessary. The lower parts of the cheeks are called flews and should not be flabby as in the St Bernard, but tight to the jawbone and the Bernese Mountain Dog should not salivate.

Smythe in his book *Conformation of the Dog* discusses the relationship of head to intelligence but comes to the conclusion that it's more the quality of the brain rather than the quantity that is the deciding factor.

MOUTH

Jaws strong with a perfect, regular and complete scissor bite. i.e. upper teeth closely overlapping lower teeth and set square to the jaws.

The mouth should have a strong jaw with a full complement of 42 teeth, which should be regularly placed with 21 each in the upper and lower jaws, made up of six incisors, two canine, eight pre-molars and four molars. Ideally they should show a scissor bite which means that the upper teeth are set square to the jaw and just overlap the lower. If the lower teeth are

a

a) Correct scissor bite. Preferred. Incisors of upper jaw just slightly overlap the incisors of the lower jaw leaving no space between a tight bite.

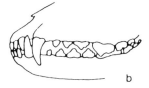

b

b) Acceptable level bite. Incisors of both top and bottom are dead level like a pair of pincers.

c

c) Unacceptable undershot jaw (fault). Lower incisors overlap upper incisors, functionally as useful but considered a fault

d

d) Unacceptable overshot jaw (fault). Short lower jaw incisors with lower canines lying behind. In time will indent into jaw and prevent dog eating properly. Lower jaw canines should be removed for safety.

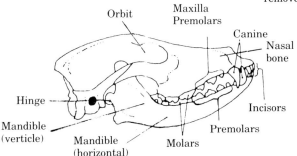

Skull structure
Closed jaw showing 1 side

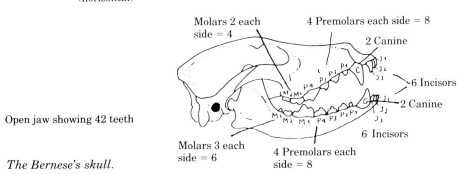

Open jaw showing 42 teeth

The Bernese's skull.

in front of the upper this is called undershot, and if the upper teeth are way out in front this is termed overshot. Both conditions being undesirable faults. Some judges have a fetish over teeth but one should remember they are only one part of the make-up of the picture, not the whole story and I would not unduly penalise a level bite though of course a scissor bite is to be preferred.

53

EYES

Dark brown, almond shaped, well fitting eyelids.

The eyes should be set at equal distance apart in the head and have no other colour, a black or light eye is unacceptable. Remember that the dog's expression whether it be hard or soft is regulated to a great extent by the eye colour and position in the head so they should not be set too deeply.

EARS

Medium sized; set high, triangular shaped, lying flat in repose, when alert brought slightly forward and raised at base.

These should be of medium size, that is about five inches long and well set on, high on the head. They are triangular in shape and when in repose lie flat but when the dog is alert they are brought forward and raised at the base.

NECK

Strong, muscular and medium length.

The neck should be well set on and there should not be any throatiness. It should also be obliquely placed on the shoulders which should slope well into the back. Too short a neck unbalances the dog's outline.

FOREQUARTERS

Shoulders long, strong and sloping, with upper arm forming a distinct angle, flat lying, well muscled. Forelegs straight from all sides. Pasterns flexing slightly.

The chest should be deep and the term 'good front' stems from the brisket (breast) from whence the legs come out on either side to give a good working movement. The shoulders themselves should be long, strong and as previously stated, sloping well into the back. The upper arm being well muscled forms a distinct obtuse angle and lies flat. The forelegs should be straight from all sides with good quality bone and the toes should neither turn out nor in, the latter fault sometimes being referred to as 'Queen Anne Legs', a reference to the furniture of that period rather than the lady herself. Pasterns (the area just above the heel of the foot) being slightly flexed so that the foot is lifted off the heel. Being 'down on the Pasterns' is a familiar fault with dogs that get insufficient road work and take most of their exercise on grass.

FEET

Short, round and compact.

The feet of the Bernese Mountain Dog are black soled, short, round and compact. As with the horse the saying 'no foot no hoss' appertains to a working dog who needs thick strong pads to cushion the jarring shocks as feet meet the ground, which a splay foot is unable to do, covering as it does too much of the floor space.

BODY

Compact rather than long. Height to length 9:10. Broad chest, good depth of brisket reaching at least to elbow. Well ribbed; strong loins. Firm, straight back. Rump smoothly rounded.

In the show ring, in recent months, I have noticed some very long bodied Bernese being shown in contradiction of the Standard, which states that it should be compact rather than long with a height to length ratio of nine to ten. A good depth of brisket (chest) reaching at least to the elbow is required because it is here that the heart and lungs need space to grow, giving room for the development of wind capacity and stamina. The term stated is that the body is well ribbed up meaning that the ribs are sufficiently separated to give room for a good lung capacity.

The topline should be level and firm and straight with strong loins going into a smoothly rounded rump. Occasionally when growing, a youngster like a horse grows up unevenly, higher at the back than at the front (withers), but this usually rights itself unless the stifle is too straight when it does not seem to be able to.

HINDQUARTERS

Broad, strong and well muscled. Stifles well bent. Hock strong, well let down and turning neither in nor out. Dewclaws to be removed.

The rump goes into the hindquarters which are broad and strong with good muscles and well bent stifles. The stifle joint is the area (see diagram) in the back leg which joins the patella (knee cap) from the femur (top leg bone) to the tibia (the lower leg bone). This joint needs to be at the correct angle to allow the body to stand square on the ground. In judges' reports the phrase used is 'a good turn of stifle'. Strong hocks are also necessary to support the considerable weight of a full grown Bernese. They should be completely straight, neither turning in, which is termed cow hocked, or out. The term 'well let down Hocks' is sometimes used in descriptions which means that when looking at the rear view of the animal the hocks are low placed, pointing directly at the judge if he is standing immediately behind the dog, and set off by the tail.

Another requirement of the Standard is that the dew claws must be removed. Bernese often have double dew claws (these are extra claws found below the hock) and if these are not taken off soon after birth they can turn round on themselves and enter the flesh of the leg, or get caught up in wire and tear out, giving a great deal of pain and loss of blood to the animal.

TAIL

Bushy, reaching just below hock. Raised when alert or moving but never curled or carried over back.

I have already mentioned the tail as being set off by the hocks and it should reach just below them. It should be bushy and carriage is very important. It seems a pity so many dogs (and bitches too) spoil what is a lovely outline while standing when they begin to move and their tail comes up to be carried over the back. The Standard allows it to be raised when alert and when moving but states it must never be curled or carried over the back. The term for such a fault is 'a gay tail' and has the appearance of unbalancing the dog. Tail carriage and wagging are the main dog communication methods.

GAIT/MOVEMENT

Stride reaching out well in front, following well through behind. Balanced stride in all gaits.

Many judges place a great deal of weight upon good movement when assessing a dog. Bernese should stride out well with a balanced gait whether running or walking, the back feet following well through behind in the wake of the front. The movement must be free flowing, neither too close, nor too wide when viewed from the front or the back. Lameness in Bernese can be a serious problem due to the heaviness of their bodies and you will find this condition more fully discussed in Chapter 6.

COAT

Soft, silky with bright natural sheen, long, slightly wavy but should not curl when mature.

This is said to be soft and silky, with a bright natural sheen which comes from the combination of full health, correct feeding and regular grooming. Although I agree with the former and latter parts of the Standard here, I do feel that a Bernese coat is not light enough to be called fine and silky in texture, especially with the coarser hair on the trousers and under the tail. If one compares it, for instance, with the Australian Silky Terrier, which also demands a silky coat in its Standard, the two types are completely different.

The Bernese coat is long and only slightly wavy and it should not curl when mature, although the puppy coat very often does, but this grows out as the dog matures. Feathering occurs on the front legs and from the hock down the back ones to the pasterns. There are different coat textures all of which protect the dog, particularly from water, and produce oily secretions which actually prevent wet penetrating through to the skin itself. Although nothing is mentioned in the Standard on undercoat the Bernese has of course got a soft coat under the top one as have most dogs, even those of short coated breeds.

COLOUR

Jet black, with rich reddish brown on cheeks, over eyes, on all four legs and on chest. Slight to medium sized symmetrical white head marking (blaze) and white chest marking (cross) are essential. Preferred but not essential, white paws, the white not reaching higher than pastern, white tip to tail. A few white hairs at nape of neck, and white anal patch are undesirable but tolerated.

The Bernese is recognised by its distinctive tri-coloured coat. Predominantly black it is set off by the brilliant white and dark tan patches, and it is interesting to note that all the four Sennenhundes are similarly marked. The main colour is jet black over most of the body with equal rich reddy brown or tan patches over the eyes (leading the Swiss to call them 'four eyes'), on both cheeks, all four legs, the anal patch and the sides of the chest, with tan hairs on the inside of the ears and the bottom corners of the mouth. The tan in fact divides the black from the white, which is found in slight to medium symmetrical blaze on the head reaching from occiput to nose, broadening out on the muzzle and the chest to form a cross which finishes under the brisket, both these markings being essential. The well marked Bernese also has white toes (but not socks, the white must reach no higher than the pasterns) and a white tip to the tail. Some dogs also have white hairs at the nape of the neck and a white instead of tan anal patch, both of which are tolerated but undesirable.

Talking to one or two breeders at a recent show the question of markings came up in discussion. All agreed that there are dogs being shown in the ring which only a little while ago would probably have been sold as pets as the markings were not strictly true to the Standard. As a breed grows there is always a tendency for some people to try their luck even if the markings are not quite accurate but the dog is otherwise a good specimen, this is a matter for each individual to decide for themselves and for judges to penalise or not as they see fit.

SIZE

Dogs: 64–70 cms (25–27½ ins). Bitches: 58–66 cms (23–26 ins).

It is very noticable that there is a great variation in size to be seen in the ring at shows. In a number of cases, and with dogs in particular, they seem to be way above the height requirement (measured at the withers dogs 64 to 70 cm/25–27½ inches, bitches 58–66 cm/23–26 inches) laid down in the Standard. No weight is given in the Standard, however a mature dog averages about 100lbs and a bitch 86lbs.

The main trouble when animals get so big is that they tend to become coarse and lose the compactness required by the Standard, Whether a Bernese is within or just outside the size laid down by the Kennel Club it must look like a dog if a male or a bitch if a female, I do not care for animals if I cannot tell their sex without having to look underneath to make sure.

FAULTS

Any departure from the foregoing points should be considered a fault and the seriousness with which the fault should be regarded should be in exact proportion to its degree.

NOTE. Male animals should have two apparently normal testicles fully descended into the scrotum.

Faults should be penalised depending on how serious they are, which is fine if one knows what faults are being considered for these are not given in the British Standard. The Americans disqualify blue eyes and any other main colour but black, while the Swiss list faults under two headings, those not serious enough to form a disqualification for breeding purposes and those that are. Under this latter heading come disqualifications like hair lips and cleft palate, blue eyes, incorrect bite, curly coat, a St Bernard head (too much stop) eye faults like entropian and ectropian (see Chapter 5), lack of tan, white boot markings and neck ring, timidity, gun shyness, lack of testicles and hip dysplasia. The British Standard tells us the dog must have two apparently normal testicles descended into the scrotum, but as the Kennel Club has now removed the restriction on showing castrated dogs and spayed bitches this part of the Standard will have to be deleted in the near future.

The Bernese's intelligence and beauty coupled with its loyalty and affection all combine to make this breed more popular by the year, as evidenced by the litter registrations annual rise at the Kennel Club. But whether shown or worked if the combination of beauty and brains is to be used effectively owners must be aware of their responsibility to harness these factors for the good of all.

— 5 —

The Puppy Choosing, Caring and Training

Choosing

'Oh dear!' many of my prospective puppy owners wail, 'They all look so alike I don't know which one to choose.' I can sympathise with their dilemma, for faced with a litter of puppies, all on first acquaintance looking so similar which one do you chose? Before ever deciding on a puppy, however, one should consider whether you and the breed are compatible and your reason for wanting to buy a puppy of this particular breed.

As a breeder I always want to know:

1) Whether the person wanting to buy the pup knows anything about dogs in general and Bernese in particular.
2) Do they have another dog or dogs at home.
3) Is this puppy to be their first canine acquisition.
4) Do they want to show or breed from the dog or are they buying it as a pet.

I was talking to a business acquaintance of mine the other day and he was telling me of a puppy he had acquired. The children had seen a friend's puppy on the Saturday morning and had come home wanting one like it, so the family all set off in the afternoon to a well know commercial establishment and bought a Westie, or for the uninitiated a West Highland White Terrier with no more thought than if they were buying a new piece of furniture. Hopefully, they are learning as they go along and I am sure the pup will be well looked after, but I could not help a wry smile when I thought of how I had taken two years to buy my first Bernese

Rase Honey Bear and Nookie Bear as puppies.

puppy after talking to breeders, watching the breed in the show ring and generally going into the whys and wherefores of owning a Bernese Mountain Dog. Talk about going into dog ownership where angels fear to tread!

If the people coming to buy a puppy already have a dog they will probably have a better idea of what to look for than someone who has never owned one, and it is often the latter group that do not know where to start when confronted by the litter. I am sometimes asked by people to chose a puppy for them but I decline to do this, unless it is one that has to be sent abroad of course, for if in the future the puppy I chose developed some fault that was not apparent at the age of seven to eight weeks it would be very easy for the disappointed owner to lay the blame on me as I had chosen the animal.

Very often one puppy will detach him or herself from the rest of the litter and seem to say 'I'm your pup chose me', a case of the pup deciding who is going to be his new owner and not the other way round. Something similar happened with the first Bernese litter I bred when I was only going to keep a bitch, but this little dog was always with me, almost as though he decided he liked it here and was not moving, so Nookie Bear stayed as well as Honey Bear. He and I have a rapport which one only gets occasionally with certain animals in life and then only for the short time of their life span, which is about 10 years if you are lucky.

THE IDEAL OWNER

Most top breeders have waiting lists for their puppies and in order to purchase a Rase dog intending owners have to satisfy me that they and this breed of dog are compatible. I also want to be certain that they really like dogs, which becomes obvious one way or the other within the first few minutes. I am told by people , that are now friends of mine, that the fusillade of questions as to their suitability as owners was equal to police questioning and very intimidating. But I whelped these puppies and watched them grow over the weeks into little characters in their own right, and although I would not say I did not like selling them, I have to be sure that they and their new owners are going to be happy with each other. The latter must also be aware of the snags of keeping a big dog that eats a fair amount, requires room at home, free exercise and needs to be with his people and not shut away because of lack of time. Also I do not consider the Bernese to be an ideal first purchase for someone with no previous experience of owning a dog.

There are one or two other generalisations too, I will not usually sell to people living in a flat unless it is on the ground floor, or to members of the forces, although having said that I have done so to a couple of officers who have been posted abroad for a four or five year tour taking the 12 week old pup out with them.

In both cases I am happy to say the animals returned to the UK were quarantined and are, at the time of writing, still living the life of Riley back in their own homes. I think long and hard too about letting a puppy go to a household where everybody works full time. It is acceptable if they are working shifts or even part time, but it is not fair to take a puppy from the litter and put him into a strange environment and then leave him on his own for long hours to become destructive because of boredom. Finally, I will not sell to someone I do not take to, though fortunately that happens very seldom, and I have made many long lasting friendships over the years with people who started out as puppy purchasers.

DOG OR BITCH

I hope you have thought seriously about the factors involved in keeping a dog long before you reach the breeder who is selling the puppies, unlike my business acquaintance mentioned earlier. Next there are a number of considerations to take into account and the foremost is surely the decision as to whether you want a dog or bitch.

These days the former is more easily obtained, partly because at present there seems to be a preponderance of dogs to bitches in most litters, and secondly because many people fancy their chances at having a go at breeding at least once. When I started breeding in the 1960's, the boot was on the the other foot and everyone preferred dogs to bitches, which could be quite slow to sell, but then suddenly the trend was reversed and now bitches command a ready market. I still get people telling me bitches are more faithful but that is simply not so in my experience. I will concede that there is an affinity between opposite sexes, men most often prefer a bitch while a woman prefers a dog, but both can be faithful and Bernese are very often one-man or one-woman dogs whatever their sex.

I usually advise people looking for a family pet to have a dog because if they do not want to breed there seems to be little point in having a bitch with the resultant twice yearly three week heat periods occurring roughly in spring and autumn to cope with, plus trying to keep the neighbourhood canine Casanovas at bay. But it should be remembered that Bernese dogs are very interested in the opposite sex, in fact anything in skirts will do, but they are not over sexed like some breeds that will try and climb up cushions or peoples' legs. They are, however, strong and very determined, especially if they have been used at stud, although fortunately they don't seem to wander.

FINDING A BREEDER

Having made the choice between dog and bitch there is only the availability of a puppy to worry about. For Bernese this is not further complicated by colour, whether to have a black, golden or chocolate, for example, for all are (or should be) similarly marked according to the Standard. Occasionally there is one that is badly mismarked in which case the breeder will usually sell this more cheaply and if one only wanted a pet then the strict show colouring is not important.

It is important, however, to obtain your puppy from a recognised breeder and not like my aforementioned acquaintance from a puppy farm, but fortunately as Bernese are not a numerically large breed, though numbers are rising steadily, one is unlikely to be able to buy one in a pet shop or commercial puppy farm anyway. If you do not know of a breeder, you could try asking your vet, ringing the Kennel Club in London, or obtaining a copy of one of the following *Kennel Gazette*, *Dog Directory*, *Dog World* or *Our Dogs*, the two latter being weekly publications. If you are hoping to show you are better going to an established breeder who has a proven line and is much more likely to guard their good name by not trying to palm you off with inferior stock. They will also offer help and advice if it is required. That is not to say you cannot do as well with a puppy from someone having their first litter, but beware of people who set themselves up as instant experts on the strength of only having whelped a bitch once and having shown for only a short while with no notable success.

PRICE

One question that obviously looms quite large is that of price, but I must admit that I do not warm towards prospective puppy purchasers whose first question is 'how much?' To my mind there are a dozen others that should come before that. It is also quite difficult to answer in general, for, as with most other prices, so too have the price of puppies risen and they are likely to go on doing so. I can only give an estimated cost that appertains at the time of writing, 1991, but remember it can vary between breeders and is even influenced by whether the litter is bred north or south of Watford. The cost of a puppy whether dog or bitch is the same these days although about 20 years ago a breeder could ask more for a dog. Even in the early 1980's, bitches cost on average about £10 more, which is odd in this day and age when all cost the same to rear. For a good healthy well marked registered Bernese puppy a purchaser could expect to pay between £300 to £450, the average being around the £375 mark. Puppies can be insured with firms like Pet Plan and Pet Protect which gives peace of mind to the owners.

It may seem a great deal of money for an eight week old bundle that closely resembles a teddy bear, but one has to remember that breeders base their prices only on how much has been spent. When one adds up food, vets fees, Kennel Club documentation, electricity, telephone expenses, plus of course the price of the stud fee which averages around £150–£200 these days there is little true profit to be made. So contrary to most peoples' ideas the breeder does not make much money and if all the hours entailed in whelping and rearing were included the cost would be prohibitive.

With my last litter the bitch had to have a Caesarean section and produced no milk for three days. The puppies still had to be fed every two hours night and day, and although I don't require a great deal of sleep, I was dropping off in the chair clutching a puppy in one hand and a bottle in the other by the end of this period.

THE RIGHT AGE FOR THE PUPS TO LEAVE THEIR MOTHER

Breeding a litter has both plus and minus sides to it but one has to be prepared to wave goodbye to the puppies as they set off into their new lives without it becoming too traumatic an experience. Some people will not breed a second time because they find the first attempt too upsetting when it comes to letting the pups leave home. Very few prospective buyers can visit the litter at regular intervals during the formative weeks, usually due to the distances involved, but I do like to meet people on my puppy list fairly early on, before they actually come to collect their new puppy. I normally let my puppies go between the ages of seven to eight weeks and veer towards the latter rather than the former as I feel puppies need the security of the litter for as long as that to give them the confidence to take new experiences in their stride.

WHICH PUPPY TO CHOOSE

As I have already stated I will not make a choice of an actual puppy for a buyer but I do point out the differences between the siblings such as puppy A is very active and an extrovert while puppy B is of a quieter nature etc, but the actual choice is a matter of individual preference. There are, however, several factors that could influence this choice, one of these is size.

In my experience the smallest of the litter could end up the largest of the lot, while the biggest dog as a puppy could be well within the Standard on maturity, but there is always the chance that he would go on growing and go over the Standard, so presenting too big a picture for most judges by the time he is two years old. One likes to have a litter that are all similar in size

A difficult choice.

but occasionally one is smaller than the rest and this one, called the runt, usually gets a fair bit of knocking about by its brothers and sisters. If you fall for this one you could be buying trouble because although usually he is a bright little thing, he obviously has had to fight for his place at the milk bar and will often take a long time to reach maturity and could be weaker than the rest, on the other hand he could be a born survivor once he gets started, and end up as has already been stated the biggest of the bunch.

Ideally though, you want to chose a strong bold puppy who is not afraid of coming up to make friends and receive a fuss from these new humans. He should have good bone in a short sturdy plump body with a well set on tail, but he should not be too fat, feet should be compact and well angled with dew claws removed. The head should be typically wide with a certain amount of stop and a good width between the ears, which should be neat and set on fairly high. The nose should be black and the eyes should be dark with an intelligent expression, tight so that they do not droop or show the haw. Neither should there be any discharge from them which could indicate a hereditary condition known as entropian where the lashes turn in and irritate the eyeball, which is very painful and requires an operation. Teeth should be correct scissor bite, mouths do alter a great deal during the early stages but there should be room for jaws to grow and there should also be a slight gap between the upper and lower teeth. The coat should be clean and should not contain fleas, lice or scurf, the presence of which are usually indicated by scratching the obvious irritation. Nor should the fur be covered in dried excreta. The coat itself should be dense and properly coloured. The pup should have that special puppy smell that is peculiar to them and should be active, good tempered and playful, coming up to receive a fuss from visitors quite freely. It should not be necessary to look far for the dam of the litter as she should be around. The bitch should be proud of her family and much in evidence, however if the sire does not belong to the breeder he may obviously not be available. By seeing the dam however, one can get a good idea what her progeny will be like once they reach maturity.

When examining the litter you may pick up a puppy and on examination find it has a soft swelling on the underside of its tummy near the navel, this is probably an umbilical hernia. They are not so common in the bigger breeds of dogs such as Labradors but in the toy breeds, especially in Yorkshire Terriers, Cavaliers and Poodles the condition appears to be inherited, but it is a difficult thing to research. However, it can also occur where a bitch of any breed bites the cord too short on the delivery of the puppy, or if she whelps standing up. The condition produces a weakening of the wall but this usually rights itself and closes the gap as the puppy grows into maturity. It does not normally cause problems, even later in life when a bitch is whelping but it is considered a fault of course if the space does not close up.

If the puppy is to be shown his markings will need to be fairly close to the Standard, as often a quality undermarked dog will go down in placings to a better marked one with other faults because he is not as showy. A surfeit of white, while flashy, sometimes produces blue eyes (most undesirable) and lack of pigmentation around the face, although a nose that still shows signs of the pink colour present at birth during the early months nearly always comes right in the end as the puppy matures.

TIME OF YEAR TO BUY A PUPPY

The best time of the year to obtain a puppy is spring or summer, autumn is not too bad as although the days are shortening there are still some pleasant weather periods when the puppy can get out into the garden. The winter is not a good time, especially for house training, and responsible breeders would not consider selling a puppy as a Christmas present unless they were very sure where it was going. But it is not usually from them that the problems arise with unwanted animals being cast out after the festive season, but from the back street breeders and pet shops in the main.

Pro-Dogs produce a car sticker declaring 'A Dog Is For Always Not Just For Christmas' to try and impress the facts of dog ownership on those thinking of giving a puppy as a present. It is enough of a trauma for a puppy to change homes at any time but when it comes at a period when there is so much excitement in the air as at the end of December it makes readjustment doubly difficult.

PAPERWORK

When the pup that is to be your pride and joy has been chosen and paid for the breeder should supply a diet sheet showing times and contents of meals to which the puppy has been accustomed. You would be well advised to adhere to this sheet, at least in the beginning, if diarrhoea and an upset

There is always something to occupy a puppy in the garden.

tummy are to be avoided due to change of food, on top of changing homes. Such a condition can be extremely serious in a puppy. Also you should receive a slip of paper showing the pup is registered with the Kennel Club but even today with the help of the computer a breeder does not always get back the registrations giving the pup's official name and number in time before the litter leaves home. Please check that the breeder has signed the back of the form so that there are no hold-ups when you want to change the ownership to yourself. The third document you should have is a signed pedigree (preferably hand written although many are now being printed out by special machines) This shows not only sire and dam but the relatives tracing back for four or five generations. Do at least memorise the former, for the first question dog people normally ask of an owner is, 'How is he bred?' which means which dog was mated to which bitch to produce this off-spring.

Pedigrees often fox people but they are not difficult to understand if you remember the sire and his relations take the top line while the bitch and her parents, grandparents and great grandparents take up the lower, producing a triangular shape (on its side) at the apex of which is your pup. It is usual to say that the pup is 'by' the sire and 'out of' the dam, so that reads that the pup is by x and out of y.

There are often abbreviations to be found alongside the dogs name on the pedigree, the most usual being Ch or Champion, Int Ch or

International Champion and JW meaning Junior Warrant winner. A Champion is often shown in red on the pedigree as it is the highest show award available. It means that a dog or bitch has gained at least three Challenge Certificates (top award at a Championship show) all under different judges. A Junior Warrant on the other hand is not an official title although a certificate is issued by the Kennel Club if it is claimed (a CC is sent to the winner by the Kennel Club without having to claim it). A Junior Warrant means that a dog has amassed a total of 25 points from first prizes in breed classes at Open shows, which are worth one point each and Championship shows which are worth three points each between the ages of 12 to 18 months in Junior classes.

I also give a Pedigree Petfoods Pet Owners Folder containing a number of leaflets on feeding, training, etc in with the rest of the paperwork, plus the suggestion that the puppy is taken to classes in obedience and/or show and the owners apply to join the Bernese Mountain Dog Club of Great Britain, or one of the area breed clubs, so as to keep in touch with breed happenings as they occur.

INSURANCE

Another service that I offer my new owners is that of an insurance cover note. For the cost of around £10, the puppy can be insured from the moment you leave the kennel premises and it is valid for a period of six weeks covering the dog for such things as death from illness or disease, theft or straying plus veterinary fees. The firm will then arrange to continue the insurance on payment of a yearly premium, which can be paid by credit card or instalments using a bankers order.

So there you are, just about to embark on the adventure of owning a Bernese Mountain Dog puppy and in the next section I will try and help improve your knowledge, but you will have to bring along two qualities, namely a modicum of common sense and a large helping of a sense of humour, in order to benefit to the full.

Caring

Having chosen your puppy from the litter, paid for it and received all the paperwork, the first hurdle to be surmounted is how to get it home as easily as possible. My advice is that two people come to collect the puppy, one to drive and the other to nurse the dog. The puppy may start off in a box at the back of the vehicle but it will not be long before he has clambered forward and climbed into the nearest lap, which can be somewhat disconcerting if you are on your own and trying to steer the vehicle at the same time. It is also advisable to have plenty of newspaper plus an old towel with you because you are then prepared if the puppy is sick on the journey. Some travel well from the word go but others take much longer to adjust. In the main however Bernese love to go out every time the car keys are picked up. If you are unfortunate enough to have a car shy dog the only cure is to take him everywhere even if it is only down to the garage, and it is also a good idea to feed him in the car until he loses the tension the car engenders and becomes relaxed, when the problem will solve itself.

On arrival home the first three things to do are

1) See if the puppy will do a puddle in the garden and praise him if he does.
2) Feed him and give a drink of warm milk as it will probably have been some hours since his last food intake (as the breeder would not have fed him before travelling and he could have been sick on the journey back).
3) Introduce him to his sleeping quarters and let him have a sniff around.

When you chose your puppy make a check list before bringing him home to make sure you do not overlook any of his needs. It is much easier then than in the excitement surrounding his arrival.

Food: Check with breeder on type and quantity.

Sleep: Puppies need plenty of it. Make sure he will have a spot that is warm and out of the way and that children understand that sleeping puppies are not to be disturbed (adults might need reminding too). The bed and bedding should be something that is disposable or frequently washable. Avoid wicker baskets as they will be chewed and the broken ends can cause injury. I find a cardboard box is as good as anything for the first few weeks.

Play: Puppies also need plenty of this. Organise your daily routine so that you can give him the time he needs, and keep him well supplied with toys (an old soft toy will do as well as some expensive item from the pet shop). He will also need something like a hide chew. Make sure children understand that he is a living creature and not a toy and that he should be treated with respect.

Socialising: Human contact is very important for a puppy's development so make sure he will get plenty and also get used to meeting strangers.

FEEDING

Any breeder will tell you if you do not put the right food into a puppy, particularly a Bernese, in those first eight weeks you will not get the bone that is so necessary in this breed. In fact, the right food for the whole of the first year is essential for a strong healthy adult so it is up to the new owners to continue the good work started by the breeder.

At the age of eight weeks your puppy will, in all probability be on four or five feeds a day and the diet sheet given by the breeder will state the correct times, quantity and type of food given to date. Do please continue to feed as instructed to start with because the puppy is accustomed to this way of feeding and changes brought about too quickly are likely to result in upset tummies, which can prove very serious in a puppy. Meal times are roughly equivalent to breakfast, lunch, early and late evening plus an occasional bowl of a specially formulated puppy milk such as Lactol.

The quantity of food intake varies with each puppy but Bernese are greedy eaters and the speed at which they can demolish a dish of food is reminiscent of a hammer mill at work. It is probably a good idea to put the puppies dish in the top of a bucket (if you can find one to fit) so that he does not have so far to get down to it, which helps his shoulder placement. These days it is possible to buy metal dish holders with legs. Actual amounts of food are difficult to estimate but I work on the two- thirds carbohydrate to one-third protein ratio and fill one of the big silver dishes (or Pedigree Petfood brown ones) full each time. I tend to say I would rather overfeed than underfeed but do watch that the puppy does not get too fat. They usually work a lot of the surplus off playing, especially if there is another dog or dogs with whom to exercise in the garden. Remember a puppy is growing very quickly and the food intake needs to be increased in direct ratio to the growth rate. As the months go on the dog may indicate that he does not want one of the meals so in that case cut it out and perhaps slightly increase the food in the next one.

I am old fashioned in my ideas of feeding, at least as far as giving the so called 'complete' foods are concerned. They may be scientifically balanced to the nth degree, quick, easy and all the rest of the arguments that are put forward in their favour, but I still believe there is a place for the old fashioned meat and biscuits in the diet. I would be telling a lie if I said I didn't use a complete food, because I do, but the main puppy meals around 1pm and 6pm and the older dogs feed at 6pm are still based on traditional methods. Food is the highlight of a dog's day and giving the same mixture day after day must be dull in the extreme, even if, in defiance of the maker's instructions other things are added to it. In any case always eating sloppy food does not encourage the growth of good strong teeth. I know from the amount of nose twitching and lip smacking that goes on in our kitchen when there is something nice such as rabbit or chicken on the menu that my dogs are like humans and are very interested in their food.

Breakfast

When our pups leave home they are having four meals a day, breakfast consisting of Weetabix or Readibrek (depending on whether it is summer or winter) mixed with warm milk. The most nutritious is goats milk which freezes well and a stock can be laid into the freezer in advance. Cows milk is permissible in either liquid or powdered form but it needs to be the full cream variety not skimmed. I also use evaporated milk (one tin plus two of water makes two pints of liquid) and Lactol (or one of the other makes) which can be bought from a pet shop and is specially formulated for dogs. I would advise against using calf or lambs starter though, as one is never sure what extra hormones have been added.

A number of people do not feed milk and I cannot for the life of me understand why this should be so when for the first fortnight it is the only food a puppy receives. Unless the dog later, in rare cases, develops an allergic reaction carry on feeding milk.

As the puppy grows I sometimes use one of the complete foods for breakfast as a change, mixtures like Wilsons, Valumix or one made up by my own wholesaler, occasionally mix in a raw egg (salmonella free of course) while a nob of marge or spoonful of vegetable oil helps to keep the coat shining and in good condition.

Lunch

As I mentioned earlier, lunch is normally some kind of meat with biscuit meal or mixer added. The meat comes from a choice of Pedigree Chum Puppy Food, best mince from the butcher, cooked minced tripe, chubb or brawn or the very small dried meat reconstituted with gravy or an Oxo or a vegetable cube. But be careful to use this meat very sparingly as it can cause scouring. To this is added puppy meal and probably Pedigree Chum small mixer, any vegetables, cooked or raw, going spare and suitable leftovers from our own meal.

Evening Meal

The early evening meal is a protein one, but if I have softened the lunch one I try to make the third feed dry so the pup has to use his teeth. Fish, chicken and rabbit (without the bones of course) scrambled eggs or even soya bits provide a selection, again with mixer added, plus sometimes a little grated cheese on top for a change. It always seems to be feeding time in our house with pups and I usually put down the last meal sometime around 10.30 – 11.30 as I am a late-to-bedder. This is another milk and cereal meal plus some small biscuits like Biscrox or Baby Boneo. I sometimes give tinned rice pudding for a change, which can often be obtained in unlabelled tins from your pet shop and is very good if your pup has an upset stomach or the scours. Another cure for the latter is corn flour mixed in the food, or water in which rice has been boiled. I usually give a drink of milk either after lunch or tea meal, and of course there is always clean water available. A big raw bone or rawhide chew lying about helps exercise their new permanent teeth which are now coming through. An odd Vetzyme or Canaval tablet can also be given, or 'Stress' mixed on the food, but do not feed too many additives as with correct feeding they should not be necessary.

It is difficult to lay down a definite amount of food to be given as puppies appetites vary in much the same way as do children's (in their individual intake of food). You will need to arrive at the correct amount for your puppy by means of trial and error, but as a rough estimate I allow 21.3 grams (¾ oz.) solid food daily to start with and then increase the amount commensurate with the growth rate.

SLEEPING QUARTERS

If your puppy is to live in the house instead of out in a kennel, remember Bernese do find modern central heating too much for them at times so if you are one of those people who like their house very warm it is perhaps kinder to house your Bernese separately, particularly in the winter.

Bernese like their comforts and if living indoors are likely to appropriate one of the arm chairs, or even your bed for their own use. If you do not mind what will eventually grow into around eight stone of Bernese taking up three quarters of the bed space that is fine. If you do you must not allow the dog to develop the habit, so train it to use its own bed instead of yours from the start.

Whether or not you are intending to let your dog have the free run of the house it is still better to start off confining the puppy to the kitchen at night. This makes it easier if he is not able to be clean through the night, which he will not be when he first comes from the litter. He is going to miss his family very much if there are no other dogs in your set- up and is likely to complain loudly of his lonely state at first. A radio left on, a kitchen clock ticking loudly and some cuddly toys to snuggle up to will help and usually they do settle fairly quickly. But I can think of one instance in our very early dog days when I bought in a puppy who attached herself firmly to my husband and had no intention of being parted from him during the night. She simply yelled at the top of her voice solidly for two and a half nights until we gave in, and she slept with us every night of her life apart from when she was nursing puppies.

The puppy will need his own bed but it is silly to lash out on an expensive wicker basket as little teeth can reduce it to shreds fairly quickly which is not only a waste of money but the sharp ends can be very dangerous. I advise people to obtain a good strong cardboard box from the grocers or local supermarket, which can be disposed of as the puppy grows and replaced with a bigger one. At the age of five or six months he should be over the teething problems and safe to move into a permanent dog bed of sorts, I would suggest the use of the plastic type which is indestructible and easy to clean or a bean bag. The box must be out of the draughts and must be on a square piece of cushion flooring or carpet, or something similar, so that it is not in direct contact with the floor, particularly in winter if the latter is of stone or concrete.

A piece of blanket or carpet is needed to line the box, but you will probably find it is pulled out onto the floor by the morning. In the summer the dog will prefer the cool of the floor, and in fact they do like to sleep out on the grass at night if it is warm. Another lining for the box is of course the modern Vetbed which is warm and able to allow any puddles made on it to drain through.

The amount of sleep intake varies with the individual puppy, some need a considerable amount and others can do with much less, for like people, dogs differ too. I should perhaps add a word of warning about placing your dog's bed too near a solid fuel boiler if you have one of these, because there have been cases of dogs being poisoned by fumes when lying too close to a stove.

Bernese and children make ideal companions.

CHILDREN

If there are children in the family they must be taught to leave the puppy alone when he is in his bed, for he must have somewhere to retire to when he has had enough play. It is during sleep that growth occurs and with Bernese this seems to be at an alarming rate.

Children should not be allowed to tug at objects held by the puppy even in play. Bernese Mountain Dogs are not terriers and these bad habits learned in puppyhood are hard to eradicate.

KENNELLING

Outside housing needs to be given careful consideration for there are quite a number of different options. If one can afford a deluxe version of a modern house and run this is by far the best bet. The puppy can be put in it while you are out, thus saving the furniture and fittings in the house from any attack of bored little teeth, plus the knowledge the puppy is out of harms way himself. If an area is being concreted to accommodate the kennel it is probably worth making it bigger than necessary in order to extend the kennelling at a further date should your dog numbers grow.

The kennel itself wants to be divided into a house and run. The house part is best fitted with a stable door so that you can stand up when you want to get in to clean. These days the flooring is usually made of a compacted material which is warm and can be wiped over with disinfectant or household bleach if an accident occurs, but do not use Jeyes

Fluid, for combined with urine the smell is all pervading, or fill the place with water, dogs hate standing around in wet conditions. If you do hose down, remove the dogs or shut them up elsewhere until it dries. The size of the kennel part should be approximately 6ft (1.8m) high and the width and length should allow the dog to turn around with plenty of room to spare. If you have a chewer it is advisable to cover any tempting wood with metal strips to prevent damage.

The run is best made of concrete or slabs both for ease of cleaning and because if it is grass you may find your dog has dug himself out. Size should be approximately 10′ by 20′ and be big enough to take two dogs at a time.

The type of bedding to provide for your kennel dogs is a matter of personal choice. Most hunt kennels put up raised benches for their hounds which can be a good idea, or a dog bed on legs can be used, or simply a wooden box containing a square of carpet or Vetbed, but I would counsel against using straw. The reason for this is that it usually contains fleas (even clean straw does) and also encourages dogs to wet in it which is not a habit one is trying to encourage. If dogs come in wet and muddy one can rub them down with straw and sponge off, drying afterwards with a towel, but it does depend quite a lot on the type of soil you have. Ours is sandy so we are lucky because the dogs dry off quickly.

However, blankets or Vetbeds used as bedding can and do get carted around the place, but they are easily washed and I prefer them to straw. It is also possible to use shredded paper but you tend to get the same problems of wetting there as you do with straw. Do not forget kennels need to have clean water always available because Bernese drink a lot of Adam's Ale. They also delight in chewing up the bucket having just upset the contents all over the run so some method has to be devised to deny them this particular diversion.

If one has a shed or garage that can be converted it is possible to save the expense of buying a purpose built kennel but the building must be draught proof, dry, light and airy. It is very important that there is a free flow of air for not so long ago a number of dogs were killed because they were shut up in an airless kennel during a heatwave.

SOCIALISING

Bernese are sociable creatures and even if confined should be able to see out and be seen so that they can be made a fuss of by visitors. The breed is given to shyness, which can be avoided if they are handled properly, particularly in the critical six to eight week stage when company is so important. Most Bernese love to be with you and are very curious about human beings and their activities. It matters little whether they are kept in or out housing-wise so long as they get the love and attention that is so necessary.

EXERCISE

Exercise can be obtained if time is of the essence by stretching a rope or wire tautly between two fixed points with a ring threaded through, the other end of which is attached to the dog who can then exercise in a controlled manner. But remember a dog is at the mercy of the elements should it become very hot or the heavens open so this method is far from ideal.

Because of their weight and size Bernese can damage their shoulders, pull muscles or lame themselves without seeming to do anything spectacular to cause it. Many people do not realise that over-exercising at an early age is as detrimental as under-exercising at a later stage. One needs to apply a great deal of common sense to this question for it is very easy to give a puppy too much activity and this can lead to a complaint known as HD or Hip Dysplasia, which affects the hind movement in varying degrees, often resulting in lameness coupled with a great deal of pain. I let pups have a free run in the garden with the other dogs, but taking care that they do not play roughly and injure themselves, and in the garden they can stop when they have had enough rushing about. I do not allow puppies to go for walks until they are four and a half to five months old and then they go out on the lead while the others tear off and gambol about. This way they have a controlled distance to cover until they are also allowed to run free at about six months, but even then I do restrict the amount of exercise, and if I think the puppy has done enough I call him up and put him on a lead.

INJECTIONS

Eight weeks is usually too early for puppies to have received any injections before you buy them. Some breeders advocate inoculating puppies at a month old with a type of measles vaccine, but this can lead to complications later in life and I would not recommend it. I suggest you ask your vet what he advises re inoculations when you get home with the puppy. A minority of vets believe in providing immunity for such diseases as parvovirus as early as possible and will inject at eight to nine weeks, but it is more usual to have them done at 12 and 14 weeks.

The pup should not go outside your house and garden until about four days after the last injection as before that he is still in danger of picking up one of the fatal diseases. The diseases that are covered these days are the old scourges of hard pad and distemper and the modern problems of leptospirosis (jaundice) and Parvo-Virus. The puppy will gain a certain level of immunity from its dam, which will give it some protection up to the time of its injections. But try to avoid putting this to the test.

At the end of the course of injections the vet will give you a card showing the serum used, the diseases immunised against and the date for the booster in 12 months. I do not usually take the puppy into the surgery for fear of infection but get the vet to come out to the car.

WARNING

Normally when you collect your Bernese puppy at around eight weeks he will have been wormed several times already. I always worm my puppies (for roundworm as tapeworms only attack animals over the age of six months) at three, five and seven weeks. But the purchaser should inquire about the last date of worming and find out when the puppy should next be treated. Treatment for worms is most important because they can cause the death of baby animals if not got rid of.

There are many products on the market obtainable from pet shops, chemists or the vets. I usually use Canoval for two treatments then get something stronger from the vet for the third dose. If one is breeding it must be remembered that the bitch needs dosing at three weeks into her pregnancy because all whelps are infected via their dam. For some reason as yet unknown to veterinary science, she harbours roundworms in the form of larvae in the digestive system where they in turn lay hundreds of eggs, which are passed on to the puppies at birth to begin the cycle all over again. Even though treating the bitch will not completely prevent roundworms in the puppies it does greatly reduce the problem. I advise puppy purchasers to worm fortnightly up to the age of four months then again at six months and from then at least twice a year in the spring and autumn.

THE DESTRUCTIVE PUPPY

Some Bernese are destructive and others are no problem at all, but I cannot tell you why one should be a problem and others are not. I have had both in my time, the fact is they are quite tall, especially when they stand on two legs and can reach up on tables and take objects one thought were put well out of their reach. It is not fair to leave objects you value in reach of the dogs because if the phone goes, or someone comes to the door, and you just drop everything to answer you may expect mayhem when you return.

One of the reasons puppies chew is boredom when left alone in the house and this is why a kennel is such a good idea where a pup can have his toys, a beef hide chew or a marrow bone to go at. But even so, if the kennel is of wood you may find the dog will chew the framework, so it is often necessary, as I have said before, to line it with metal to prevent this. It is a good idea to accustom the puppy to being left alone for periods in the day, for there are not many houses where there is someone at home all the time. If leaving a puppy in the kitchen I very often put on the radio or television to keep him company, especially in the early days.

It is also a good idea to put the dog into boarding kennels for a night or even a weekend when he gets to eight or nine months old so that if one has to rush off at a moment's notice in an emergency, or go into hospital for a bit, you have not got the additional worry of how the dog will cope having never been away from home before.

PICKING UP A BERNESE

Yet another consideration is the correct way to pick up and handle your Bernese puppy. You must remember that an eight week old dog is very heavy and must never be picked up by the forelegs as this will put undue stress on the dog's shoulders which is very bad. The scruff of the neck is the

A puppy should be correctly supported when picked up.

method the bitch uses to carry her whelps but remember if you pick up a puppy this way it must immediately be supported under the hind quarters to take the considerable body weight. I do not advocate allowing children to pick up puppies at all, but they must of course be allowed to handle them and learn how to hold them securely in both arms while supporting them under the bottom. A puppy should be lifted in and out of a car because dogs as heavy as Bernese can lame themselves very easily jumping in and out of a vehicle. They can also injure themselves jumping up to reach something held in a hand above their heads, as with all four feet off the ground landing can jar them and again cause lameness, particularly of the shoulders.

You will need at some point to teach your Bernese to negotiate stairs particularly if you live in a bungalow, but it is better to wait until they are around five months old before doing this as it can be another source of shoulder and weight problems. If it is not familiar with stairs you may find the dog faced with this unaccustomed obstacle at a later date, say at a railway station when you have about two minutes to catch a train from the opposite platform, which could pose a problem.

Good Manners

Puppies should not be allowed to jump up at people, it may be very endearing in a pup of eight to twelve weeks but a very different story if an eight stone muddy adult ruins someone's decent clothes. My husband always advised people coming to our house to wear dungarees and wellington boots to be on the safe side! While talking about inculcated bad habits I do intensely dislike dogs being a nuisance at meal times. If puppies are taught at the beginning that meal times are for humans and not canines, and never on any account fed any tit-bits from the table, there should be no problem. With my dogs any left overs from the meal are distributed in the kitchen afterwards or put aside to be added to their dinner later. If the puppy is a pest and persists in making a nuisance of himself he will have to be shut out of the dining room until he learns better manners.

ADMINISTERING MEDICINES

Giving pills and medicines can be difficult if you have not mastered the art. In the first instance pull the top lip over the teeth and put two fingers against the bottom jaw, thus extending the open mouth to its fullest extent. The pill can now be flipped or put into the back of the throat, the mouth is closed and held whilst the throat is stroked which stimulates swallowing. I always look in the mouth to see if it really has been swallowed and is not sitting under the tongue or round the gums. Some Bernese are very clever at palming the pill and spitting it out later when you think all is well and if it is a worming pill, for example, it is very important for obvious reasons that the puppy ingests it properly. Even the most difficult dog will swallow a pill if it is concealed within some titbit. Medicines are usually tipped in the side of the mouth but do make sure that the mouth is held shut and the head slightly back or else you will administer the dose all over yourself instead.

GROOMING

Grooming Materials
 1) Wire brush.
 2) Stiff brush.
 3) Bristle brush with strap.
 4) Fine comb.
 5) Coarser comb or combined teeth.
 6) Rake.
 7) Serated scissors.
 8) Ordinary scissors.
 9) Trimming scissors.
10) Stripping knife.
11) Chamois leather.
12) Grooming glove.
13) Nail cutters.

Not all the above are necessary but you will need as a minimum:

1) A good stiff brush.
2) A strong comb with wide and narrow teeth.
3) A rake.
4) Serated scissors.
5) Ordinary or trimming scissors.
6) Nail cutters.
7) Stripping knife.

Bernese are not a difficult breed to keep tidy and if you show regularly the amount of grooming that entails is sufficient to keep the coat in order. If you only have a pet a good brush and comb twice a week paying particular attention to ears and feathering is enough. Preparation for showing is covered in Chapter 8.

IN CONCLUSION

I have tried in this section to suggest a way in which a Bernese puppy can be reared to ensure he develops into a healthy and well-adjusted adult. One must always remember that he is only a puppy and like a human baby needs sufficient exercise of mind and body, plenty of good food, sleep and affection in order to grow up into a well adjusted dog that is an integral part of the family.

Training

At birth a Bernese only weighs about 1–1½ lbs (454 g) which is not very big considering within 18 months it will weigh between six to eight stones and possibly even more as it reaches maturity at between two to four years of age. With a dog of this size it is important that the owner should be fully in control at all times. To train a Bernese properly he needs to combine know-how with a certain amount of common sense. Training should start at eight weeks, or when you first collect the puppy.

Before going into detail I feel that a few general remarks on training and dog behaviour would not come amiss for it must be remembered that dogs learn by using their natural instincts, which are defined as an 'innate driving force', meaning untrained behavioural patterns. A sensible trainer will capitalise on these instincts and incorporate them into the way the lesson is taught.

Dogs do not understand what is said to them for they are not anthropomorphic but they do understand sounds and can be trained to respond to consistent commands. They cannot reason as we humans do although they usually have some intelligence, which varies with the individual, so some cotton on to what is wanted much more quickly than others.

One must realise that dogs are pack animals in the wild with one outright leader and a definite descending pecking order. When dogs become domesticated the owner replaces the pack leader and as each new dog joins, or puppies grow up, they learn to take their places in relationship to the others, not always in order of age either for position is dependent on personality. If there is only the one dog in the household then it must be able to meet other dogs as well as people for contacts with both canines and humans are equally important to a dog's balanced development.

It is worth remembering that two dogs form a pack and it is then that the old instincts rise to the fore such as chasing and hunting. For example, rarely does one dog worry sheep on his own, the damage is usually done when two get together and go off hunting in unison. It should also be remembered that herding dogs are the worst offenders if left to their own devices.

Dogs mostly fall into two categories for training, those that need gentle handling that are called 'soft' and those that need a firm hand that are known as 'hard' dogs. Both cause difficulties but of the two I would rather have an animal in the first group than the second. Bernese Mountain Dogs are fairly easy to train, although they can be very stubborn on occasions, which can lead to quite a battle of wills. These the handler **must** win if he is to gain the dog's respect. Bernese do not take kindly to being shouted at and either sulk or collapse altogether, which rather defeats the object. If it is found necessary to use physical correction the most effective punishment is to hold the dog firmly by the loose skin on either side of the neck and shake him, staring him full in the face and using your deepest voice to tell him of your displeasure. Short of using a riding crop, which is quite unnecessary, except to stop a fight, there is little point in hitting the dog for you will do more damage to your hand than to your dog. Some Bernese may actively object to correction and snarl their disapproval, in which case the worst thing an owner can do is back off, one must go forward and for heaven's sake do not show fear, for the smell of it tells the dog you are frightened of him and encourages him in his defiance. He is probably trying it on like a child seeing how far he can go before he gets a clip round the ear.

Bernese Mountain Dogs are not usually nasty, their kindly temperament is one of the attributes of the breed, but having said that they are big powerful dogs and youngsters will always test the water as the saying goes just to see whether you really mean what you say. In most cases the trainer will get the best results by the use of praise with voice and hands to show the dog that he is pleased with him. Like humans, dogs lap up praise and a Bernese dog's main aim in life is to please his boss. Each owner must know the character of his dog and how to make contact with him to gain the best result, and praise or correction must be instantaneous in response to the dog's action, because a dog can only associate immediate cause and effect. It is as bad to under-praise as over-praise, for in the first instance the dog is never sure whether he has done the exercise correctly or not. Do not shout at a dog in training, or confuse it by giving a multitude of commands all at once. They have very acute hearing but, like a child, can close their ears if they so choose. This happens especially if the handler gets nervous in competition work. Orders need to be clear and audible to the dog and of one syllable if possible.

HOUSE TRAINING

Firstly let us have a look at the question of house training. If you have got a summer puppy the task will be that much less as it is easier to encourage the right habits when the weather is pleasant than when it is wet and cold.

People who have 'Rase' dogs always say that they have very little trouble getting their puppies to be clean. This is because from about the age of three weeks (although all my puppies are reared in the house) I feed outside, weather permitting, so that they then relieve themselves outdoors after eating. This becomes a habit for the puppies and saves an awful lot of unnecessary clearing up. Dogs are normally clean in their habits and even in the first couple of weeks of their life when blind in the nest they move away to make their puddles, which is why it is better not to cover the whole area of the whelping box with Vetbed or whatever but to leave a newspaper area that can be used as a toilet. If the weather is bad enough to feed indoors do put the dishes onto newspaper so that the puppies can relieve themselves on that instead of the floor.

The new owner's attitude to housetraining is all important and for sensible people there is very little hassle, if one remembers that puppies are only babies with very small bladders so they need to relieve themselves at very regular intervals. They must be put out immediately after meals (if not fed outside), upon waking up, after a play and any number of times in between. They will probably learn to perform to order (to any phrase one likes to institute) in their favourite spot in the garden

Feeding time.

because dogs are very much creatures of habit. The droppings can then be collected up and buried to rot down, or it is possible to buy a chemical dog loo, which is fine if there are only one or two dogs performing but any more that that and it is too much to expect it to function properly so a pit then needs to be dug.

I said the puppy should be 'put out' to relieve himself but it is not really very intelligent to let him out by himself unless the garden is properly fenced in. In the beginning therefore he must be taken out and encouraged to perform, then as he gets older he can be put into a moveable puppy pen or allowed out into the garden on his own with the house door open. Pens can be bought direct from the manufacturers or one can be constructed at home from chain link fencing, but it must be strong enough to take the considerable weight of a full grown dog. If using a pen it is worth remembering that puppies, particularly Bernese, become overheated if left in the sun with no shade or water, or catch a cold if left out on damp grass, so constant supervision is necessary.

Until the puppy knows the reason why he is going outside the owner must go with him otherwise he will sit on the step and come straight back in and puddle (or worse) on the carpet, which will be your fault and not his. It is cruel to rub his nose in it, a lot of praise when he does get it right is much more likely to achieve the required result and if you actually catch him performing in the house you can grab him by the scruff of the neck and remove him outside using your voice to good effect. You must not shout, swear or cuff your puppy if you come across a pile in the wrong place as a dog does not reason as we do and he will not know why you are mad with him over something that happened some time previously.

A puppy will be able to be clean during the day much more easily than going through the night so he needs to be confined at first to somewhere like the kitchen. The floor can be covered with newspaper which is renewed when soiled and as the puppy grows older the newspaper can be put near the door. By about 12 weeks old the puppy should be clean during the day providing he can have a clear access to the garden, but he will be four to five months old before he can last all night, however a lot depends on how early the owner goes to bed and how late he gets up. A young Bernese eats enormously and often so that he has a large intake of food to process and this means he will relieve himself of a motion as many as four times a day and make a great many more puddles. House training takes time but with a sensible attitude most owners pass through this stage with a minimum of aggravation.

LEAD TRAINING

It is a good idea to get your puppy used to a collar and lead as soon as possible. He can not go out of the garden until he has had his injections, but you can start getting him used to a collar and lead around the house and garden before then. Puppies react differently one to another and here patience and tact are necessary. Some take to it with a minimum of fuss but others react like a young colt restrained for the first time, rearing up, dashing forward and digging their feet in, or sitting down and refusing to move. I do not keep collars on my dogs because they are show dogs and a collar spoils their neck ruff but mine do not go out unless they are supervised and then I use a ring or show lead.

Dogs are required by law to wear a collar when loose and it should have a disc attached with your name and telephone number on it in case the dog gets lost. If the oft-discussed proposals for ear tattoos or pellets in the neck become law then collars will no longer be necessary to identify a lost dog in future. When lead training puppies I use a leather ring lead because it is light. I encourage the pup to move forward with lots of praise and if I encounter opposition I keep going gently. It does not take long for the pup to register the fact that it is more comfortable to walk on than rebel, or if the sight of the lead is a preliminary to a walk or a ride in the car it does not take long either for that penny to drop. If you do use a collar remember to let it out as the puppy grows. To be a comfortable fit you must be able to insert two fingers in between the collar and the neck. The puppy will soon forget he is wearing a collar, even if in the early stages he does try to scratch it off.

When I have a litter that is similarly marked I sometimes use a coloured collar to distinguish one chosen puppy from another so I keep an assortment for this purpose, but unless you are intending to breed often, this is not really viable. However, as stated, I usually prefer to use a leather ring lead and although these can also be obtained in nylon or rope, the two latter can cut into your hand if the dog, especially when older and stronger, makes a sudden lunge.

BASIC OBEDIENCE

If one is to have a manageable dog a certain amount of basic obedience must be instilled in the early days before he gets too big and boisterous to handle properly. He should have been taught to respond to 'sit', 'stay', 'recall', 'down' and 'heel' commands by the time he is four to five months old. These orders are the very fabric of any training and even if you do not intend to do obedience or agility competitions the dog must be trained to sit, stay and come when told. Such a level of obedience may even save his life.

I cannot understand people with an untrained or badly behaved dog if they have had the animal right from a puppy. Even if you cannot or do not know how to get the obedience necessary from your Bernese there are training clubs in most towns where dog and owner can train together. Of course it is another story if you come into the ownership of your Bernese at a much later age, through rescue or some similar scheme, when perhaps already formed habits can never be completely eradicated.

To teach an animal anything requires patience and the maxim 'little and often' should be your guide. Five minutes four times a day is better than twenty minutes at one go, for you will bore the socks off your Bernese if you go on too long. Any training should be in an atmosphere of fun and needs to end on a high note, preferably when the dog has done the right thing and received the statutory praise. It is very important to let the dog know when he has done right and equally when he has done wrong and people who are too embarrassed to praise their dog in public end up with a very puzzled pupil. It is absolutely fundamental that correction is applied the moment the offence is committed.

Remember that punishment as with praise must be immediate and of sufficient severity to stop the 'crime' without causing suffering. Afterwards something should be immediately instituted so that the dog can be rewarded for his reaction so that training finishes on a high note. If there is any doubt that the dog has misunderstood the order rather than deliberately disobeyed do not correct him, rather ignore the behaviour or start all over again with the exercise. Remember also to always finish at a good point where the dog is praised so that he carries over the well-being to the next time.

SIT

To teach a puppy to sit gently back him up to a wall, talking to him all the time, and holding his chin with the left hand press down on the hind quarters with the right, simultaneously lifting the chin and giving the

A puppy will soon learn to sit.

command 'sit' in a firm voice, then make a fuss of him when his rump goes down. With the wall at his back he cannot move off and has no alternative but to sit. Leave him there a second or two praising him with your voice and then let him get up; before too long the word and pressure on the dog's rear end will achieve the same result without the use of a wall. This exercise can be started as early as eight weeks as long as you make the lesson short and sweet and again little and often until the penny drops. In training the tone of voice is very important and voice sounds for orders and release at the end of the exercise should be completely different so that the dog knows he is free to move.

STAY

An order to sit is often followed by the command 'stay' and this is best taught on a long lead so that if he does move away at least he will not go far. Put the dog into the 'sit' position and give the command 'stay', making a downward motion with the right hand in front of his nose. Make a fuss of the dog when he complies, wait a couple of seconds and then give the command for the release. It does not matter which word is used as long as you always use the same one, for it is not the word the dog understands but the sound association. The next time give both the command and hand signal and take a sideways step away, wait a second before returning to make a fuss of him. If he has not stayed but tried to follow, put him back and try again, but at this stage the handler must always go to the dog, never the other way round. When you can take three or four steps to the side without being followed you can then move to the front of the dog, wait, then return to him going round the back and he should stay until you give the command for release. If a youngster will not stay deepen your voice and bump him down, but if you think that the reason he has not complied with the order is because he is afraid he is going to be left behind or that something else is frightening him, then a much more reassuring approach is required. If he sees you do not go far from him and the exercise is repeated often enough the fear will subside.

Once learnt, if a command is given it must be obeyed and you must see that it is, even if it requires physical handling to achieve, but do make sure that he understands the order as against just being naughty. When you can leave the dog at the sit, move away with your back to him and return walking round behind while he remains steady then you can progress to leaving the dog while you go out of sight.

THE RECALL

The 'recall' is from the 'sit' 'stay' position and should only be attempted when the youngster is steady to that order, otherwise again you stand a chance of muddling him. Go away from the dog in a straight line, still keeping contact with the lead. Turn and face him and depending on the progress so far in the exercise wait for a variable length of time before calling him to you. He should sit in front of you, then give the command 'heel' and using the lead guide him round your legs to the lefthand side. Dogs are always worked on the left, though whether this habit stems from most people being righthanded and carrying their weapons on their right in the old days I do not know.

Some novice owners make the mistake of getting irate when they call their puppy and he runs away and plays about, staying just out of reach until he tires of the game when he comes trotting back tail wagging. If he then gets clouted by the irate owner, he associates the owner's displeasure with his return not with his running away in the first place. If he believes he is going to be punished for returning he will make sure that the owner does not get a second chance. There should not be much trouble in getting a Bernese to return to you if he knows that it means a titbit or something pleasurable but NEVER, NEVER call a dog to you and then hit it, for there is no surer way of destroying your dog's confidence. Again, many inexperienced owners make a rod for their own back because the only time they call their dog up is when he is free and on a walk and it is time to go home. If your Bernese is on to a good smell he may not want to come at that moment especially if he knows that his period of freedom is about to come to an abrupt end. Problems can be avoided if the owner calls the dog at varying times during the walk to make a fuss of him, or to give him a titbit, pop him on his lead for a minute or two and then let him go again so that the dog associates the recall with something pleasurable. If you cannot get your dog to come back you have a problem, which perhaps can be solved with the use of a friend's trained dog who will return or, alternatively, use one of the extending Flexi Leads but that should not be necessary with a Bernese who usually stays close enough to be within easy reach.

Bernese puppies should be trained to be steady to all other animals.

DOWN

The 'down' or 'lie' is an easier exercise to teach and again needs to be started on the lead. The dog will naturally adopt this stance rather than the 'sit' but do be careful not to use the phrase 'sit down' for this will only muddle him as the phrase contains two quite separate commands. Nor should you use the word 'down' to stop dogs jumping up, a better choice is 'off'. If you progress to obedience competition work and your dog is muddled then unnecessary points will be lost.

Put the dog in the 'sit' position place your left hand to exert pressure in the scruff of the neck and pull down on the lead with the right hand giving the order 'down' 'stay', or you can give the command and pull both feet out in front of the dog effecting the necessary collapse. When you get the dog to lie down without having to use both your hands, which should not be long, use the downward hand motion described in the 'stay' exercise, palm towards the dog.

HEEL

It is important that a big dog like a Bernese walks properly on the lead and does not pull. Bernese dogs are rather good at making sudden lunges if they spot a bitch, so owners ought to be prepared for this manoeuvre. The leather ring lead is ideal for teaching 'heel' work because it is light and does not cut or burn the fingers, but if you take on a dog that pulls, and Bernese are very powerful, it is probably worth buying a 'Halti'. As the name implies it is similar to a horse's halter, or head collar, and has been perfected by Dr. Roger Mogford, a canine psychologist. I believe it is quite effective although I have not tried it myself. The more traditional form of correction is a choke chain but in order to be effective it must be put on in the right way so that the chain runs back freely when pressure is released.

To teach 'heel' work, put the dog in a 'sit' position on the lead, remembering he should be on your lefthand side, and make sure that the lead is long enough to have some spare to play with. On the command 'heel' both handler and dog should move off together at a normal walk, the dog's nose at your knee and lead slack. In the beginning of course the untrained dog is likely to bound forward dragging his handler after him (which is where a long lead helps) or to hang back behind him. If the handler has his left hand, knuckles uppermost, halfway along the lead and the slack gathered into the right hand with the whole of that hand firmly in view he is in the best position to stop the rush forward, or to encourage the hanger-back by a jerk on the lead. If this has no effect use a stronger jerk and the command 'heel'.

With a headstrong dog a rolled up newspaper does not hurt the dog but does make a satisfactory sound if banged on the leg or even the dog's nose. Another way is to put the dog between yourself and a hedge or wall. With the hanger-back lots of praise and encouragement is necessary to achieve the desired position. Some dogs take a lot longer than others and one just has to persevere. Always be consistent and although it may mean one arm longer than the other in the early days, to have a dog, particularly one the size of a Bernese Mountain Dog who walks properly on the lead, is well worth all the hassle needed to achieve it.

'Heel' work is very boring and must not be done for too long. It is worth remembering too, that a big dog that gets plenty of free exercise is much more likely to walk properly on the lead when the time comes. If your dog has to be exercised under control it is worth investing in a Flexy Lead which can be played out by the handler rather like those tape measures. These are also a Godsend if your dog is not too good at coming back when free, but this would not apply to a Bernese except in very exceptional circumstances.

RETRIEVING

Some Bernese will carry objects with no trouble at all but others are not interested in the slightest. With the latter a modicum of patience is required to try and discover an object that they will recover and that sometimes takes time.

When teaching the retrieve, never snatch the object from the dogs mouth but teach it the command 'dead' or something similar, so that it can be taken gently from the mouth. It is a very bad practice to chase a dog or play pulling games with any dogs (except maybe terriers who do it naturally) so do not let the children tug at objects in the Bernese's mouth because that only makes the animal hang on tighter. If your dog will pick up but not return to you use one of those extending Flexi Leads so you can reel him in. Another command that is very useful is 'hold', to teach the dog to continue to carry until asked to give up the object, as one is not always in a position to stoop down and pick it up off the ground.

Do remember that youngsters of any breed get very easily bored and it

Some items need more than one to retrieve.

is by far the best policy to train little and often rather than in concentrated sessions, so a few minutes twice or three times a day is better than twenty minutes or half an hour at one time. Training needs to be consistent, a little each day is needed and not just once a week.

NOISE AND BUSTLE

Young Bernese need to acclimatise to people en masse, whether they are going to be shown and/or worked. For a young puppy (or older youngster) to go out into the wide world unused to present day hustle and bustle, in and out of the home, is very unkind and quite unnecessary. The best way of combating this problem is to rear the litter indoors or, if kept outside, to bring the pups indoors every day so that they become used to commonplace sounds like the TV, Hoover, washing machine, telephone and people coming and going. Once the pup has had his injections he can be taken, for short periods, into areas where there are numbers of people. A small country town is ideal for this purpose with the traffic, noise and smells as well as shoppers and pavements to negotiate. A Point to Point where one's car is handy alongside the course is also a very useful training ground because the pup can then be put back into the car or tied alongside it when he gets tired. Of course it goes without saying that no dog should be left in a car on a hot day, even with the windows open, because the heat on the metal turns it into an oven and the dog is literally cooked to death, which does happen from time to time through thoughtless owners.

TRAINING CLUB

Once the dog reaches the age of four months it is worth attending a local training club of some sort, whether it be for show and/or obedience. For it ensures your dog meets others and learns to interact in a working atmosphere. After all it is no good saying (as so many people do) 'oh he never behaves like that at home.'

No, he does not, because he has not the temptations that there are when in company in the artificial set up at home with no distractions to bother him.

JUMPING

Before ending this general introduction to training I ought to mention the Bernese addiction to jumping, Porky (Rase Nooky Bear) for example can take a five barred gate from a standing start, and with higher fences manages to climb them and jump down with no trouble! Being able to clear obstacles is a very useful accomplishment, especially if when out for exercise the only alternative to a long walk round is to negotiate a stile.

If you want to do agility work, which necessitates clearing various jumps on the course, your dog must be able to perform. To teach a Bernese Mountain Dog to jump start with a low obstacle with the dog on

A Bernese jumping while carrying a dummy.

a lead. Giving the command 'over' the handler runs round the side and encourages the dog to clear the pole. If the penny does not drop the handler can encourage the dog by jumping it themselves. Another method is to use a narrow passage with two people one at each end and the jump in the centre, when the dog is encouraged by food or petting to travel from one to the other. Do be careful, though that your Bernese does not jar himself on landing for they can become lame very easily. It is, therefore, advisable to wait until the dog is over a year old to teach this activity, but one has the added bonus with this breed that they are naturally agile and for big dogs, very light on their feet.

— 6 —
Management of the Adult Dog

A healthy dog is a happy dog and this condition can be seen in the shiny state of the coat, loose skin, brightness of the eye and general look of well-being. In a Bernese it is not something that can be obtained externally, it has to come from inside the dog by correct feeding, training and exercise plus, of course, affection. The Bernese Mountain Dog by virtue of his ancestry is a fairly hardy canine specimen, coming from the cold of the Swiss Alps they have a natural penchant for snow and prefer cold weather to hot, often being happier kennelled outside than in the modern over-heated houses that many people seem to prefer these days. Of course they do need plenty of warmth as puppies in the nest.

Without doubt the most common disease which affects canines and humans alike is cancer in all its many forms. This condition causes the highest number of premature deaths in Bernese Mountain Dogs, as in many other breeds, and despite the sterling work being done in Cambridge by Camvet and in Newmarket by the Small Animal Trust cures are still rare for most forms.

ACCIDENTS

In discussing ailments it is important to differentiate between illness and accidents for the latter can happen at any time, usually when you least expect them and at the most inconvenient time. The Berneses' thick coat protects them from the weather, or from attack by other dogs, but does not help if the dog is injured for any reason. Many people keep handy a first aid box specially for their dogs, taking it with them to shows. If you do not keep a box then you should have to hand things like cotton wool, disinfectant, thermometer, scissors, sulphanilamide puffer for cuts, tube of eye ointment and bottle of Optrex. Canker powder, flea spray, shampoo, worming pills and liquid paraffin are also useful additions on the veterinary list which are best obtained from either your vet or pet shop. If you are not happy about your dog for any reason you should consult your vet as soon as possible rather than waste money trying cures (that usually do not work) suggested by well meaning people . Vets are, of course, very busy people and get little enough time with their families anyway, so if you have a problem try to go to the surgery at the times stated and do not leave matters so that you have to ring up on a Sunday evening. Most vets prefer to be called upon sooner rather than later for there is more chance of the trouble responding to treatment if dealt with early.

FEEDING

To grow at the speed that a Bernese does requires sufficient of the right type of food. It is important for the owners to realise that as a puppy develops in both mind and body at an alarming rate the food intake must be increased in quantity to compensate for this. It is my considered opinion that conditions such as torsion (twisted gut) could probably be avoided by feeding two or three smaller meals rather than one large one a day, and in fact I do this even when my puppies are grown up, in order to avoid overloading a dog's stomach. Torsion can kill a dog very quickly as some people have found out to their cost. Also exercise should be taken **before** food not after, as this is another contributory factor. Good bone is a fundamental requirement and the only way of getting it is by feeding good food. The full g own Bernese Mountain Dog weighs seven to nine stone, or more, and must have the frame necessary to carry this. I have not found them to be scavengers and they will usually clean the plate before the proverbial 'knife' can be uttered, but if you do have one that for some reason (post operative lassitude for example) is being a bit picky, some cheese grated up or a tablespoon of cider vinegar on the top of its food may do the trick.

On arrival at his new home the puppy is usually on four feeds a day and I tend to keep to those four for as long as the puppy seems to need them. It is not good to get a puppy too fat but with all the activity of which they partake this extra weight is usually taken care of naturally. But as an adult is not so active we need to take care that they do not become overweight. A Bernese does better if he eats his food with the dish on top of a bucket as he does not have so far to go down to the food an action which can damage their shoulders. The breed tends to grow upwards for the first two years and then do what we call 'body up' or mature for another two not reaching full maturity in the case of the dogs until the age of four or five. Bitches usually mature earlier and often have their first litter around the age of two which helps to 'finish' them earlier in the maturity stakes. However, it is worth remembering that individual dogs do vary in food intake and some need more than others and owners do have to look at their dog and recognise the difference between 'need' and 'greed'. Of course, a dog being used regularly for stud or a bitch in whelp or feeding a litter will need extra food as does a dog being used for work in any way.

I feed my adult dogs three times a day at breakfast, at 6pm. and a movable feast somewhere around 11 pm to 1 am. Breakfast is a complete food with milk and probably a small amount of dried or tinned meat added if there is none in the mixture. The 6 pm meal is usually tinned or butchers meat, fish, tripe, brawn, chubb or scrambled egg with biscuit meal added. I never feed uncooked tripe or meat. The biscuit meal is wheatmeal for example 'Laughing Dog' and is usually alternated with mixer of the Pedigree Chum or Omega variety. The late evening meal varies between a dried, complete extruded pellet like 'Omega', 'Go Dog' or 'Oko', which sometimes has Oxo or gravy poured over it and I usually add a grating of cheese or any other left-overs from our own meals. I normally feed a third meat to two-thirds biscuit or mixer and here again a common mistake of the novice is to reverse the amounts giving far too much protein. Many people feed only 'complete' foods of which there are many good ones on the market, Wilsons or Valumix to mention two, and they no doubt are very convenient, time-saving and all the rest, but I feel scarcely likely to raise much enthusiasm in the dog's gastric juices. Again, as mentioned previously some people do not feed milk which always leaves me with my mouth open, for unless your dog has an allergy to it I cannot imagine why. But I would counsel care and only use goats' or cows' milk and not use calf or lamb starter for they are treated with various additives that might prove harmful to a dog long term. In conjunction with a number of well-known dog people I am of the opinion that many dogs would benefit from a return to the good old fashioned way of feeding leaving the scientific concoctions for the experimental institutions.

No dog can do justice to his food if his teeth are faulty and like children, dogs need to have good strong white teeth. One way of maintaining good teeth is to give a big marrow bone, but do make sure that it is not splinterable, nor raw pork which is very conducive to worms. Of course, cooked rabbit, chicken or chopped bones should never be given as these can splinter in their stomach and can penetrate the intestine with dire consequences.

Dogs do not suffer from dental problems as we humans do who get food lodged into and around the crevices, but where we are similar is that both dogs and humans can suffer with tartar deposits on teeth. This is aggravated by eating too much soft food. Tartar can easily be removed by the vet and this should be regularly carried out for if allowed to collect it will not only produce bad breath but inflammation of the gums (gingivitis) and a premature loss of dentition.

GROOMING

Turning out a dog for the show ring needs a little more attention than is necessary for a pet but good condition depends on the correct food being given. If you feed him right then the healthy shiny coat condition comes from within and it can only be acquired this way. Grooming, of course, is important and with a breed like the Bernese we are lucky that we do not have to put in the hours of preparation prior to a show that, for example, the Afghan people do. But there are certain things that need doing and for this purpose you will of course need a brush and comb, scissors, trimming shears (scissors with a serrated edge) stripping knife and a chamois leather or hand glove, kept together for convenience. I use a zip pouch which started life as a soft pencil case which is always left in the showbag. There are dozens of accoutrements that you can buy, combs of various tooth thicknesses, rakes and scissors of all shapes and sizes but fortunately for the pocket Bernese do not need many tools and are shown naturally, although there are tidying bits to be done. If you are not intending to show, a good brushing and combing each day is sufficient.

Bernese like other dogs lose their coats in Spring and Autumn and a bitch also after having had a litter. Grooming is best done outside to prevent the flying hairs finding their way into food, bed, bath, etc. as being a long haired breed they do get rid of quite an amount, as our light bedroom carpet proved (we should have known better but it was a gift and you know what is said about gift horses!). Bernese need to have tidy cat-like feet, and to get these the untidy wisps in between the toes need to be thinned with shears starting from the bottom upwards. The whole foot is then trimmed round with ordinary scissors not forgetting the underneath fur. The ears too need to be neat and the old hair can be pulled out with finger or thumb or a stripping knife. The hocks can look very untidy if the hair grows unevenly here and again the best way to tackle these is to use thinning shears working from the bottom up. The thinning shears are serrated so that they do not leave a ridge as do ordinary scissors.

I do not bath the dogs I own very often for like the comic song 'too much bathing weakens you'. It is an established fact that bathing too often removes the coat's natural oils which are needed for protection against the winter's cold and rain. I do bath for Crufts and also occasionally during the summer if the coat looks dusty or at other times for medical or social reasons. For show preparation one can often get away with washing the dog's white feet and shirt front only, or alternatively using a dry shampoo preparation. The medical reasons could be to combat a flea or mite plague which can be worse in some years than in others producing scurfy or flaky skin, or some skin conditions such as mange or eczema which requires a special veterinary shampoo. Social reasons cover the extraordinary pleasure Bernese Mountain Dogs get from rolling in pungent fox or other equally obnoxious odours, including jumping into stagnant water and proceeding to shake the surplus all over you. Bathing Bernese, because of their size, is not an easy task so unless there are two hefty people around to lift the dog into the bath my advice would be to bath outside using a hosepipe. If you can fix the pipe to a mixer tap so that the water is warm, all the better. I usually use a Vetzyme shampoo (unless I have to use a special medical one) which in addition to getting the coat clean has a pleasant smell. Do not get soap in the dog's eyes, for like us he does not appreciate it and do make sure the soap is well rinsed out afterwards with plenty of clean warm water.

EXERCISE

Correct exercise also comes into management and I would like to stress that Bernese do need a daily free run, a trot around the block on a lead is not enough particularly for a boisterous youngster, but they do not require five miles a day. Road walking is useful combined with a free run as it helps to build up muscles. My dogs have a large pen in which they can run free and I also have a large enclosed garden, but I know everyone is not so lucky. However, I do also try to get them up to the woods every day and their internal clocks tell them when it is the usual time to go if I am engrossed in what I am doing.

Bernese do not want much exercise. Mine cover about half the distance of my Flat Coats when out together, but all dogs need a free run daily unless there is a fenced area at home where they can run free in which case the daily run can be cut to every other day if time is pressing. If you can exercise in woods or moors or on the seashore the dog will use his nose effectively in investigating the interesting smells. Steadiness to stock can be taught with the dog on a lead and any tendency to set off in pursuit firmly discouraged.

Bernese Mountain Dogs usually love water and will swim easily, learning to retrieve from water almost in passing, with most it is not getting them in but keeping them out that is the problem, especially if you are going somewhere in a hurry when a dripping Bernese is not the ideal companion. If your dog is not over keen on water he will probably go in alongside another dog, but tread carefully and **never** throw or push a dog into water, you could put him off water for life by such a silly action. Encourage your dog to get into shallow water first, maybe even going in yourself (so I would not try this in the middle of winter) for a paddle. A stream is the best starting point and the dog is encouraged to go to a deeper part as he gains confidence. If a suitable stream is not available, a pond, lake or the sea would do instead just so long as the bottom does not suddenly shelve away and the dog finds there is nothing under his feet.

Teaching the dog to retrieve from water is best done with a canvas dummy, although a plastic washing up bottle filled with sand would serve, and preferably another dog standing by to rescue the dummy if there is a current or your dog shows no interest. If another dog is not available tie a light nylon cord to the dummy but do remember to hang on to the other end when you throw it into the water. A foot or two away is sufficient to start off, slowly increasing the distance if no obstacles are encountered en route.

A well turned out dog in the peak of condition is the best advertisement one could have proving to all and sundry that you are able to 'manage' your stock to the best advantage.

INJECTIONS

As a puppy your dog will have been inoculated against distemper, hepatitis, leptospirosis and parvovirus. The dog should have an annual booster to ensure its immunity to these fatal diseases is maintained.

WORMING

Round worms occur in puppies and adults and all youngsters should be treated on the assumption that they are infected. There are many proprietary treatments on the market these days and if the manufacturer's directions are followed no real difficulty should be encountered.

Although it eats well a badly infected puppy will waste and even die if some cure is not quickly obtained. The stomach becomes abnormally large whilst the rest of the animal wastes to grotesque thinness. Rickets, enteritis and even death can result from neglect. At any time during its life a dog can become infected with round or tape worms and worming should be a routine six monthly precaution. Also any symptoms, such as bad breath, dragging of the bottom, loss of weight, staring, rough coat, biting the back or hindquarters, or evidence in the motions should be acted on immediately.

Certain dogs have a habit of picking up the droppings of other animals and this should be prevented especially on sheep land. The flea can be a source of infestation which is another reason for keeping the dog free from this parasite.

KENNELING/SLEEPING QUARTERS

See section in Chapter 5.

GENERAL HEALTH

In the following pages I have tried to cover common and not so common conditions that can be met with during a dog's lifetime. Obviously one dog will only suffer from a certain percentage of problems, but the longer you are in dogs the more problems you will come across and we never stop learning. A dog in the peak of fitness has a loose skin and one should be able to pick up a handful and feel the ripple of the muscles underneath. Other signs are bright eyes with no discharge in the corners, ears that are dry and clean with no sign of either wet (causing the ear to crackle) or dry canker. In the mouth breath should be odourless with pink gums and strong white teeth. In male dogs the rectum should not be inflamed nor should there be any discharge from the penis or vulva in a bitch.

Abscesses

Bites or grass seeds can cause abscesses which are inflamed septic areas of the skin that are very painful due to bacterial infection. They are full of pus and swell until they burst after which healing occurs. The best treatment is to bathe in very hot water and Dettol, both before and after bursting, but if that does not happen the vet may have to lance it and treat with antibiotics.

Anaemia
Can be caused in a number of ways but basically is a condition of the blood giving a reduced red blood cell count. It is shown by very pale gums and eye membranes and results in lack of energy and appetite, sometimes with laboured breathing. Diagnosis can be difficult but treatment is usually iron tablets and liver added to the diet.

Anal Glands
These are pear shaped sacs situated one each side of the tail or anus. When the dog defaecates they should empty, at the same time providing scent to mark the soiling area in the form of dark brown secretions. If these openings to the sacs become blocked they swell and become very painful and if not squeezed out can form abscesses. I would not advise you to try emptying these glands yourself for they are very deep seated and can cause great pain, rather take the dog to a vet who will do the job in a few seconds with little discomfort to the dog. Bernese do not often suffer from overfull anal glands but they can do so and the symptoms are continual nagging or licking at the tail region, dragging themselves along the ground or even chasing their tail. The condition can be exacerbated by too much sloppy food with overmuch protein and will be improved by using food containing more bulk so that the faeces are firm instead of sloppy.

Bad Breath
The most usual cause of bad breath, or halitosis, is bad teeth. If the dog has been eating something nasty his breath will be temporarily affected, for example if other animals' droppings have been consumed, notably cat and horse, though fish meal is awful too. The latter can be neutralised by Amplex tablets, while a visit to the vet, to perhaps have the teeth scaled and bad ones removed, will help the former condition. In older dogs bad breath can be a sign of something more serious such as liver or kidney diseases, or may just be indicative of worms.

Bites
The most frequent cause of bites are those inflicted in a fight but Bernese (at least the English bred ones) are not quarrelsome dogs and unless you have to cope with kennel jealousy you will probably not have to meet these at all. If you do, depending on the severity of the wound, clip away the hair and wash thoroughly in warm water and disinfectant or salt and puff in some sulphanilamide powder. If the wound is more serious it may mean a trip to the vet for an antibiotic jab in addition. Bites from cats can be nasty and often develop into abscesses while snake bites (adders) need veterinary treatment at once, if possible the vet coming to the dog as movement will cause the poison to spread and Bernese are too big to be

carried. If the bite is on the leg put a tourniquet above the wound but remember to release it every 10 minutes for a while. Sucking out the poison is no help but the wound can be cleaned with a soapy solution.

Bowel Inflammation
Manifested by an extended abdomen and an insatiable thirst this condition is often caused by sharp chicken, rabbit or chop bones which should never be given to a dog. They can sometimes be found where people have picnicked and left litter behind to be rooted over by a scavenging dog. Cold, too, can cause a bowel infection as can worm infestation or bacterial infection and the dog can suffer from diarrhoea or constipation as a direct result.

Burns and Scalds
With luck you will never have to deal with either of these conditions but one never knows. Burns are most likely to occur if your dog sits too close to the fire, the electric variety being worse. Fortunately the smell of burning coat permeates the air before the skin is affected and it is therefore possible to move the dog sharply from the heat. Bernese are not too prone to doing this as they are not the type to want to lie in front of the fire as they get too hot, but there is always the possibility of being caught in a house fire, for example. The affected part should be doused in cold water for a long time and gently dried. Within a day or so blisters appear and sometimes break into nasty open wounds which need treating as for abscesses.

Scalds come from boiling water or boiling fat being upset and can cause nasty wounds as the dog's coat tends to hold the heat thus increasing the seriousness of the injury. When scalding is from fat, wipe as much off the coat as possible and again douse in water. One of the main problems with both burns and scalds is the shock factor and in each case the animal needs to be kept warm and veterinary expertise obtained as soon as possible.

Be on your guard if your dog is a fire lover in case of burning.

Canker

Known to the veterinary profession as Otitis this is the blanket name given by the layman for troubles in ears. Noticeable because of the unpleasant smell, excessive scratching and/or head shaking, the head can also be held down on the painful side. Canker can be caused by a grass seed or other foreign body in the ear canal but is more usually attributed to ear mites or a fungus infection. Often appearing in the form of wet canker, the ear is hot and painful and crackles to the touch producing a waxy dark reddish deposit. To treat canker, gently clean out the affected ear with a cotton wool wedge. The ones for babies little places are ideal, then opening the ear flap as wide as you can, drop some powder from a teaspoon as deep as possible, pull the flap over the ear and gently massage the base of it to spread the powder within. Although there are a number of branded products for treatment of canker on the market I have found this old recipe to be the best of all:

	1 part iodoform
110 grams.	2 parts zinc oxide
	8 parts boracic powder or boric acid capsules.

Your chemist should be able to make this up for you even if you live in a large town for my last lot was dispensed by Boots which is, I am sure, the largest chemists chain. Parasitic canker due to lice or ear mites can usually be picked up from cats and can just be seen with the naked eye. They need to be killed before the eggs can be laid and the fumes of the iodoform will do this if the ear flap is held down long enough for them to permeate. To prevent canker, do inspect your Bernese's ears regularly and see that the hair on the underneath of the ear flap is combed out. Any excess hair in these places should be clipped out but do be gentle as it can be tender, but failure to allow the air to circulate is one of the main causes of Otitis. Another cause can be failure to dry the dog's ears after a swim. Bernese being water dogs in the main do enjoy going into water but make sure it is not retained in the ear canal afterwards. If the ear trouble is not immediately apparent it may be due to a seed from long grass being lodged in the canal. In this case veterinary help is required to remove the offending object which if deep enough may necessitate a local anaesthetic. It is better if you do not attempt to do the job yourself.

Choking

Choking to death is quite feasible if the windpipe becomes blocked. I would counsel against ever playing with a Bernese with a small ball for this reason, although the cause may be also a large piece of food, often meat, a stone or piece of bone that becomes lodged. It is obviously important to remove the offending object as soon as possible before the animal dies of asphyxia and this can sometimes be done with fingers or forceps but if you cannot see the obstruction get the dog to your vet quickly. If your dog keeps brushing his paw across his mouth or shaking his head continually it is possible that a piece of stick or bone could be wedged across the roof of the mouth or between the teeth so check to see that the mouth is free of obstructions first.

Constipation

Constipation is the name given to the difficulty in passing faeces which are hard instead of soft. This condition affects a dog as much as it affects a human and needs attention before it results in a stoppage of the bowel. It usually arises from dietary problems when not enough carbohydrates are being given or too many bones which give the faeces a hard white appearance, but can also occur when the dog is left in the house and knows he must not make a mess indoors and therefore holds it back. Bernese are also very funny about relieving themselves in unfamiliar places and will often wait till they get back home after a show to perform, which can be a very long time. If the problem is due to diet a change in the food given very often has the desired effect and brown bread and green vegetables are a useful addition here. A dose of liquid paraffin too is a good idea at about one dessertspoon per 30lbs of Bernese. Most of the well known canine brands also produce laxatives which are sold by pet shops or chemists. With an older dog, however, constipation may be due to an enlarged prostate gland which blocks the rectum and only allows the faeces to exit in a ribbon development. This obviously needs veterinary treatment as abnormal straining can lead to a hernia over a period of time.

Cuts and Bleeding

Simple cuts occur quite often and can be treated easily with warm water and disinfectant, or salt (two tablespoons to the pint) and water, finally smearing with disinfectant ointment. The dog will probably lick it and this is usual, unless the licking becomes excessive when he may have to wear a plastic collar or even a big bucket with the bottom cut out to prevent him reaching it.

Venous or arterial bleeding is a more serious problem however. The former shows as dark red blood that spreads slowly and the latter is bright red blood that spurts from the wound. The bleeding needs stopping first and here a pad of lint and cotton wool is used to cover the cut topped with a bandage or adhesive tape and you should then get the dog to a vet for stitching as soon as possible. Bad arterial bleeding may need a tourniquet but a tight bandage or even a large handkerchief would do in an emergency, applied to a pressure point as near as possible above the wound. It could be tightened by a Biro or piece of wood but remember to slacken it off every 10 minutes or so or the blood will be cut off altogether.

Cystitis

Bladder infection is often caused through a cold or stones (formed from mineral salt deposits) in the kidneys or bladder the size of which can be as large as a nut. Another cause is if a clean animal can't get out to relieve itself and won't soil inside. The bladder becomes distended and eventually the dog is unable to empty the bladder which causes inflammation. This is a condition most often found in bitches rather than males and can be observed when the dog strains to make a puddle in obvious discomfort and only pass a few drops at a time. Very often these drops of urine are bloodstained and smell strongly of ammonia. The cure in severe cases is an operation for the condition is recurring, although for a milder case citric acid should effect a cure.

Cysts

These swellings take several forms but most are painless, unless infected, when abscesses can be formed. The most common type is the interdigital cyst that occurs between the toes and that should be bathed in hot water until it bursts, then once clean, the skin of the foot should be hardened. There is a waxy substance that forms a hard protective layer over the skin if your dog suffers from tender feet but I would not recommend Friar's Balsam which is an alternative as it is so sticky. Antibiotics may help to contain the problem. Cysts contain a secretion of fluid and are often found on old animals as the sebaceous or skin swellings that can be felt under the coat. Bitches sometimes get ovarian cysts which usually require surgery to remove. In younger dogs cysts can mean the animal is short of vitamins and needs a course of tablets.

Depraved Appetite

This habit is sometimes called Coprophagy and means that the dog eats its own and other animals droppings. It is natural behaviour for a bitch to clean up after her puppies but they might then imitate her and develop the habit, which is difficult to stop if it once starts like all habits. Given the opportunity most dogs eat horse and sheep manure at sometime and will roll in cow pats and seem to treat cats faeces as a great delicacy but few eat their own faeces. The eating of manure may be due to a lack of certain vitamins in the diet, which can be gained from droppings of other creatures, or it could be due to the type of food given. Worm infestation is another cause, alternatively boredom might be the cause if the Bernese is left alone for long periods with nothing to do.

If you notice your dog has a tendency to eat faeces try and pick them up at once if at home. If out for a walk keep him away from places where other dogs have defaecated and here the command 'leave' comes in very useful. You can put pepper on piles at home but by far the best plan is to remove them as quickly as possible and thus remove the temptation.

Diarrhoea

This is a very debilitating condition and affects dogs much the same as humans when they are continually passing liquid faeces. It could be caused by a complete change of diet or by eating carrion, while in puppies it can be caused by worms, a cold or chill, dirty feeding dishes or too high a content of protein like liver in the diet. The latter is fairly easily changed and it is probably a good idea to starve the dog for 12 hours before giving any food which then contains cornflour plus water in which rice has been boiled. Hard boiled eggs, fish and rice are some foods that can be given in small quantities to restart eating. Remember always to have clean water available even if the dog is fasting. Veterinary help must be sought if the condition does not respond to treatment as given above.

Distemper

This can be a killer in puppies. It is the common name for a group of viral diseases that affect the nervous system because of secondary bacterial infection. Luckily it is not seen much these days due to vaccination but can leave after effects like paralysis or St Vitus Dance (Chorea) in bad cases which often prove fatal. Varied symptoms in the early stages such as a cough, high temperature, cold, lack of appetite and/or diarrhoea and sickness make detection difficult and the disease is very infectious, being passed to other dogs by the inhalation of contaminated air particles. It is not even necessary for your dog to be in actual contact with the sufferer to catch it either. Vets will inoculate against distemper usually from 10 to 12 weeks, in some cases earlier but then a third injection is usually necessary. Do remember to leave about four days after the final jab before taking a puppy out amongst other dogs to allow time for the immunity to work. Treatment is by antibiotics and usually involves skilful nursing over a long time. If your dog does catch distemper all affected areas such as a kennel and even the house have to be thoroughly disinfected and left open to the air and sunlight. Sometimes the condition leaves thickened pads and nose which has earned it the name 'hard-pad'.

Eclampsia

This term means a shortage of calcium in bitches suckling a litter. Often due to the fact that the dog has not received the extra calcium necessary whilst carrying the puppies, it can occur at any time in the first three weeks nursing a litter. A large number of puppies in a litter make heavy demands on their dam in the calcium intake which is present in the bitches milk. If she runs short she suffers from conditions much resembling shock and trembles and shivers, panting hard. It can be fatal for the bitch if not treated immediately, for she needs a heavy dose of calcium given by intravenous injection by your vet as quickly as possible when recovery is spectacularly rapid.

Eczema

Usually takes the form of acute inflammation of the skin causing irritation, resulting in scratching which makes the condition worse. Causes are varied, most often being due to fleas, lice or ticks to which your dog is allergic or to actual allergies themselves, but overheated blood in hot weather can be another factor, while self-inflicted skin lesions on the flank may be due to painful anal glands as that is the nearest the dog can get to the affected part.

To the layman there seems little difference between eczema and mange but of the two the latter is by far the most difficult to treat and is highly contagious while eczema can be contained more easily. Do not try patent cures yourself but get the dog to the vet for injections and a cream relevant to the specific cause. You may need to provide a collar or plastic bucket to prevent your Bernese scratching the affected part whilst it is healing.

Ectropion
This condition sometimes termed 'loose eye' is more often found in breeds such as Bassets and Bloodhounds. It is the turning out of the lower eyelid which inflames the conjunctival membrane and can be a hereditary fault, luckily not very prevalent in Bernese.

Entropion
This is a condition where the eyelids turn in either singly or jointly, rubbing the eye lashes against the eyeball giving constantly running eyes and subsequent pain and discomfort. It, too, is considered a hereditary fault and although the vet can operate affected animals should not be used for breeding. Again, luckily, not often found in Bernese more usually in some of the retriever breeds.

Eye Conditions Generally
I always wonder at owners who allow their dogs to travel with their heads out of car windows or sit too close to a blazing fire staring into the flames. In both cases it is not good for the dog and conditions such as inflammation and irritation can be caused. Yet another root trouble is sleeping in a draught or being in a place like a farm where there are dusty particles in the air. The inflammation of the inside of the eyelid known as conjunctivitis produces pus which can gum up the eyelids with discharge and could be the result of the presence of a foreign body affecting the third eyelid, which is extra protective skin found in the corner of the canine eye. Inflamed eyes will often respond to bathing in Optrex lotion or to the jelly from an opthalmic tube but the vet will need to be consulted if the condition does not clear quickly. Also see PRA.

False Pregnancy
Why some bitches suffer from this condition sometimes called Phantom Pregnancy and others do not is a question even vets can not answer. The affected bitch produces milk and behaves to all intents and purposes as if she is carrying a litter even to preparing a bed and collecting objects like soft toys, etc. which she cuddles to her. Often she has been nowhere near a dog, or if mated has not held. It occurs four to eight weeks after a heat and is usually due to a hormone imbalance. If a bitch is subject to false pregnancies she will probably go on having them, unless treated and the deficiency redressed either by injections or in the last instance by spaying the bitch.

Treatment of the condition varies but the toys, etc. should be removed and the bitch given no sympathy. Water and carbohydrates should be reduced and exercise should be increased as should the protein content of the diet to balance the cut down of biscuit and water intake, the latter two things contributing to the milk production.

I have used bitches who have produced milk in sympathy with another that has a litter, to help feed a large number of puppies with no ill effects to either foster mother or babies, so sometimes there is a bonus in false pregnancy but in the main it is an unsettling nuisance.

Fights

I loathe fights, they leave me emotionally drained and usually far more upset than the protagonists. Not that they occur very often, thank goodness, but there have been times in the past when kennel jealousy has reared its ugly head and that spells trouble.

Bernese are not usually aggressive dogs, at least not in the British Isles, but the position on the continent and in Switzerland itself is a different story for they like a more dominant male.

If your dog does get caught up in a scrap it is not such a difficult job to separate the fighters if there are two of you and each can grasp the collar of his own dog and twist pulling his fore-feet off the ground in order to make him let go of his opponent. Buckets of water are not much use for usually the contents go all over the thrower and not the dogs. A stick thrust between the teeth of the aggressor will also make him relinquish his hold but that can be difficult if you are simply trying to keep two warring dogs at arms length. Another method suggested is to fling a heavy coat over both antagonists but I have never had time to go and find one! If you are on your own and there are several dogs about remove these bystanders first before trying to sort out the main fight or you will really have a 'gang bang' on your hands. Luckily it is seldom that lasting harm is done as Bernese having such heavy coats are well protected.

Fleas

These parasites affect both humans and animals although the two strains are somewhat different and dog fleas do not always bite humans. Plagues of fleas occur, particularly in summer and some years are worse than others. One of the main problems with fleas, apart from biting your dog and causing him to scratch, is that they act as intermediate hosts for tapeworms, for flea larvae swallow tapeworm eggs and if the dog ingests a flea the worm larvae get into the small intestine where they grow up into mature tapeworms. A flea can be almost any dark colour, depending on whether it has fed on blood, from black to red and is about $\frac{1}{16}$th of an inch in size, only just about visible to the naked eye. They move very quickly round the dogs skin, especially if you are hunting for them, and only jump when out in the open, when on the dog they mostly prefer to run through the coat and can be found especially on the head, ears and neck although the stomach is also a good place to look. They show up on the white and tan colours of a Bernese coat more easily than on the black but even there they are detectable as their bodies shine and they leave fine excreta in the coat that is hard and black.

Fleas lay eggs usually in dog bedding but also in carpets or upholstery, these eggs then hatch out around about 10 days into larvae which take another week or so to pupate, the adult emerging after a further period of time to find a recipient host. Treatment for fleas includes sprays, powders and insecticidal bath lotions used at regular intervals as directed by the vet. In serious cases of infestation the dog's scratching may cause nasty skin sores which can develop into abscesses. Flea collars can be obtained if your dog seems to have a recurring problem for this protection lasts for several weeks. It is necessary to wash dog bedding regularly and hoover carpets and upholstery around the house where the infected animal has been lying, to prevent re-infestation.

Gastritis

Stomach noises and breaking wind causing obnoxious smells can be a social embarrassment for the dogs owner but probably only means the animal has colic or indigestion, although it could be more seriously associated with the condition known as 'Pancreatic Deficiency' so if it continues veterinary opinion should be sought. Dogs, like us, sometimes eat too quickly, eat things that disagree with them, become pregnant, or grow old, all conditions that have an effect on both digestive systems, our own and our Bernese.

The dog will probably eat coarse grass causing it to be sick and vomit up bile a short while later. Vomiting is a common occurrence in dogs and owners should not get too uptight about it as it is nature's way of ridding the body of excess food, but, of course, persistent sickness especially if containing blood should cause you to seek prompt attention for your pet.

Haematoma

Ears which have filled with blood often cause the dog to shake his head because they can be quite painful. They can be caused by a bite or be self-inflicted through head scratching. It is no good trying to drain the ear yourself because it only fills again, it will go down in time and if not causing too much trouble to the dog this is the best way, but usually the ear retains the extra thickness and does not return to its original size. If the dog is in obvious discomfort contact your vet for treatment.

Heatstroke

Bernese are very prone to heatstroke and one has to be very careful in the summer because of this. The sun does not need to be shining either for a dog to be overcome, and I well remember Tara being affected one sultry humid day at a show when she was quite young. She suddenly lay down and her eyes became glazed; luckily I recognised the condition and got her into the shade, where with the help of a trained nurse and the application of ice to pressure points and dousing in water kindly fetched by a concerned judge, we managed to save her life, but it was touch and go. Some dogs are affected more than others but Bernese should not be left out in the hot sun while their owners gossip together and if being judged it is sensible to get your dog into the shade out of the ring whilst waiting for your time. A number of people also use damp towels to keep the body temperature down.

Leaving dogs in airless cars in the sun can cause a particularly nasty death from literally, being cooked alive, and cases do occur. Even at dog shows, where you would think exhibitors would have more sense, there are calls for owners of dogs in distress left in cars on the car park. A word of warning, though, do not lower the dogs body temperature too far, 10 to 12 minutes of applying ice and water is sufficient to cool him off without causing complications.

Hepatitis
This condition is in no way similar to the same named disease in man. In dogs it is a viral infection spread by urine and is highly contagious, being still carried in the urine up to six months after contracting the disease which often proves fatal. Puppies are most often affected and can get hepatitis by swallowing contaminated food or even faeces that are infected causing high temperatures, vomiting, diarrhoea and abdominal pain when death can occur from dehydration. Some dogs when recovering develop 'blue eye' when the eyes cloud over and gain a blue haze but this should disappear. Obviously veterinary treatment is necessary but the conditions can be negated by early vaccination.

Hernias
The most usual result of a weak place in the inside of the stomach wall which causes the abdominal organs to protrude in a soft swelling particularly visible in young puppies. It can be caused by the bitch biting the abdominal cord too close or it can be an inherited fault. Usually it closes of its own accord but occasionally requires veterinary attention to put in a stitch. If a groin hernia is apparent, particularly when found in bitches, do not breed with the animal as the womb may be affected and therefore whelping would be affected.

Hip Dysplasia or HD
Some breeds seem to be more affected than others and unfortunately Bernese are one of the former group which includes a large number of the bigger, heavier breeds. Put simply, HD means that the femur or long leg bone does not fit properly into the socket in the pelvis thus causing lameness in the early stages, or at the very least awkward hind movement visible at between four to six months and arthritis later in life. The very bad cases are obvious to the naked eye but in many instances it is impossible to tell that a dog has HD until it is X-rayed and some people maintain that the way a dog has to be pulled about and put out by anaesthetics to do the X-ray will give it hip problems if it does not already have them.

Most Bernese owners particularly of breeding stock do have their stud dogs and brood bitches scored by their own vet or at a special session arranged by the Club. A dog has only one chance to register his score which is done at around 18 months of age by the X-ray plates being sent to the British Veterinary Association for assessment. In the first instance the panel awarded a pass or fail by assessing the nine different parts of each hip joint up to the mark of six making a score of 54 for each hip, a total of 108. Border line cases were given what was termed a 'Breeders

Ball and Socket joint

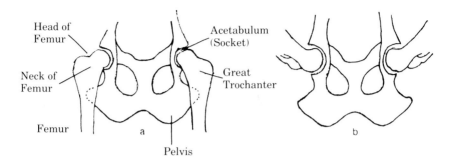

a) Normal
  From front, normal hips showing the head of the femur balanced equally in the socket.

b) Normal
  From back, normal hip joint with bent legs. Head of femur fitting snugly to allow the maximum amount of movement.

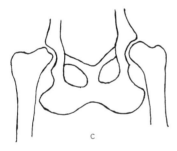

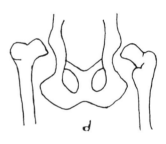

c) Dysplaced
  Head of femur in very loose position showing osteo-arthritic condition with flattened joint.

d) Dysplaced
  Head of femur completely distorted. Socket joint flattened and there is no connection between the head of the femur and the pelvis: complete dislocation.

Hip dysplasia.

Letter'. This scheme was later amended to 53 points per side and each hip actually scored with its total. Obviously the lower the score the better the prognosis, so a 0–0 total is the aim. But here let me just sound a word of warning, hips are one part of the whole and when choosing a stud dog for your bitch do remember that type, temperament and markings also play an important role and to go on hip scores alone makes a nonsense of the standard. On the other hand to breed from a dog or bitch that have bad hips is only perpetuating the condition within the breed and is equally damaging. HD is sometimes thought to be inherited but veterinary opinion is divided on this, but certainly with a puppy that has HD tendencies if it is over-exercised when very young and also fed to excess causing overweight problems then hip dysplasia is exacerbated.

Hypomyelinogenesis (Tremblers)

A very long name for a very recently diagnosed inherited condition (1986) where it has been found that the nerves of the spinal cord have insufficient insulation which causes dogs so affected to 'tremble'. But it has only been found in a very few dogs when one thinks of the numbers of Bernese Mountain Dogs there are altogether. See Appendix 4.

Inoculation

Sometimes called immunisation it makes an animal able to resist a disease so it is very important that puppies receive protection at an early age from such scourges as Distemper, Parvovirus, Leptospirea and Hepatitis. One has only to read the old canine journals like *Hutchinsons Encyclopedia* (1935) to realise how rife these diseases were at that time, when kennels were wiped out at a stroke. Vets today vary in their views as to what age to give these injections, some advocating a jab much earlier than the 12 weeks, followed by a second one two weeks later, that my vet advises. I always allow around four to five days after the second jab before taking the puppy out into public places. Up to this time the pup has a natural immunity gained from its dam but this needs to be topped up by one of the branded vaccines available, the information as to which one has been used will be found in the booklet issued by your vet along with the dates for booster shots in 12 months time.

A word to the wise, a vet's surgery sees all sorts of illness and disease and puppies are very vulnerable so ask your vet to inject your puppies in the car instead of going in. If you do have to do so, do not put the puppy down anywhere at all, carry him at all times which is a tall order with a Bernese pup but I have known two cases of people thinking that they knew better and thereby losing their puppies from diseases picked up in the vet's surgery.

Jaundice

Like humans, dogs suffering from too much bile in the blood find the skin around the eyes and inside the mouth takes on a yellow tinge. Most usually caused by an affected liver, suffering from Weils disease or leptospirea. This condition is transmitted by the dog drinking water in which rats have urinated or getting bitten by a rat and can prove fatal if not treated, which is why puppies are immunised against it.

Kennel Cough

This is usually caught during the summer months by being in contact with infected dogs and breathing airborne infected particles, most often at a show. It seems to have come to the fore in recent years and takes the form of a husky repetitive cough that can pass to every dog in the kennel, adversely affecting the very young and those under par who can die from it, but mostly it is just an annoying few days for a fit animal which should be segregated from the others and taken to the vet if it persists. Caused by both virus and bacteria it is possible to inoculate against this condition but do not take an infected dog into the surgery or go to shows or other kennels.

Kidney Disease (Nephritis)
Inflammation of the kidneys is caused by infection and can occur in dogs of all ages although chronic inflammation affects mostly old dogs when the waste products are passed back into the blood stream occasioning poisoning from the failure of the kidneys to act as a filter. This gives rise in the early stages to an increased thirst, lack of appetite and listlessness, which goes on to produce an inability to keep food down and very bad breath, which usually ends up in the dog being put down. It is worth remembering that Bernese are not long livers, 10 being about the average age and nephritis is one of the main scourges at this age. Weils disease can also cause kidney problems resulting in leptospirea but this condition usually responds to veterinary treatment.

Lice
These are tiny round white creatures in the early stages, which become light brown and fat on drinking the host's blood. They are passed from dog to dog on contact and live on the skin laying nits or eggs attached to the coat hairs, they cannot exist without a host and are found mainly around a dog's ears. They, like fleas, carry tapeworm eggs which are ingested by the dog, causing worms. Signs that your Bernese has these parasites are excessive scratching of the ears and neck which can be treated with shampoo, spray or powder and the eggs combed out. If found on puppies in any numbers they can cause anaemia.

Mange
This condition can be transmitted to humans and other dogs in the form of mites (tiny parasites) and takes several forms. The most common being Sarcoptic Mange in which the microscopic organism burrows under the skin where it lays the eggs which then go through the same life cycle as the flea. The ears, thighs and forelegs are the most usual areas of infection and if caught early can be treated successfully but if left can spread all over the body forming intensely irritating scabs.

Demodetic Mange is more serious and therefore more difficult to cure. It is not transmittable and usually affects the short haired breeds rather than long coated ones like the Bernese. The mite lives deep in the skin layer and singly causes little trouble so long as there is no irritation but if there is an increase in numbers the glandular system of the infected dog can be probed and severe dermatitis set up. Puppies can inherit the condition if their dam is infected so do not breed from your bitch if demodetic mange is diagnosed.

Mastitis

Most usually heard of in connection with cows and occasionally in humans but suckling bitches can also be affected if they are producing a lot of milk. The condition means the inflammation of the milk glands and is an extremely painful swelling of the affected teat (usually only the one) causing the bitch to have a high temperature and loss of appetite and can prove fatal if not treated.

In my early days of breeding we did come close to losing a nursing bitch with this problem. Because the puppies will not suck the teat as the milk is all clotted there is no chance of it improving. The bitch was obviously in pain and the vet said he dare not open the teat in case of infection which seemed to me to be stalemate, but the bitch solved it herself by biting open the affected member and licking out the infected milk but that was some years ago and the advance of science means the condition can now be treated rather more effectively.

It was interesting to note, however, that the affected teat was not usable when the next litter came along. As I gained experience I learned to look for signs of hardening in the teats and milked that one out myself. Some people also advocate the use of warm wet towels, if the puppies are not using all the milk produced, to reduce the flow.

Medicine Administration

I am also including under this heading pill giving for there is a knack to both. Liquids are best given in a spoon through the gap in the back of the teeth at the side of the jaw, holding the mouth closed with the other hand, the muzzle pointing upwards. Pills alternatively need the mouth wide open and if you can flick them (or place them if not) to the back of the throat close the mouth and massage the gullet till they are swallowed you have the problem solved, but do make sure the pill is not palmed into the cheek pouches to be spat out later, as Bernese are very adept at doing.

Osteochondritis Dessecans (OCD)

This is quite a mouthful to say so it is usually referred to by the initials OCD. What it means is that for some reason, and vets seem unable to say why, the bone growth in the puppy's front legs (Humerus) is faulty, causing bits to flake off, mostly in the form of cartilage which causes lameness and often a thickening of the shoulder and elbow joints. It seems to affect those dogs that grow very quickly, almost as if they are outgrowing their strength, and is more often found in dogs rather than bitches because of this. It cannot be said to be hereditary because that cannot be proved but it does seem to be prevalent in certain lines. Another cause can be lack of calcium and also too much food with too little activity which leads to problems of overweight. It is not a good idea to use an affected animal for breeding but the condition itself can be operated on, usually successfully, or with some dogs protracted rest will bring about a cure.

Parvovirus Infection (CPV-Canine Parvovirus)

This has become one of the modern day canine scourges and seems to have surges in an area and then die away only to start up again sometime later. It affects young puppies causing dehydration and is usually fatal. If it attacks the heart muscle of puppies, which are affected once they start to become active in later weeks, it is called Cardovirus but this is not so common as the virus which attacks the intestinal lining, affecting food absorption. One of the most tell-tale signs of this is very bad diarrhoea containing blood plus a vomiting which goes on and on. Puppies with the latter parvo infection are usually about a month old but it can affect youngsters up to and around a year and once infected an animal is liable to reinfection in later life.

The disease can be transmitted in faeces which carry the virus as also do humans on clothes and shoes, while another source of infection is by contamination by infected objects. The virus can remain active for up to 12 months in the home or kennel and, therefore, all the members of the family whose dog has had parvo must stay away from contact with dogs for around six months to be on the safe side. The affected puppy must be isolated from any others in the litter and will probably require drug treatment by your vet. Puppies usually gain some immunity from their dam and it is possible now to vaccinate pups from the virus earlier than the usual 12 weeks. It is prevalent at certain times in towns and cities and the most effective disinfectant is household bleach.

Poisoning

These days with so many agricultural sprays, rat and mice concoctions, weed and slug killers plus other lethal poisons, all able to be bought over the counter, it is not surprising that this method of death in dogs is increasing year by year. Puppies of course are particularly vulnerable so do not leave anything of this nature where they can get it. Warfarin, which is the stuff used to kill rats, must be placed inside some container like a drainage pipe for safety, because this causes internal haemorrhaging. In fact we nearly lost a dog from Warfarin poisoning and knowing we had none on the property we came to the conclusion that it must have been dropped by a bird. Be careful too of carrion as the animal may have died from a poison. In towns dustbins are a hazard so do not allow your dog to go scavenging for that too is a potential danger source. If you suspect your dog has been poisoned some signs to watch out for are foaming at the mouth, vomiting, fits, although these can also be signs for other conditions, a general lassitude and loss of healthy red looking gums to almost white. He must be made to vomit (a tablespoon of salt in half a cup of water) and veterinary attention sought at once keeping the dog warm meanwhile.

A recent addition to this section is Blue Algae poisoning. This can prove fatal and is found in some lakes and reservoirs during very hot summers.

Progressive Retinal Atrophy (PRA)

Another condition which is better known by its initials and as it implies, gets worse and worse affecting the light sensitive tissue in the eye causing failing sight which ends in blindness. It affects a number of the gun dog breeds but to date has not been reported as affecting the Bernese. The Kennel Club in co-operation with the British Veterinary Association have set up special schemes whereby animals can be specifically examined for PRA which is deemed to be hereditary and for which there is no cure.

Pyometra

This condition occurs most often about a month after a bitch has been in season and takes the form of pus in the uterus which can be fatal if veterinary help is not sought at once. It is thought to be caused by a hormone imbalance in bitches of middle age. It gives rise to a great thirst and consequent frequent trips to make puddles, raised temperature and a tight tummy. In the less serious cases, which may well respond to treatment, a dark brown smelly discharge comes from the vulva. In the main though, the only answer is to spay the bitch removing the uterus (womb) and ovaries.

It is to avoid pyometra that people think their bitch ought to have at least one litter and although very often it is found in maiden or barren bitches it can occasionally affect those that have had puppies. We found this to our cost when a bitch of mine having had three litters developed the condition as did her daughter at the age of 10 having had five litters. In both cases it was prompt action by my vet in carrying out hysterectomies that saved both old ladies, who carried on for several years after that.

Rabies (Hydrophobia)

The thing that worries me about the Channel Tunnel is the fact that the dreaded scourge of rabies is only just across the sea in France and could be carried through the tunnel by foxes and rats. It is a virus infection found in an infected animal's saliva and is transmitted by a bite, or by entering an open wound, from whence it travels to the nerves of the brain causing fits and then on into other organs.

There seems to be two types of rabies in animals, both affecting personality changes. The first, or 'dumb' rabies, causes wild animals to become tame and affectionate while the 'furious' type causes domesticated animals like the dog to become extremely savage, attacking people and animals for no reason with paralysed jaws producing dripping saliva which of course transmits the disease. Dogs with rabies hide from the light and eventually die from paralysis in a coma. For rabies in dogs there is no cure, for humans affected by the disease there is an extremely painful treatment of injections into the stomach which has a limited success rate, although research is being done. If exporting puppies, almost all countries require a certificate to say that the animal has been vaccinated 30 days before departure so this puts Bernese youngsters at the age of 12 weeks or more before they can leave for new homes abroad.

Importing a dog into Britain means quarantine for six months and there are very heavy penalties for anyone stupid enough to try and smuggle animals onto these shores without going through the proper channels.

Scurf

This often goes hand in hand with continuous shedding of hair which is most often associated with the fact that modern dogs live in centrally heated houses. I have also known scurf occur temporarily with a youngster waiting to go into the ring almost like a nervous condition and one which they seem to grow out of. These dry flaky scales can be found in puppies' coats too, there being several causes. The first, if they are out of condition from not having been wormed, second the result of infestation by a tiny skin mite or thirdly failure to rinse the coat properly after shampooing. Some forms of scurf can manifest itself as dry eczema and the vet's advice must be sought.

Teeth

Like humans, puppies first have a set of 28 milk teeth coming through at about three weeks of age which in their case are like little needles they are so sharp. These are replaced by the 42 permanent teeth by the age of about six months giving a white shining healthy mouth. Providing the dog is not fed too many sweet things like chocolate and biscuits and given a good bone and hard biscuits he should keep these permanently until old age. Incorrect food often produces a hard brownish crust of tartar which causes gum infection and bad breath often culminating in tooth decay.

The total of 42 teeth is made up of 12 incisors, 4 canines, 16 premolars and 10 molars – 4 in the upper jaw and 6 in the lower jaw are for tearing food, therefore dogs do not get tooth decay like humans whose teeth are adapted for grinding.

Bernese should have a scissor bite to be correct, this is where the position of the upper incisors just covers the lower incisors when the mouth is shut, this is the most usual mouth arrangement. A level bite should not be unduly penalised as should an undershot or overshot mouth, which are distinct faults and where found, that animal should not be used for breeding.

Ticks

Adult ticks live on their natural hosts sheep, although there is also a type that lives on hedgehogs, they lay eggs on grass in summer and autumn which hatch into larvae and it is these that affect the dog. These parasites are whitish to start with but when gorged with blood swell to the size of a pea and change colour to brownish red. They live by digging their heads into the dogs skin, usually round the head and ears, and sucking through a type of proboscis. One needs care in removing the tick, so as not to leave the head attached, as this can cause an abscess so do not just pull it off the skin, use cotton wool soaked in surgical spirit, disinfectant or oil. A cigarette end is definitely not recommended as you could burn the dog.

Travel Sickness

This condition is very often brought about by failure to relax on a journey or even over-excitement at the start of a car ride, very similar in fact to those conditions affecting humans. Human travel sickness pills should not be given to dogs, there are animal tablets made by most of the proprietary brands of pet care firms available at pet shops for just this purpose.

If a puppy is taken in the car from an early age there is usually no trouble with vomiting or salivating excessively and I can only think of one of our dogs out of all the many we have had in the last 30 years that has been a problem in the early stages. If you do experience an aversion to car travel by your Bernese you will need to spend some time getting him used to it. To start with the car needs to be stationary and the dog left in it for short periods, fed in it and made a fuss of in it. Then you can progress to taking the dog out at every opportunity even if it just down to the garage when you fill up with petrol, or up to the corner shop. When you extend the range a bit, a free run somewhere can be included, so that the dog knows that the car ride is pleasurable. When taking youngsters out for the first couple of months I use a wire mesh cage as it provides a form of protection for the puppy. Do remember not to feed a puppy before going on a journey, although as the dog gets older this does not generally worry them and with perseverance and time almost all grow out of the difficult early stages.

Torsion or Gastric Bloat

This can be fatal if not treated early enough, for the stomach suddenly fills with gas and expands and the gas stops the heart. Very often the condition is complicated by the intestine twisting (torsion) to block both exits and most often it occurs after feeding. The dog experiences great pain and is in evident distress with his breathing and if he does not receive immediate veterinary attention to release the gas, will die very quickly. It is for this reason that my dogs, even when adult, are fed three times a day on the old adage 'little and often'. I always exercise **before** not after food and I do not encourage them to drink large amounts of cold water after food, particularly if the meal has been a dry one. The cause of torsion has still not been discovered but all the above reasons have some credibility and I would rather be safe than sorry. It is most prevalent in the large breeds and thought by some to be hereditary.

Worms

So much has been written about worms in the last few years that there can hardly be many people who are not aware of the dangers associated with not worming puppies. Perhaps most, too, treat their adult dogs, but all animals suffer from infestation regularly during their life span and easily become re-infested if not wormed at least once every six months. Dogs catch worms from animals such as sheep or rabbits, ingesting eggs found in droppings, nuzzling dead birds or carrion and, as already stated earlier in this chapter, fleas are also carriers.

113

In this country there are two main types of worms, round and tape, although Africa has many more. We are lucky also that we do not suffer from the heartworm which is such a scourge in America. Both our types of worms are found in the stomach and intestines of the dog and live on digested food.

Roundworms are, as the name suggests, round white worms of up to seven inches in length, mostly found in pregnant bitches and young puppies. When excreted after treatment, a bad case of roundworms can look like a tin of spaghetti and a badly affected puppy can also cough up roundworms en masse. The pregnant bitch experiences hormonal changes and these hormones activate roundworm larva that have been lying dormant in the tissues, some of which move to the womb (uterus) and others to the developing puppies while some continue developing their lifecycle in the bitch's intestine. By the time the puppy is two weeks old the larvae it has acquired via the bitch, either through the milk or prior to birth, have travelled via the bloodstream into the stomach, intestines and the lungs where they hatch into adult worms, yet other larvae lie dormant in body tissue awaiting their chance of development. The adult worms lay eggs in the intestines which are passed out of the host in the faeces and can remain quietly in the grass or soil for up to five years until another host, dog or sheep comes along and off the whole merry-go-round goes again. It can be seen, therefore, how desperately important it is to worm the bitch at about three weeks into her pregnancy and to then worm puppies fortnightly from the age of three weeks, ie at five, seven, nine etc. until three months old. The treatment is only effective on the adult worms so the newly hatched larvae need to be killed in their turn, hence the need for repeated treatment.

It is not always possible to tell if a puppy has worms, he may look perfectly healthy but although you may not see anything even after treatment, take it from me that there are always a few. A badly affected puppy looks pot bellied, can cough, suffer from diarrhoea and is often small with a harsh staring coat. In very bad cases the worms can affect the bodily systems causing death.

Many people have spoken and written about the dangers of toxacara canis where children are concerned, for if they pick up the eggs from their coat or their faeces and ingest them the eggs which hatch out as larvae can travel in the circulatory system throughout the body. Should they reach the eyes and the brain blindness and other conditions can result, but although such a lot has been said about this disease the chances of infection are very very slender. However, it is obviously common sense to pick up worm infected faeces and burn them or put them down the loo, do not bury them for as already stated they can live on in the soil for years.

The second type of worm is the tapeworm and this affects adult dogs, developing in the small intestine. It is made up of white segments, each carrying ripe eggs and all joined together, reaching about twenty inches in length and attached to the intestinal wall by hooks from the head. Simple segments carrying eggs are excreted live in the faeces but die off

114

once they are in the air leaving the eggs to be picked up by birds, sheep horses, rabbits and fleas, ingested, grown into larvae and the life cycle repeated once more. As earlier stated the tapeworm requires a host and this most often is the flea although sheep are also one of the main intermediaries. It is, therefore, obvious that if this parasite is to be killed the head must be removed and not just the segments or the whole cycle starts again. My advice is to get tablets from your vet for those obtainable from the pet shops are often not strong enough for Bernese and the dog needs to be wormed at least twice and probably three times a year, the number of tablets depends on the weight of the dog.

Zoonoses

Diseases transmitted from animals to humans are termed Zoonoses. These can be caught from all domestic animals but as most people are in closest contact with dogs and cats these are the most common sources. The risk is minimal providing precautions as to hygiene are taken when dealing with such things as washing dog dishes, cleaning up faeces and preparing and storing food. One should always wash ones hands after dealing with or petting dogs, wear gloves when picking up droppings, dissuade your dog from licking your face and refrain from letting your Bernese lick your plate after a meal. Zoonoses cuts both ways and humans can affect dogs by giving them fleas, bacteria such as salmonella, TB and sore throats to mention but a few, while dogs can transmit rabies, toxacara canis, leptospirosis and other things. Veterinary surgeons are particularly at risk from fleas, mange and even brucellosis from infected cows or sometimes, though rarely in Britain, from whelping bitches. However, do not panic it is very rare that cross infection occurs in this way, you are much more likely to catch something from your nearest and dearest, but seriously, if you need the vet's services do call him sooner rather than later for in that way he has a chance of arresting the disease in plenty of time.

— 7 —
Breeding

Since I started breeding in the 1960s the greater demand for dogs in those days has given way to the one for bitches today the reason for the change I have not really solved. Many people claim that bitches make better companions, do not roam and are less aggressive in comparison with a dog. These are all good reasons but not necessarily true for it depends a great deal on the dog itself and also on whether the speaker is male or female. It is a recognised fact that many of the former prefer a bitch while women often achieve more rapport with a dog. Basically, it may well be that more people want to try their hand at breeding a litter which is certainly a most interesting aspect of keeping dogs. However, there are many pitfalls, especially at the present time when there are already so many puppies about needing good homes. The old adage that all bitches ought to have at least one litter for the good of their health is a fallacy. The condition known as pyometra (pus or fluid in the womb) can occur whether the bitch is a maiden or has had several litters. The cause of this septicaemia is not really clear but vets think it is due to a hormone imbalance and it can be fatal if not operated on, which usually means a hysterectomy, but with the marvellous drugs and antibiotics available to veterinary science a great deal of the danger has now been alleviated.

People who want to breed ought to acquaint the breeder selling puppies of this fact. Buying the last puppy in the litter, that is both undersized and mismarked and consequently reduced in price, would not be an auspicious start to any breeding career. It is of the utmost importance that the choice of bitch as a brood is as good an example as possible. Many people think the dog to be the most important factor in a mating but this is not so for it is from the bitch that the dominant features come and to produce good stock one must have a first class bitch. She needs to be physically and mentally sound, marked according to the standard, friendly but neither nervous or aggressive and correctly put together with plenty of heart room. The genes of your bitch and the chosen stud dog pass on to the puppies the attributes of both in the ratio

116

of fifty-fifty resulting in a recognisable type that will, with luck, make your name as a breeder of good sound stock, should this be what you are aiming towards.

Before entering into the world of the dog breeder the pet owner should stop and think. Firstly, one has to sell the puppies produced and even if Aunt Emily would love one what about the other seven, eight or nine in the litter? What are you going to do if they have not got new homes lined up by the time they are seven to eight weeks old? Puppies rampaging round the place and eating you out of house and home can be both expensive and time-consuming. It is no good relying on other people to sell them for you, or expecting the stud dog owner to do the necessary advertising either. Secondly, can you afford to breed. Can you afford the stud fee, the food for the bitch and the puppies, increasing amounts being necessary to assuage the ever growing appetites? Thirdly, have you the necessary time to give to them, and can you provide a suitable place to house them once they are up on their feet? It is no good thinking of all the money you are hoping to make either, because there is very little profit in producing puppies if all the effort, expense and time expended is taken into account.

THE BITCH'S SEASON

Bitches can only mate when they are in season. They reach pubity some time after six months of age and have their first heat between six and eighteen months. This means that the bitch's vulva becomes enlarged followed by blood being lost in varying amounts. Some bitches clean themselves up very well so that there is very little mess, others seem to leave a trail of fluid behind them everywhere they go. Domesticated bitches usually come into season twice a year, but in the wild a bitch will only come into season or oestrum once a year in the spring. The heat sometimes causes discomfort, probably a tummy ache. A lessening in appetite and an increase in excitability are also signals in some bitches and certainly the first heat can have these and other effects on a youngster. The appearance of the blood signals the commencement of the heat proper and is called 'showing colour'. Although in fact it is the second stage of the oestrus it is the period when dogs become very interested in the female but the bitch is not yet interested in them. This latter stage usually comes after about 12 days when the blood gives way to a colourless discharge which is when the bitch will stand to be mated. She indicates her readiness for mating by turning her tail to one side and the breeder can also gain this reflex by rubbing the area above the tail.

This of course will not be necessary if more than one animal is kept for bitches will mount each other, the one usually on the top being the in-season bitch. If a dog is kept he will leave no doubt as to the impending situation. A bitch in heat usually sends a dog off his food so he loses condition, sometimes for as long as a week. It affects different dogs in different ways for some go quite mad and tend to tear round the place noses to the ground and others take it much more calmly but watch every opportunity to get to the bitch. We have had both types in the past but luckily at the moment my stud dogs fall into the latter category, which is much more conducive to a quiet life.

If you are intending to mate your bitch it is usual to approach the owner of the stud dog you have chosen sometime before she comes into season and ask if he or she is agreeable to their dog being used. When the bitch first comes into season contact the person again so that arrangements can be made for your bitch to visit the dog in plenty of time. Many books will tell you that you must mate your bitch on the 12th day, which always causes me to smile for as far as I know dogs cannot read. In my experience, although this tends to be about the average, the actual day of mating can be anywhere between the 4th and 30th day so you just have to wait and see when your bitch is ready to stand, for there is no hard and fast rule, bitches are like people, individuals.

Novice owners often ask at which age they should first mate their bitches and my answer is that I do not consider Bernese bitches to be sufficiently mature in themselves until around two years of age, and as this usually coincides with about the third heat this is when I first attempt to mate. Certainly by the age of three, if you are thinking of having puppies, you ought to be seeing about it, but having said that I do know of bitches as old as five who have successfully produced and reared a first litter. But as in humans the older the mother the more chance there is of something going wrong. A bitch can easily produce three litters in her lifetime and again I have known four or five produced quite happily at a rate of one a year or every other season. It is not good for the bitch to mate her at every season, she is not a breeding machine.

Many breeders consider that the first three litters produce the best results and they will not go beyond this number. In anycase recent Kennel Club legislation has now restricted people to breeding a maximum of six litters from any bitch.

THE STUD DOG

I mentioned earlier about approaching the chosen stud dog owner when your bitch comes into season but this begs the question 'how do I choose the right dog for my bitch?' This is not an easy question to answer even for established breeders. At least Bernese Mountain Dogs are not so numerically strong in this country that there is the temptation to use the dog down the road irrespective of whether the pedigrees match. When thinking of mating you need to start looking at the dogs available some time in advance of your bitch's season. Perhaps one particular dog takes your eye at a show or the 'Garden Party' by its achievements and certainly it is easier for a novice to sell puppies that are sired by a well known dog. The stud dog owner may get enquiries for puppies which can be passed on to you from prospective customers, but it is not an inherent right so do not take it as such. Some people think there is easy money to be made if they keep their own stud dog, for whose services owners will pay, plus they will save stud fees when mating their own bitches, but a dog has to be seen to be winning in the showring and also to be attractive to would be users before there is a queue at your door.

Another point to consider when choosing a stud dog is that you need to like the dog yourself, or you are unlikely to like the type of puppies he will sire which rather defeats the object of mating in the first place. I reckon a dog should be around 14 months of age before he is used for the first time but I know there are people who disagree with this and tend to use them earlier. The reason why I like them to be over a year old is because once they have been used at stud they know what it is all about and tend to be keener on the bitches whether they are in season or not, and Bernese dogs are very keen, in fact one might suggest that they are interested in anything 'in skirts' at any time. It is better to use a young dog on an experienced bitch the first time as she is more likely to stand while he experiments, but that is not to say that two maiden (unused) animals are not well able to get on with the job in hand but it does depend a bit on the temperament of both dog and bitch.

INBREEDING, LINE-BREEDING AND OUTCROSSING

It is very necessary that whichever stud dog is chosen the pedigrees of dog and bitch are compatible. They can have some closeness of forbears but it is asking for trouble in the main to breed too closely, so avoid putting a father to daughter or father to sister for this is what is called **inbreeding** and it is not advisable as faults are magnified as often as not. It is, however, permissible to miss a generation and put grandfather to granddaughter, for example, if you wish to double up on a particular trait or good point. This is called **line-breeding** and means that there are similar connections on both sides of the pedigree often showing a line of descent. The system known as **outcrossing** is where a suitable dog is chosen for a stud from completely outside one's own line or pedigree.

THE MATING

I do not usually feed before a mating and I also make sure that both animals have relieved themselves for obvious reasons. If you are the bitch's owner do allow her out somewhere en route to the dog so that you do not wait until you get outside the stud dog's home to let her make a puddle, it is not a very considerate gesture.

Right then, let us suppose your bitch is full in season and standing and you have taken her to the dog of your choice to be mated, which is the usual procedure although there is in fact no hard and fast rule about this. It is usual to get the vet to take a swab for streptococci in the bitch at the beginning of the heat for, if it is present, the germs kill the sperm and there will be no puppies. It is the main cause of failure to conceive in bitches in my experience.

Introduce the dog and bitch for the first time on leads so that the dog can be pulled away should the bitch snap at him, if all is well slip the lead and let them indulge in a little pre-mating play. Mating usually takes place in a stable or other confined space such as a garage but care must be taken, especially if the bitch seems upset, that she does not escape in the excitement. She does need to be free and relaxed for she will not accept the dog until she is. When she allows the dog to mount her then the serious business in hand can start. The owner of the stud dog should know his own dog so that if he needs help he can guide him into the bitch, but at the same time helping to support the bitch (who is bearing all the dog's weight) under the loin. The bitch's owner in the meantime is holding the animal's head to prevent her swinging round to snap at the dog or move away as he enters her, for with some maiden bitches this can be painful while others accept it without comment. The stud dog owner should not stand there and say that he never interferes but lets the dog get on with it on his own, if one owns a stud dog one should find out how best to help the dog and not just leave it to chance, after all you are collecting the stud fee for the service.

If the bitch persists in being awkward and sitting down or snapping at the dog she is probably not yet ready or it could be that she dislikes the suitor. There is no point in letting the dog wear himself out with his efforts if he is getting no co-operation so he may as well be removed until a more suitable occasion occurs which may be on the following day or in two or three days time. If on trying again the bitch is still not playing you are left with two options, firstly you can give up the idea of mating your bitch with this dog and either try another stud or you can allow the bitch to remain unsullied. Secondly, the bitch can be force mated which I do not really like for dogs like humans have their own likes and dislikes. Two illustrations spring to mind here, Tara my original Bernese bitch, was forcibly mated first time and it took four of us to do it for she did not like the dog, consequently I was not really surprised when she did not hold to him although there seemed to be no reason for this. The other example was when I wanted to mate a bitch of mine to a dog I also owned but she just did not want to know and would have nothing to do with his overtures, so we brought out the dog who sired her first litter and we had a tie inside two seconds flat, which only goes to prove the mutual attraction theory. In my experience if a bitch will not mate normally there could be a reason for the incompatibility and it must be remembered that a dog and a bitch sometimes just do not gell. Another factor to consider is that some maiden bitches can be difficult and it could be fear that is causing her to try and savage the dog, in which case a muzzle might help and this can be fashioned out of a tie or a bandage if the proper thing is not available and the bitch held by the owner at the head end.

Stud dogs vary in their approach to a bitch some will throw themselves at her after a mere cursory introduction while others will play for a while before getting down to business. Providing the bitch likes the dog and is willing to be mated he should have no trouble, but most mount several times before beginning to thrust. As I mentioned three paragraphs back, the stud dog owner should know whether his dog will require help to guide him into the bitch for some dogs will come off at once if the owner tries to guide their penis. Most, as it should be, are quite well able to manage on their own, instinct here being the guide.

If the bitch is a good deal smaller than the dog you may have to put her on some raised surface, like a small bank, to facilitate mating. It is just worth mentioning that if the dog does not appear to be getting anywhere fast it may be that he is not really trying to thrust and this could have its roots in a psychological problem. You see, if he has been shouted at for getting on bitches on prior occasions, for whatever reason, he might not just believe his luck that this time is for real and he is expected to go the whole way. I had an example of this very thing with a dog and at his first mating I could not understand why he would not get on with it for the bitch was standing rock steady and then the 'hang-up' idea occurred to me. I rang a doggie friend who came over at once and with me out of the way he tied in a matter of seconds.

The Tie
The tie usually occurs after mating has taken place and the muscles in the bitch's vagina contract and hold the dog, preventing him from withdrawing the penis. It is at this time that the sperm is pumped into the bitch, and if you look you can see the juddering as the bitch draws in. Try not to touch her during this time as this can prevent the flow of the dog's semen. With a maiden bitch it is important that she does not struggle to free herself at this time as this could damage the dog so the bitch's owner must hold her head firmly. Many dogs step over the bitch naturally whilst others need help to get their leg over her back and turn so that they are standing in a back to back position. This state of play, so to speak, can last from 10 to 60 minutes although 25 is about the average until the penis retracts and the dog is able to withdraw. This wait can be rather uncomfortable if you are down on your haunches holding the bitch in particular. But you must be alert in case you need to frustrate any attempt to lie down by either party, although it is most likely to be the bitch who may try as this can injure the dog if allowed to succeed. It helps if there is a box or a bale to sit on during the wait when all sorts of topics can come up for discussion.

Some dogs do not tie but enter and come out at once. This is not usual but if this happens with your dog it does not mean that the mating has necessarily been unsuccessful. I had a Labrador cross dog once, that I ran in obedience, who could smell a bitch on heat for miles and was like Houdini in his attempts to get to her. He was as quick as greased lightning when mating, never seemed to tie and yet successfully sired a number of litters without it seeming any effort at all. As I said before, it is a matter of knowing your own dog.

But to get back to the tied mating, when the dog and bitch come apart I 'wheelbarrow' the newly mated bitch, that is pick her up by the hind legs and gently shake her, to prevent the fluid containing the semen from coming back. This may well be considered rather old-fashioned these days but it has never been proven whether or not it is effective and I am a great believer in doing all I can to ensure a satisfactory end to a mating.

The bitch should then be put back quietly into the car and not allowed to relieve herself for at least a couple of hours. The dog does not usually require much attention and will clean himself thoroughly. If you have other dogs at home it is probably a good idea to wash him before allowing him back with them as it could cause trouble otherwise. He may require a drink but a young healthy dog will quickly recover and be ready to do it all over again inside a short time.

The Stud Fee

It is now that humans retire to the kitchen for a well earned coffee and the bitch's owner must pay for the service just received. The money is normally due when the bitch is covered and not when the litter is born. The stud fee at the time of writing is about £175 for a Bernese but this can vary somewhat depending on whether the dog is a Champion or not. Alternatively the stud dog owner may, instead of a cash fee, ask for 'pick of the litter' so being entitled to the first choice of dog or bitch before anyone else, including the bitch's owner. Should the bitch not hold and there are no resulting puppies it is usual for the stud dog owner to offer a free return to the dog but this is not obligatory. This point, like that of fee or puppy, must be discussed when arrangements for the mating are taking place to avoid any misunderstanding. Unless you are super-stitious (like me) remember to ask the stud dog owner to sign the blue form necessary to register the litter with the Kennel Club at the same time as you pay the stud fee. I tend to wait until I have the pups delivered safe and sound before I tempt fate by counting my chickens, if you will forgive the mixed metaphor. You will also need the dog's registered name and number, or stud book number, and the date of the mating for the form.

An Unplanned Mating

Although the bitch has been mated it is up to the owner to make sure that she cannot be raped unofficially by another suitor until she is past the danger point, which usually happens quite quickly if she has conceived to the planned mating. But occasionally the bitch will go on discharging even though mated, however, this does not seem to affect the conception and soon stops. I had a case recently in which a bitch belonging to a farmer had come to one of my stud dogs and we had a successful mating. Three days later the phone rang and a voice told me that the bitch had got out and had been covered by a neighbours' dog and asked what should he do. My reaction was sharp and to the point 'get the bitch to the vet and abort both matings'. This would have the effect of causing her to come into season all over again. I then told him to bring her back to the dog the next time she came on heat for a free return and ended by adding a few choice words on the carelessness of allowing such a thing to occur. If this happens to you and you get the bitch to a vet within 48 hours of the mismating it can be stopped by an injection once but not the second time, and it is obviously better if it does not happen in the first place.

It has in fact been known for a bitch to produce a litter normally and then two or three days later to produce a second batch having held to two separate matings but this is not usual. If the bitch is mated twice she usually has all of the puppies at one go and not in two completely separate whelpings.

Many people like to bring their bitch to the dog a second time, on the next day or a couple of days after the first mating, but providing the first mating produced a good tie it is not usually necessary. However, if they wish to do so I usually agree for at least the dogs enjoy it.

THE BITCH IN WHELP

Pregnancy in a bitch produces roughly the same body changes as in a woman and like in them it is a perfectly normal happening. It is often difficult to tell whether some bitches are in whelp until they begin to show about the fifth or sixth week. Others change almost from the word go and become more sedate and careful with themselves increasing their food intake and exhibiting other signs of the forthcoming pregnancy like morning sickness. It is sensible at about three weeks to treat the bitch for roundworm, to start a course of extra calcium and vitamin supplements and to increase the food intake commensurately as the weeks go on. Do not change the diet of your bitch from what she is used to under any circumstances for many vets believe that this is a fundamental cause of early abortion of the fertilised cells.

A pregnancy lasts for 63 days or nearly nine weeks, but can be as short as 57 or as long as 69. In most cases the condition becomes noticeable between the fifth and sixth week, but prior to that the nipples begin to fill out giving a good sign that your Bernese is in whelp. Here perhaps I ought to give a word of warning because it is sometimes difficult to decide whether your bitch really is in whelp or if she is having a false pregnancy. The vet can only gain some indication of whether the bitch is in whelp by palpitations around three weeks after mating and if this opportunity is missed and the bitch gives every indication of having puppies it is perhaps not surprising if people think that she has held when in fact it is a false pregnancy. This can occur if the bitch fails to conceive having been mated or produces a lot of symptoms of pregnancy even though the dog has not been near her. The first signs appear six to eight weeks after the bitch has been on heat when she produces milk and starts to collect toys or other objects into her bed and treat them as if they were her puppies. Some bitches even go through a phantom birth restlessly panting and straining as if in actual labour. Bitches that are prone to false pregnancies usually repeat the process after each heat with symptoms of increasing severity. This coming into milk, however, can be quite useful if another bitch with puppies is experiencing problems as some of the pups can be fostered. But if you want to stop it quickly remove all the accumulated objects and reduce the carbohydrates (biscuit) and water available. In serious cases hormone injections or tablets can help and the ultimate cure is to have the bitch spayed if all else fails. However, let us take it that your Bernese has held to the dog even though it may be difficult to decide whether or not she is in whelp, for some bitches carry the whelps high up in the ribcage not letting them down until later on in the pregnancy. There have been cases of the vet declaring that a bitch is not in whelp only to have his opinion confounded on the birth of a hearty litter a few days later.

Rearing good Bernese puppies comes with firstly, feeding the mum-to-be correctly and this starts with the increase of the bitch's food intake between the third and fourth week. I am assuming that you normally feed good quality meat and biscuits or complete food but if you do not you will need to do so from the beginning of the pregnancy. An occasional raw egg in milk can be poured over food or drunk separately and plenty of other protein should be given, particularly good meat whether from the butcher or the tinned variety e.g. Pedigree Chum or Prime etc., plus other examples like rabbit, fish, chicken or tripe in conjunction with good quality wholemeal biscuit meal or mixer. If a complete food is given make sure it is of the best quality and has a high protein content and other things are added to supplement the bitch's extra needs. If you usually feed twice a day then increase this to three times and do not experiment with foods she is unused to for this is the wrong time to be upsetting your bitch's tummy.

Do make sure your pregnant Bernese gets some free exercise daily. As the weeks go on a gentle stroll is probably all that is required, especially if your bitch is one of those who takes care of herself during this time, like my Tara who was quite content to amble round a small area in the woods at her own pace while the others ran miles, so I took them separately at this time.

About the sixth week you will notice distinct bodily changes in your Bernese as she grows rounder in outline and her teats become more prominent, with milk being produced about 10 days before she is due to whelp. Once you know your bitch is in whelp you will have to think about where you are going to have the family so she can be introduced to the place before the actual event. If your bitch usually lives in then you will probably have the puppies born in the house as a normal progression, but if she lives out you may well wish to have the puppies born inside and move them out later at about three weeks of age. All our dogs live in the house so our puppies are reared in but of course do go out if the weather is suitable during the day, when they are older. I like to have the puppies where I can both hear and see them easily.

THE WHELPING QUARTERS

But wherever you chose, the whelping quarters must be draught-free, warm but not hot, light and airy and with an adjacent electric plug so that if an infra-red heater is needed it can easily be plugged in, although opinions on the advisability of using a lamp are mixed. If you use a lamp it should be adjustable and of sufficient height that the heat can be regulated according to the age of the puppies. Too much heat is just as

WHELPING TABLE
TABLE SHOWING WHEN A BITCH IS DUE TO WHELP

SERVED JANUARY	DUE TO WHELP MARCH	SERVED FEBRUARY	DUE TO WHELP APRIL	SERVED MARCH	DUE TO WHELP MAY	SERVED APRIL	DUE TO WHELP JUNE	SERVED MAY	DUE TO WHELP JULY	SERVED JUNE	DUE TO WHELP AUGUST	SERVED JULY	DUE TO WHELP SEPTEMBER	SERVED AUGUST	DUE TO WHELP OCTOBER	SERVED SEPTEMBER	DUE TO WHELP NOVEMBER	SERVED OCTOBER	DUE TO WHELP DECEMBER	SERVED NOVEMBER	DUE TO WHELP JANUARY	SERVED DECEMBER	DUE TO WHELP FEBRUARY
1	5	1	5	1	3	1	3	1	3	1	3	1	2	1	3	1	3	1	3	1	3	1	2
2	6	2	6	2	4	2	4	2	4	2	4	2	3	2	4	2	4	2	4	2	4	2	3
3	7	3	7	3	5	3	5	3	5	3	5	3	4	3	5	3	5	3	5	3	5	3	4
4	8	4	8	4	6	4	6	4	6	4	6	4	5	4	6	4	6	4	6	4	6	4	5
5	9	5	9	5	7	5	7	5	7	5	7	5	6	5	7	5	7	5	7	5	7	5	6
6	10	6	10	6	8	6	8	6	8	6	8	6	7	6	8	6	8	6	8	6	8	6	7
7	11	7	11	7	9	7	9	7	9	7	9	7	8	7	9	7	9	7	9	7	9	7	8
8	12	8	12	8	10	8	10	8	10	8	10	8	9	8	10	8	10	8	10	8	10	8	9
9	13	9	13	9	11	9	11	9	11	9	11	9	10	9	11	9	11	9	11	9	11	9	10
10	14	10	14	10	12	10	12	10	12	10	12	10	11	10	12	10	12	10	12	10	12	10	11
11	15	11	15	11	13	11	13	11	13	11	13	11	12	11	13	11	13	11	13	11	13	11	12
12	16	12	16	12	14	12	14	12	14	12	14	12	13	12	14	12	14	12	14	12	14	12	13
13	17	13	17	13	15	13	15	13	15	13	15	13	14	13	15	13	15	13	15	13	15	13	14
14	18	14	18	14	16	14	16	14	16	14	16	14	15	14	16	14	16	14	16	14	16	14	15
15	19	15	19	15	17	15	17	15	17	15	17	15	16	15	17	15	17	15	17	15	17	15	16
16	20	16	20	16	18	16	18	16	18	16	18	16	17	16	18	16	18	16	18	16	18	16	17
17	21	17	21	17	19	17	19	17	19	17	19	17	18	17	19	17	19	17	19	17	19	17	18
18	22	18	22	18	20	18	20	18	20	18	20	18	19	18	20	18	20	18	20	18	20	18	19
19	23	19	23	19	21	19	21	19	21	19	21	19	20	19	21	19	21	19	21	19	21	19	20
20	24	20	24	20	22	20	22	20	22	20	22	20	21	20	22	20	22	20	22	20	22	20	21
21	25	21	25	21	23	21	23	21	23	21	23	21	22	21	23	21	23	21	23	21	23	21	22
22	26	22	26	22	24	22	24	22	24	22	24	22	23	22	24	22	24	22	24	22	24	22	23
23	27	23	27	23	25	23	25	23	25	23	25	23	24	23	25	23	25	23	25	23	25	23	24
24	28	24	28	24	26	24	26	24	26	24	26	24	25	24	26	24	26	24	26	24	26	24	25
25	29	25	29	25	27	25	27	25	27	25	27	25	26	25	27	25	27	25	27	25	27	25	26
26	30	26	30	26	28	26	28	26	28	26	28	26	27	26	28	26	28	26	28	26	28	26	28
27	31	27	1 (MAY)	27	29	27	29	27	29	27	29	27	28	27	29	27	29	27	29	27	29	27	28
28	1 (APR)	28	2	28	30	28	30	28	30	28	30	28	29	28	30	28	30	28	30	28	30	28	1 (MAR)
29	2	29	3	29	31	29	1 (JULY)	29	31	29	31	29	30	29	31	29	1 (DEC)	29	31	29	31	29	2
30	3			30	1 (JUN)	30	2	30	1 (AUG)	30	1 (SEP)	30	1 (OCT)	30	1 (NOV)	30	2	30	1 (JAN)	30	1 (FEB)	30	3
31	4			31	2			31	2			31	2	31	2			31	2			31	4

bad as not enough and Bernese Mountain Dog puppies easily become dehydrated, but the bitch will show by her panting and moving out of range if she is too hot.

Before the date the puppies are due, which you can work out from the

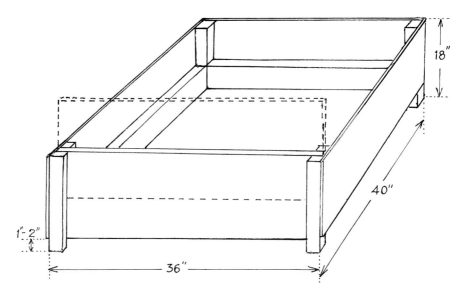

A typical whelping box.

chart, the bitch will need a whelping box in which to produce and rear her family. It is best made of wood and raised off the floor on a base of an inch or two but not too much as there is the risk the puppies can fall out and roll underneath in the early days. A box can be fairly easily constructed but it must be big enough for the Bernese bitch to be able to lie comfortably on her side, which in measurement means her length plus a half and the width must allow for the height at shoulder plus eight inches. So the measurement of the box to house a Bernese comfortably needs to be about 36 x 40 inches (101.6cm x 92cm) with three sides of about 18 inches (45.7cm) and the fourth divided into two parts of nine inches each so that the top part can be lifted out when the pups are climbing in and out. A rail around the inside edge of the box prevents the bitch from lying on a straying puppy but do make sure it is strong enough to take the considerable weight of your Bernese. Newspaper can be crumpled up and stuffed round the sides of the box to form a temporary pad if there is nothing else handy.

I usually line the box with samples of cushion tile flooring but polystyrene tiles are equally good and then on top place newspapers and a large piece of the type of bedding called originally Vetbed, although there are now several similar proprietary brands available these days. This is like sheepskin except that it is made of nylon backed fur fabric with polyester and allows the damp to drain through to the newspaper underneath leaving the top surface warm and dry. It can easily be machine washed and you really need three pieces, one on, one dirty and one in the wash although two will do at a pinch – they cost about £10 a piece.

The bitch can produce her family as much as a week either side of the sixty third day but they are usually early rather than late. However, it is wise if she goes more than two days over her due time to give the vet a call or maybe take her in for an examination, because occasionally inertia sets in and the bitch does not begin her labour at all. Then a caesarean may be necessary to get the puppies out alive. A caesarean section is said to be so called because it was first carried out on one of the rulers of Rome.

WHELPING

As the time draws near for whelping bitches behave very differently, but when their temperature drops to approximately 37°C then birth should be within the next 24 hours. Unless you take her temperature you cannot be sure of the timing. It is quite common for a bitch to refuse to eat before going into labour but not always, some may rip up newspaper and others may dig enormous holes in inaccessible places. So keep a close eye on your bitch when her time is near for we have had one or two close shaves in the past when the bitch thought she would prefer to rear her litter under the shed or some other equally unacceptable place at the eleventh hour. There is often a grey or white discharge from the vulva within 24 hours of whelping which is normal but if the discharge is dark or smells of pus you need to get your bitch to the vet as there could be a problem with a dead puppy.

Nine times out of ten the actual whelping commences in the early hours of the morning, the reason why I have yet to fathom. Probably for several hours prior to actually lying down to get on with the job your Bernese will have obviously been unsettled, she could have been tearing up paper to make a bed, getting down in the box and getting out again, following you around like a shadow and probably refusing food, though not all of them do any or all of these things.

This first stage can last several hours or be over quite quickly, no two bitches are alike, but she will probably begin to pant as the birth becomes more imminent. Before things really start to happen make sure that you have a cardboard box with the bottom covered with a small piece of Vetbed, in case you need to move the puppies from the bitch at any point, also a pair of scissors, a couple of dry towels and a kitchen roll just in case of need.

Bitches should take birth in their stride but Bernese can be difficult. A maiden bitch very often takes longer in producing her litter than a brood that has been through the experience before, when all you might see is a ripple down the body followed by a thrust and out pops a glistening wet bag containing one Bernese puppy while another bitch might strain and lick herself for some time before getting her first out. The puppy is followed by the liver-like placenta. If the strain goes on for some time, for example an hour or so with no result, it is better to let the vet take a look for you could have a breach birth where the puppy is presented the wrong way on. My vet likes patients to go to the surgery if at all possible for there everything is to hand, and in the case of Tara's first litter she had been trying to expel a puppy for an hour and a half so I whipped her into the car and set off for the surgery at around two in the morning. I do not know whether it was the car ride or what, but just as the vet arrived she gave birth, took one horrified look at the mess in the car and jumped out of the back of the estate and would have nothing to do with it at all. I hurriedly had to open the bag clear the mouth and nose and break the umbilical cord, because otherwise the puppy can drown all in the space of a few seconds, and rub the pup dry in the towel I had brought along in case. The vet gave him a quick jab and we set off back home with the pup wrapped in a towel where Tara proceeded to have seven more at regular intervals.

Puppies first appear in a water filled bag, all weighing about 1lb to 1½lb, which the bitch removes biting off the umbilical cord in the process. She will then stimulate the puppy by thoroughly licking it so that within a very few minutes this little wet gleaming object is squirming around hunting instinctively for the milk bar, for all pups are born blind. Following the pup should come the placenta or afterbirth (similar in texture to a liver-like substance) which the bitch will eat endeavouring to clean up the mess, one might say bloody mess but it is also green and brown in colour, that has been expelled with the birth fluids, before settling down to produce the next one. This gives her faeces an almost black colour for a day or two but is quite usual. She may have several puppies in quick succession in the early part of whelping and then she may need some help to cope. Do make sure that the puppy's face is clear so that it can breathe and the cord is severed, which can either be done with the fingers or with a sterile pair of scissors, but make sure as far as possible you cut it in the middle or you could encourage a hernia. Some breeders will remove puppies born earlier to a box under a lamp or containing a covered hot water bottle (making sure it is not too hot) so as to leave the bitch freer to produce the next one and also making sure that none are buried whilst she is producing another. If your bitch becomes agitated it is better to leave them with her only moving them out of the way if she starts to fling herself about. The times between delivery of each puppy can vary from between 10 minutes to two hours, but on the whole Bernese bitches can make the whole affair a fairly long drawn out event. I know Tara's first litter took 27 hours overall, I thought she was never going to finish. You may offer your bitch a dish of warm milk with a dash of water during proceedings but do not be surprised if she refuses it until she has finished whelping. She may also get up to relieve herself in the garden in the middle of it all, but do make sure if she does go out that you go with her plus torch just in case she drops a puppy en route which has been known to happen. Usually they will not move until they have finished and then you have the chance to remove the puppies into the side box and clean up the bed putting in fresh paper and covering. It is now that you can remove any dead pups with the least amount of hassle because this needs to be carried out without the mother seeing you. If there are two of you available one can take the bitch out, even if it means putting her on a lead and insisting, and the other can tidy up, having a quick look in the process to see what proportion of girls there are to boys and also weighing them if you wish. Before the new mother is allowed back into the whelping box sponge down her trousers and vulva with warm disinfectant water and dry her off then settle her down and put the pups to her. She will lick them all again, for this stimulates their bowel and bladder movements, while they hungrily devour the vital colostrum or first of the milk that is so necessary to get them off to a good start.

You need to stay with a bitch the whole of the time she is whelping for if there is any trouble you are then right on hand to cope, but in the case of problems too big for you to handle call the vet earlier rather than later whatever the time of day or night. Providing the birth is normal I do not want the vet visiting the new litter because of infection, and although he is a friend I would rather not have him around at this vulnerable time. It is quite normal for a bitch to have a slight discharge for a day or two after the birth but this can be sponged away with a soft cloth.

Weeks One and Two
Bernese puppies are born with dew claws both front and back and some of them are double ones. These have to be removed within the first five days which can be a shock to the youngster's nervous system. It is better if the bitch is taken away at this time because the pups do yell and she may try to defend them. But if your operator whether self, friend or vet is skilled there should not be any blood spilt and the pups soon get over the trauma, but of course, they need to be kept warm to prevent shock. When Bernese puppies are born they are very pink around the muzzle but this gradually disappears. But to return to the hours after birth, as the bitch and her new family settle down there should be very little sound from them except perhaps contented squeaks. Any prolonged sounds like a high pitched mewing means there is something wrong. This could indicate that one is cold or unable to get to a teat or ill in some way. The bitch may not have enough milk to start with and, particularly if it is a large litter it may be necessary for you to bottle feed the pups in the first few days until they are sucking. This action stimulates the teats and produces the necessary fluid. Another problem may be that the milk is not rich enough or even may be infected in some way when again veterinary help must be sought. A prolonged loud squeaking generally means that one of the most adventurous of the whelps has got on the wrong side of mum and needs rescuing and returning to the bosom of the family.

You may find that one puppy is continually being pushed out from the milk bar by his stronger brothers and sisters and if so you are faced with two alternatives. You can help by bottle feeding the weakling which should then get it on even terms with everyone else within a few days or you can allow it to become weaker and eventually die. If this puppy is a bitch it is very tempting to try and rear it and often with additional feeding it will gain strength. It may have been the last to be born after some length of time and the others having got well established before its arrival it started off at a disadvantage. It is possible that it may have a deformity of some sort and often the bitch recognises these puppies as having a problem and pushes them away by herself. I would definitely try with any puppy but sometimes nature knows best. I never cull my litters (put some down) due to their size as usually the bitch is well able to cope and if not, because of the size of the litter, it should be possible to find a foster mother for some of them for instance a bitch with a small litter or one having a false pregnancy, even a cat has been known to fill the gap. There is a rule in Switzerland and Germany that the maximum size of a litter is six never mind how many the bitch has had. I wonder how many potential Champions have been destroyed because of this piece of bureaucratic legislation?

In the first couple of days after giving birth I feed my bitches on light high protein foods like chicken, fish or rabbit along with plenty of milk, the odd egg and vitamin extras in either pills or powder form mixed with the food or given straight. I leave the family in peace as much as possible just seeing that she goes out at regular intervals and the bedding is changed night and morning. The puppies will soon settle into a routine of sleeping and eating. I do not encourage visitors for the first fortnight partly because of infection and partly because the puppies are better left quietly. Although people do stand in the kitchen and look they are not allowed into the scullery where the whelping box is until the pups are on their feet. This happens after their eyes open at around a fortnight old.

Weeks Three and Four
At about 18 days I start them on solids for if you do not put the right foods in you will not get the necessary bone and the process starts early. I commence feeding with the baby food Fairex and for the first few times protective clothing is necessary as your shoes and trousers, to say nothing of the pups themselves get covered in a sticky porridge. The puppies will need washing thoroughly after the feeding operation, but it is not long before they clean each other and of course mum is always keen to be in on the act. I give one feed for the first two days increasing to two after that then adding best minced beef, given by hand individually about the fifth. By the end of the first week on solids the puppies are on a milk food night and morning and a meal of minced raw beef, cooked flaked fish, minced cooked chicken or scrambled egg and the very fine puppy meal in the middle of the day. By the end of the second week the litter will be on four or five meals a day, two or three of milk and cereals such as Weetabix or Readybrek or special puppy cereal and two of meat etc mixed with a fine meal. Puppies can be fed from either one or two big containers or individual bowls, it does depend a bit on the size of the litter. At least with the latter method everyone gets a fair share especially those that do not eat as fast as some of their greedy brothers and sisters. I do not leave food down once it is obvious that all are satiated, I pick up all the remains as I find they are then ready for their next meal when the time comes whereas if food has been left around (a) it gets stale and (b) it blunts the pups appetite and you really have no idea how much each individual is actually getting. The amount of solid food is rather dependent on how much milk the bitch is still producing and

whether she will allow the pups free access for as long as they want it. Some bitches get fed up quite quickly and leave the litter, only going in to feed and then drying up early. Others are much more maternal and will allow the puppies to go on feeding without restriction.

Weeks Five to Eight

By the time the puppies are about a month old they can be on a very varied diet but basically it remains at the two meat two milk ratio. The meat can be butcher's mince, Pedigree Chum puppy food, cooked fresh rabbit, fish, or chicken (without the bones of course), scrambled egg, the chubb like sausages, cooked tripe or tinned pilchards all make interesting meals mixed with puppy meal or small mixer.

For milk, goats is the best of all, or full cream cow or special puppy milk powder, mixed with Weetabix or Puffed Wheat, Cornflakes or a complete food such as Wilsons or any of the other proprietary mixes. 'Beta' and 'Go Dog' produce a high protein pellet that is useful from about five weeks when their baby teeth are forming. To produce good bone it is necessary to put in good food and this is expensive, but well reared puppies cannot be produced on the cheap for the end product is there for all to see the success or otherwise of the venture. They need a diet of high protein and low carbohydrates not the other way around. Do remember that puppies also need access to clean water, many people forget this is necessary from the early days as the pups grow.

Some people remove the bitch from the pups at around five to six weeks. I do not wean them from the bitch as in my experience she will stop them suckling herself when she dries up, and I do not see any point in removing the source of what is after all nature's most natural of foods, which the breeder should by then be supplementing with four to five meals per day.

It is incredible how quickly the puppies develop and this is especially noticeable once their eyes are open. Up to this time they mostly sleep (in a pile) and eat, but once they begin to focus they are soon moving about lying stretched out in a line to suck at the milk bar, beginning to play, fight and use their voices. If at all possible weatherwise, from about the age of a month I try to feed outside so that the pups get into the habit of relieving themselves outside after feeding, but even when they are in the nest in the first fortnight they leave the rest of the litter to make a puddle etc away in the corner, which is why the whelping box needs to have a Vetbed that does not cover the entire surface. By a month old, they will know you and know you bring food and I love to watch a litter scampering up to their bowls to the cry of 'Puppies, Puppies'.

WORMING

I worm my pups at the age of three, five and seven weeks so that when they are ready to leave home at seven-and-a-half to eight weeks they will need worming again within seven to nine days. Puppies are born with round worms which are transmitted from the bitch, even if she has been wormed in pregnancy. Round worms are white in colour, about four to six inches long (10 to 15 cm) and will stunt growth and even, in extreme cases, cause the death of the puppy. Sometimes, outward signs such as staring coats, pot bellies or lack of weight are present, but often it is difficult to tell if the puppy is infected unless you spot worms in the droppings, or even if badly affected, in the vomit. I usually treat the condition by tablets, Canaval produce a palatable wormer tablet which can be broken in half and the puppy will probably eat it by itself after two dosings. Half a pill is given at three weeks and a whole one a fortnight later. These can be obtained from your vet or petshop. About the seven week stage I get those tablets necessary from the vet in order to make sure that the dosage is right. Here may I say two words of warning over worming. Firstly, do make sure that the puppy does digest the pill and does not palm it down the side to spit it out later. Some Bernese are very clever at this so put it right down the throat, close the mouth and massage the throat if the dog will not take it voluntarily. The second point is that you must devise some foolproof method of separating the dosed from the undosed because it is not a good thing to do one puppy twice and the next not at all. We have a system whereby each puppy is popped outside as he is dosed and cannot get in again until the barrier is lifted and the last pill has been given.

REGURGITATION

It is quite normal for nursing bitches to regurgitate food for their puppies, but although this is a natural form of weaning the bitch will soon begin to lose condition if it is allowed to continue. Not all bitches do it and in fact in all my long experience of breeding I have only ever had one that did. If yours has this trait make sure she is kept away from the pups until an hour or so after she has eaten.

UNSUPERVISED EXERCISE

It should not be necessary to explain that Bernese Mountain Dogs are nosey little souls and put their oars into all sorts of places that are not good for them. They should not be left out by themselves unsupervised in the garden unless in a confined area like a kennel and run where they really cannot get up to mischief very easily.

POSSIBLE PROBLEMS

While not going into all the possible difficulties encountered in whelping I felt I should mention one or two points of general interest. Most Bernese have their litters with no complications but there are some who for one reason or another do have difficulties. One of these is an only bitch living in a house as a pet and used to being the centre of attention, she may refuse to push or help at the birth at all to try and keep the owner's attention on herself. These bitches do not make very good mothers and often have to have their litter by caesarean section.

BREEDING

Breech Birth
Another problem that can arise is if a puppy is wrongly presented. Normally they come head first but occasionally there is one that comes hind legs first for what is termed a breech birth. If this occurs early on in the whelping when the bitch is pushing strongly it should not be too difficult for her as long as both legs come down together and the puppy has not been too long travelling down the birth canal. This condition can be suspected if the bitch strains for some time and produces nothing and unless you are very experienced I would advise calling the vet, although the bitch can be assisted by the owner using a cloth to hold the puppy as far up as possible and using a downward pressure every time the bitch strains. If the bag breaks before the puppy is out, it is likely to drown in the fluid contained therein so it is important that any breech puppy's nose and mouth are clear. This can be done with a soft cloth or even to make doubly sure the puppy can be turned upside down and swung gently by the hind legs.

Inertia
Occasionally the problem of inertia occurs. After straining for some time unsuccessfully, the contractions seem to retract until the bitch gives up and can even go to sleep. This may be due to fear on the part of the bitch in which case a trot around the garden with lots of encouragement may get her started again or, it may be due to a puppy being presented sideways and blocking the entrance to the vagina and the vet's help would be needed promptly.

Fading Puppies
It can be very worrying when apparently healthy pups stop feeding at about three to four days old, moan continuously, feel clammy to the touch and possibly die. The vet may be able to give an injection and will take swabs to try and ascertain the trouble. But in the meantime you are desperate to save the litter so I suggest you try the following mixture – 2 oz of water, one teaspoonful of honey (not sugar), one teaspoonful of whisky, giving half a teaspoonful per puppy every half hour, which could prove to be a full time job with a big litter!

Mastitis and Eclampsia
Mastitis can also cause difficulties if it occurs a few days after whelping. This is a form of milk fever when the bitch, either from producing too much milk or from having a blind teat, gets a hard swollen nipple from which the puppies will not suck and which can be very painful. I remember one of my bitches had a really bad one which the vet said nothing could be done about immediately as opening the swelling up was too dangerous and an injection would take time to reduce the milk. The bitch obviously had not read the same book as she bit it open herself and licked out all the pus and clotted milk, but the teat was a blind one ever afterwards. To treat this condition blind teats should be massaged, the food decreased and fluids increased, milk the bitch yourself and apply a

warm wet cloth to the teat for as long as necessary. With a well fed bitch the condition known as eclampsia should not occur at all. This is due to a lack of calcium and can happen very suddenly. It is most likely to occur with a large hungry litter who are too much for a poorly fed bitch and draw off her vitality at any time up to the first month. The symptoms are heavy panting and a shaking, somewhat reminiscent of a fit, and she will need prompt veterinary attention and a large calcium injection as soon as possible or she will die. In the meantime she should be removed from the puppies and kept warm and quiet. It may be necessary to wean the puppies early as a result.

Nails

Many novice breeders do not think to cut their puppies nails with the result that the bitch can be very sore from the action of the constant kneading of their little feet as they feed. Ordinary nail scissors are all that is necessary but do be careful only to blunt the nail and not cut it to the quick so that it bleeds for that causes pain to the puppy. This can be done weekly from two weeks of age until they leave for their new homes.

Scurf

I do not know why some litters suffer from scurf and others do not but the condition can be treated by a special medicated shampoo obtainable from the vet. Sometimes the cause is fleas, especially if the litter is being kept in straw, and this is detectable because, of course, the puppies scratch and bring themselves up in lumps which can be felt when they are handled.

THE DEVELOPING PUPPY

As the litter grows up and changes, the different characteristics of each puppy emerge and as you watch them develop into independent beings you should be able to pick out the extroverts and the quieter ones so that if you are keeping one yourself, theoretically the choice should be made easier. It is a common assumption that seven years of a human life equals one of a dog, but to be more accurate we need to take the ratio of ten years to one. That means that when the puppy leaves for his new home, he is, in equivalent human terms, already two years old. Half the fun of breeding a litter is to see them off to their new homes with their excited new owners, providing you are happy with the pairing up, ready to start a new life, while you look forward to, after a rest, starting the whole procedure all over again.

SELLING PUPPIES

The best time to plan how you will sell your puppies is before you decide to mate your bitch. If you are unsure of the market, it is best to wait until the prospect of sales improve.

Summer Puppies
Although it is easier to rear summer puppies than those born at other times of the year, it is often difficult to sell at this time. Many people are thinking of their own holidays, and perhaps prefer to buy a puppy when the holidays are over, and it will not be easy to kennel a very young puppy while they are away, especially with the risk of infection at an early age. You can offer, if you have the space, to look after puppies of your own breeding while the owners are away, and this will sometimes clinch a sale.

Winter Puppies
Puppies born in the winter are much harder to rear, requiring more time and attention. If born in October, and ready to leave the nest in December, they may attract Christmas buyers, and these sales need very careful vetting. A dog of any breed, and particularly a Bernese, is a most unsuitable impulse buy for Christmas. A puppy brought into a house on Christmas Day, when there is so much activity and excitement, will be in far from ideal circumstances. Children may play with the puppy for too long, and it may not receive proper rest or even the recommended diet. After Christmas, interest may pall, and as soon as the puppy has made a few messes or chewed up a few shoes or toys, the impulse owner wants to be rid of it, thereby creating further problems. So avoid this sort of sale at all costs.

However, there are genuine buyers at Christmas. People who have had dogs before, particularly dogs of this or a similar breed, know what is expected in the rearing of a puppy and will usually make good owners.

Returning of Puppies
If the new owners of a puppy find for whatever reason that they cannot keep it, they may approach you to ask if it can be returned. If the puppy has no defect, there is no legal reason why you should take it back, nor is it necessary for you to return the purchase price. But most responsible breeders will take their own stock back. If the puppy is still young, it may be possible to sell it to a new owner. In this case, it is usual to give the second fee obtained to the first purchaser after deducting the expenses incurred in looking after it, such as feeding and advertising. More often, owners are only concerned that the dog is found a good home.

Unsuitable buyers
It is well worthwhile getting to know something about prospective buyers so that these situations are avoided as far as possible. I find the following groups of people unsuitable:

People who are out at work all day. Bernese need company, and if left can become bored and destructive. This may lead to the owners not wanting to keep the puppy.

People who are excessively house or garden proud. This can be all right if a separate part of the garden can be fenced for the dog.

People who live in unsuitable places such as city centres or flats. Such people would have to be really dedicated to take the dog to an open space for exercise.

People who are not 'walkers'. Part of the pleasure of a dog is the daily walking.

People whose work may take them abroad for a time such as the armed forces, or employees of overseas companies.

Very elderly people. Will the new owner be able to care for it throughout its life?

Suitable buyers
The best prospects for successful ownership are:

People who have had Bernese or dogs of similar type before, and have kept them throughout the dog's life.

Someone who has just lost a much loved dog through disease or old age. These people will be animal lovers.

Families with children, where the mother is home all day, and enjoys the 'caring' side of looking after a puppy. These lucky puppies will become part of the family unit.

Someone who already has a Bernese. Two dogs are company for each other, and the older dog keeps the puppy in check.

Advertising
If you have not got a waiting list you can advertise your puppies in the dog papers or newspapers, and prepare your copy when the puppies are about two weeks old. It usually takes about a week from the placing of the order until publication. Try to arrange for the advertisement to come out when the puppies are about a month old. Buyers can then visit the puppies, possibly make a choice, and then come back for the puppy later. This gives the buyer a chance to think again, and also to get ready for the puppy. It is better for a buyer to back out at this stage rather than later, and if they do so, there is a better chance of finding other buyers.

You can also make use of reputable agencies, such as Dog Breeders Associates. These agencies will require you to meet certain criteria before they will accept you as a member. They will wish to be assured that the puppies are properly registered and that an authentic pedigree has been provided, and that the puppies have been wormed at the correct intervals.

They advertise widely, and will direct suitable buyers to you, so that you, as the breeder, will deal direct with the buyer. This will enable you to ensure the buyer is someone you are prepared to sell a puppy to. Usually, the sort of people who come to you via these reputable agencies are the ideal owners, people who have taken a good deal of trouble to find good quality home-bred puppies. In return for this service, the agency will expect a commission on the sale. This will vary, but will probably be in the region of 5 to 7% of the sale price.

Paperwork associated with a sale
Finally, to ensure a satisfactory sale for both the new owner and yourself as breeder, make sure that all the paperwork associated with the sale is ready when the puppy is taken away. The new owner is entitled to an accurate pedigree. Although these can be typed, or photostatted, a handwritten document looks better. You can buy pedigree forms on good quality paper at any of the major dog shows, or you can see them advertised in the dog press. They can be supplied over-printed with your prefix, name and address if you wish, although it is not worth going to this expense unless you are expecting to breed on a regular basis. Use the period when the puppies are only one or two weeks to write up your pedigrees. You may find it difficult to find the time later.

You can obtain from your veterinary surgeon, or from one of the major pet food manufacturers, some folders containing a number of leaflets which will be useful to the new owner. They cover such things as toilet training, diet, innoculation etc. You can add to the folder your own pedigree and a diet sheet based on the way the puppy has been fed prior to leaving you. It is helpful to give the new owner a 'starter pack' of the foods you have been using which will help both the puppy and the owner to settle down.

Ideally you will have completed the registration with the Kennel Club of your litter before they are sold. If you complete the necessary forms, and send them off when the puppies are about two weeks old, they will normally be returned within four weeks. If there is any delay, you will need to send the registration papers on to the new owners at a later date.

Keep a careful record at the time of the sale of the name and address of the new owner. You cannot rely on your memory, and you may need to contact the new owners later, not only for the purpose of passing on registration documents, but in case any defect develops in other puppies which you might wish to follow through to check the whole litter.

It is very satisfying to complete the rearing and sale of a good litter to the right owners, with every detail of registration and advice to the owner correct, and it is this attention to detail, and this responsible attitude, which makes for a good reputation.

CHECK LIST

WEEK BEFORE THE PUPPIES ARE DUE

Advise your vet of the expected date.

Prepare the whelping box, and the infra-red lamp.

Introduce your bitch to the box.

WEEK ONE

Phone the owner of the stud dog to report on whelping.

Put down any deformed puppies.

Get dew claws removed.

Inform Bernese owning friends of litter in case they get enquiries for puppies.

WEEK TWO

Prepare pedigrees, and plan any advertisements.

Start to wean puppies.

WEEK THREE

Worm puppies for the first time.

Place adverts, if necessary.

WEEK FOUR

Make sure someone is available to answer the telephone.

WEEK FIVE

See visitors to the litter.

Worm the second time.

WEEK SIX

Complete all paperwork for the litter.

WEEK SEVEN ONWARDS

Puppies start to leave for new homes.

Worm the third time.

WEIGHT CHART

Birth	1 – 1½ lb
1 week	2 – 3 lb
2 weeks	5 – 7 lb
3 weeks	8 – 12 lb
4 weeks	12 – 16 lb
6 weeks	16 – 20 lb
8 weeks	24 – 28 lb

— 8 —
Showing

People enter into the show world for many reasons, many often have no intention of doing so when they first buy a puppy, which is why dogs that have been sold originally as pets are sometimes to be seen in the ring even though they are mediocre specimens of the breed. Most people have heard of Crufts but have no idea of the complexities of the show scene for there are thousands of shows held all over the country during any year. They are held mostly at weekends, but during the main season from April to September they are very often held on many week days as well.

People who show dogs for a hobby are quite mad, at least that is usually the verdict of those who sit on the river bank for hours in pouring rain or walk miles around a golf course following a small white ball. Those of us who do get up at various unearthly hours summer and winter and charge up and down the motorways, north, south, east and west just to put a dog in a ring in a hall, a field or a tent in competition with others, in all sorts of weathers, might be forgiven for concurring sometimes and wondering just why the devil we do do it. One either hates or loves dog shows, there seems to be no middle road, and it can almost become a way of life.

I have always thought how difficult it must be for those people who break Kennel Club rules and find themselves in the equivalent position of the Jockeys' Club 'warned off' state, not allowed even to attend shows let alone show or judge. Their life must stretch emptily before them for the foreseeable future. There is certainly quite a large turnover of exhibitors as people start showing and then find they do not win at once and drop out. But the hard-core of exhibitors go on showing, win or lose year after year.

Whether you get bitten by the showbug depends on a number of factors; looming large amongst which is whether, despite poor handling, your dog is good enough to get placed. There is nothing like the spur of winning a card (and any card will do in the early days, later on one gets more selective) to drive one on. Then there are the friends one makes in

139

showing, it is very much like joining a club which meets regularly. If one enjoys motoring round England and seeing the countryside it gives a perfect opportunity to travel to Scotland, Ireland and Wales in pursuit of one's hobby.

It is a time-consuming, expensive and sometimes frustrating hobby. Those of us who have been at the game a long time keep on going whether we are at the top of the line one week or bottom the next with the same dog. You have to learn to accept the judge's opinion with equanimity, after all that is what you have paid for, and if you can not lose gracefully find another less competitive hobby.

CHOOSING THE RIGHT DOG

You may already own a dog which you would like to show, or someone may have suggested to you that the dog is suitable for showing. You will find it helpful to ask another owner or breeder for an opinion, or best of all, the breeder from whom you purchased the puppy. Breeders usually like to get their stock shown in the ring, but are naturally anxious that only good specimens are exhibited. If the dog has very noticeable faults you will not win top honours, but you could gain a little experience of showing, and this would help you with a subsequent better specimen.

The important thing to remember is that no dog is perfect, but good handling and presentation will compensate for some weaknesses. If you are choosing a puppy with the intention of showing it, make sure that the breeder is aware of this, and seek his help in choosing a suitable one. At about eight weeks, it is usually possible to spot good conformation and marking. Look also for sound temperament, for a shy puppy may not have the necessary outgoing personality for the show ring.

TRAINING

As soon as you get your new puppy, start training straight away. This early training consists of a daily session of about one to two minutes teaching the puppy to stand still while you hold its head in one hand with your thumb above the nose and fingers under the muzzle, while the other hand strokes its back, and when it is calm, gently hold out the tail. Puppies usually object to this rather unnatural procedure and will wriggle and complain, but patience will win in the end, and the earlier this routine starts the better. Always reward the puppy with a titbit and a cuddle after it has stood still for a few seconds, and say the word 'stand' during the exercise several times, so that it will eventually know what is required when you give it this command. Start by trying to teach it to stand still for about five to 10 seconds, and slowly work up to a minute. Adult dogs will need to stand quite still for as much as five minutes in big competitions.

The next lesson will be to walk on a loose lead. An ordinary collar, with a clip on lead is quite suitable for ordinary walks, but for show training you will need a slip type lead, without a collar. The dog must learn to

An outgoing temperament is needed for the show ring.

walk without pulling, responding to a gentle tug to correct its pace or direction. I usually start very short sessions on the lead from about 12 weeks. Do not use any type of metal choke, as this spoils the coat. You can get leather, nylon or soft cord slip leads, and these are much kinder.

There are many ring craft clubs all over the country, and your next step should be to locate the nearest or most suitable one for you. The Kennel Club will give you the address of the clubs in your area if you cannot find one by recommendation.

It is essential to give some training in a classroom atmosphere, for even if you can give the training in standing and moving yourself without help, you cannot provide the environment of noise, lights, people, other dogs and so on, which the puppy must learn to cope with. Bernese are sensitive dogs, and early exposure to all these things is essential to a young puppy if it is not to be frightened on its first trip to a real show. Clubs are friendly places, where you will get help with the training of your puppy, and he will enjoy his evening out, and will make friends with other dogs. Most clubs have regular 'matches' which are like mini shows, and which provide practice both for dogs and handlers in competition and form part of the training pattern.

SHOW REGULATIONS

There are many rules, both written and equally important unwritten, that can trip up a novice exhibitor. I am going to make a few general observations that apply to all dogs before going on to qualify them with our breed particularly in mind.

In the U.K. all but the types of dog event known as an Exemption show are for pedigree dogs only and all are under the complete blanket of the Kennel Club whose rules and regulations govern procedures at the 4,000 events scheduling classes that are licensed annually. There is no closed season and although Championship shows (where one can make up a Champion) usually start with Crufts in January and end with the Ladies Kennel Association in Mid-December, the busiest months are June, July and August. Although others of Open or Limited status take place at weekends right throughout the year.

Show regulations stipulate that puppies must be six calendar months old before being shown, so that means if the dog was born on say the 24th of the month he is not eligible to enter the show until the 24th of the sixth month, even though he may be a week or more into his sixth month. The dog must be registered at the Kennel Club as owned by you, which means transferring him from the breeder into your ownership. The name given him by the breeder is unalterable except to add the owner's affix or registered kennel name at the end. Should your dog not have been named it is up to the new owner to remedy this omission and any entry forms must then carry the letters NAF after the name meaning 'Name applied for'. This application can of course be altered should the Kennel Club in their wisdom turn down your first choice of name. Sometimes 'transfer applied for' or TAF is also seen in a catalogue which means that the change in ownership is in the process of being effected.

TYPES OF SHOW

Canine societies put on shows that are divided into seven types all of which have to be licensed by the Kennel Club. They range from an **Exemption** to Championship, the first is usually run for charity, often in connection with a local agricultural show or gymkhana and it is divided into two parts, the first four classes are for pedigree dogs, not necessarily registered and not Challenge Certificate winners, and the other eight are for any dogs and can be entered on the day, the only type of show where one can do this.

A **Match** is usually held as an internal club competition between a number of breeds and involves pairing off dogs by drawing numbers from a hat. They are eliminated one each time rather in the nature of a knock-out competition and you might find that a Bernese could be drawn against a Chihiuaua. Next on the list comes the **Primary** show which can only schedule eight classes for dogs not having won a first in any class but puppy, it is very rarely held as it is too restrictive. Show number four is entitled **Sanction** and unlike its predecessors must produce a schedule. It limits classes up to Post-graduate to 10 for one breed or 25 for all breeds and a dog's wins to five firsts at Championship show level at Post-graduate class or above. **Limited** shows mean that they are restricted in entry, usually to members of one canine club, with up to 50 classes scheduled for non CC winners, to become eligible for entry one only has to pay the subscription. Catalogues must be produced with the judges name thereupon, one usually doing all classes.

The most common type of show held by societies is of the **Open** variety which is, as indicated, open to all whose breeds are scheduled whether CC winners or not. Many are of one day's duration but more are being held over two days with a number of judges, usually breed specialists, to officiate. It is at Open shows that a point can be gained toward the Junior Warrant if a youngster wins a breed class after the age of 12 months.

Championship shows are the top of the scale and these can be either restricted to one breed, or group of breeds, for example the National Working Breeds or the general variety scheduling classes for most breeds held over two, three or four days such as Windsor, Ladies Kennel Association, Bath etc. with specialist all-round judges.

Bernese Mountain Dog classes are scheduled at 24 general Championship shows throughout the year, three group Championship shows (National Working Breeds, Working Breeds of Scotland, Working Breeds of Wales) and our own three breed shows which offer tickets or Challenge Certificates for the breed. Three of these CCs under three separate judges will qualify a dog to put the magic letters Ch (Champion) before his name. A CC is awarded to the top dog and the top bitch on the day and from these two comes the ultimate Best of Breed which goes forward to compete against the winners of the five other groups. From these winners of the Working, Hound, Terrier, Gundog, Utility and Toy groups is chosen Best in Show. Group Winners and of course Best in Show and Reserve Best in Show, Best Puppy and Reserve Best Puppy do usually receive monetary awards, as do the winners of sponsored stakes classes, but very few of the Championship shows these days give money prizes, and those that do only award £2, £1 and 50p for the first three places. The man in the street imagines that one must be rolling in money if you do have a winning streak, but nothing could be further from the truth for by the time you have paid Championship entries of anything between £8 and £12 per dog for a first entry, the petrol to get there and back plus

Benched and bored at Crufts.

numerous animal expenses like food and the goods you buy whilst you are there you could end up the year being hundreds, if not, thousands of pounds out of pocket, if you dare to keep account of the money spent. Shows are big business and in 1990 (the latest figures to hand) 581 Championship shows were licensed by the Kennel Club with 5,207 shows in total ranging from Crufts at the top down to Exemption level.

Crufts was the only Championship show to be held in London. It takes place in January and is both the beginning and end of the show season. It is the beginning in that it is the first Championship show of the new season and the end because it is the result of all the qualifying shows held during the previous 12 months. It began in 1891 at the Royal Agricultural Hall in Islington under the auspices of Charles Cruft, its founder, and after the war was held for 30 years in Olympia moving to Earls Court in 1978. It has increased from a two day to a four day show over the last decade with world-wide media coverage. It was thought that it was immovable from London as it is the Kennel Club's own show, but in January 1991 (Centenary year) due to all sorts of unforeseen circumstances it moved to the National Exhibition Centre in Birmingham, much to the delight of most exhibitors for whom access and travelling will be made easier.

ENTERING A SHOW

What about the novice owner of a Bernese who wants to show and does not quite know where to start? My advice would be to try and start at

Limited or Sanction level before plunging into the deep end of the Championship show but this is not always possible. The first step in practical showing is to obtain a schedule for with it comes the entry form. These are all roughly of the same format and will, therefore, be accepted by any secretary if you do not happen to have the one for a particular show. It requests information on your dog's breeding, your ownership and the classes you wish to enter. Do read it through carefully for mistakes are expensive and time consuming if a secretary has to ring to clarify incorrect information. If you make an error, say in the name of the dog, the Kennel Club will remove any prizes won whether you inform them or the mistake turns up later.

The closing date for entries is given on the form and although two or three days' leeway for postal delays are normally allowable once the entries have gone to the printer it is too late to accept any more. Any forms received after that are returned to the sender along with the cheque.

I have mentioned entry forms for shows and I can hear you saying 'where do I get these from then?' Once you start entering your dog you will pick up local schedules at shows on the secretary's table or on some of the many stands selling all the accoutrements of dogdom. Other sources of supply are the weekly canine dog newspapers, *Dog World* and *Our Dogs* and if you have entered a show the previous year you will probably be sent a schedule for the following event.

A novice sometimes finds it difficult to fill in the correct classes in which to put his dog, particularly if the dog is aged two or three before being entered for competition. Minor Puppy, Puppy and Junior classes are limited by age, the former up to nine months, puppies to 12 months and junior to 18 months. Wins in any breed classes, from 12 to 18 months count towards the award known as Junior Warrant which can be claimed from the Kennel Club on the acquisition of 25 points, one for a win at Open show level in breed and three for a Championship show win.

Puppies are now restricted from gaining points for a Junior Warrant until they are 12 months old, then all the winning has to be crammed into the last six months. It is an odd award as although it is recognised by the Kennel Club it does not carry any official kudos nor does it benefit the holder in any way but exhibitors will travel miles to gain the points necessary.

After Junior classes it depends on what the dog has won previously and the definitions for each one is listed in the schedule. Often Championship show classifications jump from Junior to Post-graduate, because of the Crufts qualifier, and with a young dog it is probably a good idea not to exhibit at Championship shows for four to six months after he comes out of Junior. This gives him a chance to mature as Post-graduate in Bernese usually has a very large entry in both dogs and bitches these days.

When entering a youngster in a Championship show there are no restrictions as to the number of classes for which he is eligible, apart from those of age stated above. But if you are wise it is better to limit entries to two or three at the most, for a young Bernese can tire very quickly and boredom also sets in if he has to wait about, often in the heat of the sun. In Limited and Open shows, classes are more usually spread out, particularly in Varieties, but I would advise refraining from entering the latter with a youngster until the dog is older and better able to cope. An Open class means just that it is open to all, but entry is not obligatory so again wait until your dog is mature before entering. Where Bernese classes are scheduled you must enter in the breed class first, you may not just enter Varieties alone.

Do not forget to sign your entry form at the bottom to the effect that your dog has not been in contact with any contagious or infectious disease over the previous six weeks nor is it liable to disqualification due to its being blind or deaf. A dog with only one testicle descended (monorchid) or with neither (cryptorchid) down is not actively banned these days, but if your dog is so affected it is not worth spending the entry fee because both conditions are serious faults and no judge would give them a second look. It is worth noting that sometimes a youngster who is having trouble dropping one of his testicles can be helped with a hormone injection if the vet can feel it further up the scrotum. In 1991 the Kennel Club rescinded the disqualification of spayed bitches and castrated dogs.

Another thing not to forget is your address and those printed sticky address labels can be very useful if, as on some forms, you need to write it three times in order to allow notification for the next show schedule etc. Fees must be paid at the time of entry and do remember to use first class post and get the form off in plenty of time, the earlier the better from the secretary's point of view. With Championship show entries it is sensible to get a certificate of posting as, if they go astray, you then have proof of the date on which they were mailed and this is the only proof that is acceptable to the show committees.

Championship shows usually send passes and car parking tickets a week to 10 days before the event and this is the only notification that you will get that your entries have arrived, unless you have enclosed a stamped addressed envelope with your form. If your passes have not come five days prior to the show telephone the secretary to check she has received your letter. If you have not been entered in the catalogue you will not be eligible to compete and will have a wasted journey, unless you can prove posting with the stamped certificate. Some Open shows these days also have passes, particularly if they are run in conjunction with an agricultural event, like Wetherby or Bakewell, so check your schedule to see if passes will be sent out or not. If you are entering only one dog mark on the schedule the classes entered then you will not have to rely on your memory. It is when you come to enter two or three dogs it is important to put names to the entered classes and not just indicate them.

It is usually discernible from the schedule the times at which the breed will be in the ring as all Championship shows and most Open ones these days give an order of judging but even so the society has a right to alter these times and cannot be responsible for you missing your classes should they find need to do so. Judging usually commences in this country at Championship and Open shows at 10 am, although in Europe it can be as early as 8 am. Even here when there are large entries for some of the popular breeds like Dobermans and German Shepherd Dogs etc you can expect a 9 o'clock start, which can mean a very early departure from home unless one can run to a hotel or has friends in the vacinity and can travel the night before. Smaller shows start judging anywhere between 11 am and 2 pm depending on the classification. Removal times at the big shows are stated in the schedule and can range from no restrictions at all to 1, 2 or 3 pm right up to the 5 pm removal time at Crufts. These rules are much more relaxed these days than of old as most people want to get away once they have been in the ring, often not even waiting to see which dogs take the top awards. In the old days when life was not such a rat race, exhibitors had the time to socialise after the judging and all was much more relaxed. Showing then was much more fun than today's rush to get there and rush to get back but it must be remembered many now have no help at home with the dogs. Exhibitors may not go before the official removal time unless there is a dire emergency and show secretaries can recite a list of excuses for wanting to leave an event early as long as your arm, some quite amazingly intricate. If you do slip out through a hole or over the fence you face the risk of being reported to the Kennel Club and may be fined, but due to the easing of restrictions the temptation to do so these days is much less than it used to be.

UNWRITTEN RULES

I said earlier that I would mention the unwritten rules on showing and first among these is that it really is not done to show dogs under the person who bred them. I know on occasions this is done, but it leaves the judge open to criticism either way, if they put up the animal the critics say 'Oh well, it is her own stock' and if they put it down the commentator says 'Oh, doesn't like his/her own breeding'. The Kennel Club lays down that if the dog has been kennelled by the judge or he/she has owned the animal previously, 12 months must elapse from the change of ownership date before the dog is eligible. It is also rather pointless to exhibit a dog a second time under a judge who has already given him a CC for it does not count towards his title and you are barring the way for someone else to win. The only exceptions are Crufts which is dogdom's shop window or if due to illness or some other unforseen circumstance the original judge is unable to carry out their appointment and a replacement has already judged you. It is possible in this case to withdraw and reclaim entry fees but if it is your only dog you may not want a wasted journey. It really is most unfair to take a bitch to a show in full season, Bernese being what they are with regard to the love stakes, they take a great deal of holding once they have the aroma, which cannot really be masked 100% even by a spray or ampoule, and it is very difficult to show a dog who is permanently trying to get his head down to the ground.

PREPARATIONS

So you have completed your entry forms for your Bernese to appear at a show and sent it off to the secretary in plenty of time. So now all you have to do is await for the appointed day and time. In the intervening days you will probably need to wash his white shirt front even if you do not go the whole hog of a total bath. He will need to be well brushed and combed out and also tidied up. Bernese Mountain Dogs do not need much titivating and certainly should not be barbered but the old hair between the toes needs scissoring (remember to use serrated not ordinary scissors for this) so that the foot is neat and cat-like. The ragged growth on the back of the hocks also needs the same treatment so that it lies flat. The ears are a moot point, some people like to see the old hair in streamers but personally I like my dog's ears to conform to nature's shape and add to the overall tidy picture so I pull out the old hair with the help of a stripping comb. If one attends enough shows the amount of concentrated grooming is kept to a minimum for one is doing it constantly to keep tidy.

By show day your dog should look a picutre of health with gleaming white shirt front and shiny black coat, while correct feeding and exercise should have produced bright eyes and a cold nose. He should be able to move freely on a loose lead and stand still for the judge to examine his body and teeth without fidgeting or collapsing. The ring is not the place for training your dog, this should be done either at home or at your dog club but having said that, there are occasions when, if your dog misbehaves, he must be corrected at the time, in the ring if necessary, for they are intelligent enough to know the difference and some only play up in front of an audience.

Prior to going into the ring the dog needs a last brush and comb and a rub over with a soft chamois leather also helps. All grooming equipment should be kept together and I use a soft pouch which I think was originally intended for a pencil case. You will also need a show bag of some sort. When you are successful enough to win Best of Breed at a Championship show, Pedigree Chum will provide one of these but till then you will require some sort of a bag. In this you will keep benching chains, water bowl, food and water dishes, towel, kennel nameplate plus a show lead or even two to be on the safe side. You can buy these show leads in nylon, leather or webbing and of these I prefer a leather ring lead, which serves as both a collar and lead, for nylon can cut into your hands especially if your Bernese lunges at a passing bitch. Nylon leads are produced in various colours, which seems to attract some people, and a number are sold for this reason.

Another necessity if the show is benched is a cover to put on the bench, some people use carpet squares (which can be awkward to carry), an old blanket, an old electric blanket with the wires removed, Vetbed or a synthetic furry cover, some of which can be purchased at one of the many show equipment stands. Benching must be provided at the larger shows or where breed entries top the 200 mark. Benches are three- sided metal partitions making a frontless cage in which the dog must be chained short whilst not being shown or exercised. Kennel Club regulations stipulate that proper chains not leads must be used and it is inadvisable to ever use a choke chain as a dog could hang itself if it falls off the bench and cannot get back. Over the top of the bench is the number of the exhibit which coincides with your own ring number, usually worn in the front and secured by a special clip. There are some very nice clips with Bernese heads on them readily available these days.

Where there is no benching provided, for example at smaller shows, exhibitors have the option of tying their dogs to a convenient fixture

In the ring.

indoors or buying one of the metal corkscrews that can be twisted into the grass to provide a standpoint outside. Providing it is not too hot dogs can be left in cars too, until the appointed judging time, but remember Bernese do suffer quickly from heat exhaustion.

The number of your dog is listed in the catalogue under your name in the Bernese Mountain Dog section and is only relevant for this particular show. It lists the dog's registered name, sire, dam, date of birth etc, as per entry form so that the particulars are easily available for those interested. Exhibitors numbers can usually be obtained from the ring steward when it is time for your class, but sometimes they are found on the bench or they may be sent by post with passes prior to the show day by some of the bigger societies, whilst smaller events tend to have them on the table by the entrance. There is no hard and fast rule, each show is different and one has to wait and see what pertains on the day when you arrive at the venue.

Depending on how organised a person you are in the mornings it is worth getting everything required for a show the following day ready the night before. Then when one comes to start, often in the early hours at 5 or 6 am, they have only got to be picked up as you rush out. Do not forget schedules and passes, purse, pens, leads and showbag plus food for the period of absence. Make sure that your Bernese Club badge and showclip are pinned to your jacket and the car has been refuelled in plenty of time. If one has friends in the show vicinity or own a caravan it makes a very pleasant break to be able to motor down the day previously to get to the showground in a civilised manner the next morning without the worry of traffic hold-ups making you miss your class. It is much better to arrive in plenty of time at the ground giving your dog time to relax rather than rushing straight into the ring from the car. Try and stop en route so that your Bernese can relieve himself somewhere other than on the showground or worse still in the ring. The exhibitor is responsible for cleaning up after his dog on the showground, including the officially designated exercise areas too, these days.

After making the dog presentable it is worth spending time considering your own turn out when showing a Bernese. Because they are mainly black in colour it is not very sensible for the handler to dress in a black skirt or trousers so that the dog's outline cannot be seen, contrasting colours are much more to the point. There is always a fair bit of running to be done when showing so make sure you have on sensible shoes and leave at home any jangling chains or jewellery, including dangling earrings which are sometimes a temptation for a puppy to pull off. Also empty your pockets of change which can clank when you are on the move and also weigh you down.

ON ARRIVAL AT THE SHOWGROUND

On arriving at the showground obtain a catalogue and check your entry to make sure no mistakes have found their way into your dog's details. If he is not entered in the correct classes go at once to the secretary and get the matter put right before entering the ring for if it is allowed to go unchecked and you win, or are placed, the Kennel Club can withdraw that award when the mistake is discovered.

If you are not around when your class is called you stand a chance of missing it so do be ready to go into the ring. If you happen to be showing another breed or entered in the stakes it is a pound to a penny having hung around for hours you will be in both rings at the same time often at opposite ends of the showground. Judges are usually very accommodating but they cannot wait for ever so do inform the breed ring steward if you are likely to be in this position.

IN THE RING

The apprentice does not need to confide to her neighbour (I say 'her' because 7 out of 10 of the people who show are women) 'I have never been in the ring before' the fact is very obvious, for like all skills although there appears nothing to it when an expert is handling, when a novice is doing so the contrast is marked.

On first entering the ring take up a position with the unseen dogs, it does not matter where in the line you stand but if you are a novice it is safest in the middle. You can then see what is expected whereas if you are on either end it is possible the judge may start at the opposite end to where one expected them to begin on occasions. Do make sure your dog is under control at all times in the ring, particularly in a mixed class where the Bernese boys can sometimes get rather amorous if their

The author showing.

neighbour happens to be a girl. Many people give titbits to their dog in the ring, if this is your practice make sure it is done as unobtrusively as possible and avoid rustling plastic bags which can distract the dog in front of you, often at a crucial moment. Do not give food when the judge comes up to look at your animal so that the dog's head is jerking round in the wrong place at the wrong time, one of the things I hate to see when I am judging.

When the class are all in the ring and the steward has checked the numbers some judges will work down the line before looking individually at each dog, whereas others will ask the exhibitors to move round the ring first. This movement is carried out in an anti-clockwise direction (probably because most people are right-handed) and gives the judge an overall picture of the dog's gait. Do remember always to keep your dog on the judge's side, after all it is the dog's movement not your own that is of interest. Leave room to move easily and keep in single file using all the ring space available. Do watch for the judge's signal to stop, which is, thankfully, usually only after one round, Bernese not being like the German Shepherd Dogs who seem to go on pounding round forever.

Each dog is 'set up' in front of the judge which means that you place your Bernese full square with front feet apart and back feet comfortably extended for the judge to go over. Do not over-handle and keep out of the way, coming round to the dog's head, whilst the judge goes over the rest of him. You will probably be asked your Bern's age but you may not make general conversation whilst in the ring. When the judge has finished his examination you will be asked to move your Bernese in one of two formations. Do listen to what the judge requires. I know how irritated I get if having asked specifically for a triangle I get a circle instead of the three distinct corners. When you have moved join the line of seen dogs behind the dog originally in front of you. It is permissible now to chat or 'coffee house' with your neighbour but keep an eye on the judging so that you can set your dog up once the judge has finished looking at them all.

If your Bernese is nervous in the ring it can affect the way he stands and the way in which a dog is presented to the judge can make or mar his chances. A clever handler can make a good dog look even better or disguise the faults of a poor one just by the way he is shown. One common fault is not standing the dog full square so that his toes turn in or out and he appears cowhocked or to have a dip in the back. Never draw attention to a fault in your dog by touching the offending parts and when setting him up turn his best side to the judge not the other way round. Concentrate on the judge whilst you are in the ring even if only with one eye whilst discussing the canine world with your neighbour so that if he requires you to do something else you are ready. Unlike America we do allow our dogs to relax once they have been seen and on a hot day many exhibitors wait in the shade out of the ring altogether.

The final positions in the class varies with the person doing it. Some judges pull out a selection for a second look, mostly on movement, some pull out in similar order but state they have not finished and you get others call out dogs in their final order straight away. If you are on the short list it is worth remembering that you have not won first, second or third until you have the card in your hand and the judge is writing the result in his book, so go on showing until then as the places can easily be changed even in the line-up. If you are not selected the judge usually says 'finished with the rest' and you then leave the ring. Do not then grumble about the result, you paid your money for the judge's opinion and that's what you have got. There is nothing in the contract about liking it so think to yourself there is always the next time and keep mum. Everyone has good and bad days although if you have been doing well and then get left out it comes as a bit of a shock, but it serves to bring you down to earth. If the same people won every time there would be no point in showing and if you hate being beaten you had better take up a less competitive hobby. The steward then hands out the prize cards and notes the numbers of the winners for the records while the judge writes the critique, usually only on the first two dogs placed at a Championship show and the winner at an Open show. This normally appears in the dog papers at some later date.

Prize cards are awarded according to position in the line-up. Red for first (in America blue is the top colour), blue for second, yellow for third and green for fourth which is often termed 'Reserve'. Very often a 'very highly commended', 'highly commended' and even 'commended' (down to seventh place) are also given and the colours for these vary. At far too few shows these days prize money is also awarded although some sponsorship by firms like Pedigree Petfoods does help make stakes classes worthwhile. At Championship shows, breed class wins in money can be claimed from the treasurer on production of the serrated slip torn from the prize card filled in and signed. But do not put your card up over your bench leaving the counterfoil still attached as some people have taking ways. In Open shows the money is usually in an envelope stapled to the card itself for ease of administration.

Most shows award rosettes in addition to prize cards in the same colours as the cards. Championship shows usually only give them to the Dog C.C., Bitch C.C. and Best Puppy winners, although occasionally all first class winners will get them, but other shows usually give rosettes from first to fifth place. Some pretty coloured ribbons are usually available for Best of Breed, Reserve Best of Breed, Best Opposite Sex and Best Puppy on almost all occasions and these rosettes make a great splash of colour if you put them up on a wall at home. Championship shows usually only have trophies for the top winning dog, bitch and puppy overall. Most other shows, even the lowly Exemption events, provide them as well as cups, plaques, tokens, shields or bowls to be held from show to show for Best of Breed, Best Working, Best Gundog, Toy etc., and many other classifications. These have to be returned but sometimes on special occasions replicas are presented to the winners that they can keep. If you have had a good day it is worth checking the catalogue for cups and trophies awarded as there may be one for Best

Working, Best Working Puppy or whatever and if your dog is eligible to compete, it would be a pity to miss the chance.

But to go back to the ring if you are entered in the second class the steward will indicate where the seen dogs are to stand, and it is usual to keep out of the way until the class has been judged and then join the line, to be considered with them for the new set of awards on offer.

At the time of writing placings from first to third in both Limit and Open class at a Championship show qualify your Bernese for entry into the Kennel Club Stud Book, plus also qualifying for an annual entry to Crufts show. The Kennel Club award the dog a special number which should be quoted in preference to the original registered number when filling in pedigree forms or writing to the registrations department. If the Championship Certificate or the Reserve Championship Certificate winners come from classes other than Limit or Open they also qualify for the Stud Book. The Kennel Club does tend to alter the Stud Book qualifying classes from time to time so it is worth checking what is in operation at the time your dog is entered.

At a small show to find the eventual Best Dog in the Show all unbeaten dogs line up for the judge's final decision but it is more complicated at a Championship show which is worked on a group system. In the Working Group for example, all Best of Breed winners compete for Best of Group and there are six groups each choosing their top dog. The final line-up for Best in Show is made up of the winning Toy, Hound, Utility, Gundog, Working and Terrier from which one dog overall is chosen with a runner-up in Reserve position. If your Bernese wins Best of Breed and you have also entered in Variety classes, at the moment Kennel Club rules allow Best of Breed and Best Puppy winners to compete in the Varieties but do remember to remove the earlier won rosettes before going into the ring again. If awarded Best of Breed, it is courtesy to your judge to remain at the show for Best in Show judging if you possibly can, otherwise there is no representative of the breed in the big ring at the end of the day. There is a great deal to learn for a novice exhibitor and this has been covered in more detail in the previously published book of mine (*A Concise Guide to Dog Showing*) but I hope I have answered some of your questions. A great deal can be gleaned from watching and listening and most of the old hands at the showing game in Bernese are very helpful and will point newcomers in the right direction. Some people ask the judge at the conclusion of the judging why he did not like their dog and most will explain their point of view, but remember it is only that, and a dog that one judge dislikes one week another may praise on the following. Each show is sufficient unto itself and the experienced exhibitor remains optimistic and looks forward, not back, to glories yet to come as each show finishes.

— 9 —
Working

Placed by the Kennel Club in the Working Group for shows in England it is only occasionally that the Bernese is able to prove how it got that classification. As I have already explained in the chapter on the history of the breed its job in Switzerland was as a draught animal, pulling a cart for the farmer, butcher or basket maker and it is in this direction that its working abilities are most often seen in this country.

A few Bernese are also worked in obedience and agility competitions, showing an aptitude for both once the difficult early stages have been overcome. Working trials are also a possibility, at least at their lowest levels, but I do not know of any Bernese taking part. Bernese Mountain Dogs are not natural retrievers so this is quite difficult to teach for obedience and in the agility tests the stubborn side of their nature can be very much to the fore if there are jumps they do not wish to tackle. But they are naturally agile for so big a dog and do enjoy it once they are convinced there is a purpose to these games.

Bernese are good but not aggressive guard dogs, they will let you know if there are people about with their deep resonant bark and will also guard the car but I do not really know if they would defend their owner if attacked, for the instinct to run away if thoroughly frightened is still much to the fore.

In Switzerland today the Bernese Mountain Dog is also used for tracking and rescue work, particularly in connection with people buried under snow in instances such as avalanches in the Swiss Alps. Competitions are held annually by the Swiss Kennel Club with tests set with people actually under the snow. Bernese have also been trained as 'earthquake' dogs, but I do not know of any trained for these tasks in Great Britain so I am going to restrict this chapter on working ability to the three avenues open to most UK Bernese owners, those of carting, obedience and agility work.

155

BASIC OBEDIENCE

Before commencing working your Bernese Mountain Dog in any discipline he must know the basic commands of 'come', 'sit', 'stand', 'down', and 'heel'. He must also be able to walk on a lead without pulling. This standard is necessary for whatever branch of work you wish to try. Carting and agility have their own vocabulary and that has to be learnt in addition, but as the saying goes 'you cannot make bricks without straw' and it is not possible to work your dog in either discipline unless you first have the basics of obedience on which to build.

CARTING

Of the three different types of work in which Bernese Mountain Dogs are involved in this country, the most usual is carting whether for display or competition. Some Bernese take to this activity like the proverbial duck to water and seem to know what is required of them almost by instinct, while others need a great deal of patient persuading before they will pull at all and some will have none of it at any price.

The best age to start the training for pulling a cart is about 18 months as prior to this the dog is not sufficiently mature to be able to pull any weight. The first thing necessary is to have a properly fitting harness and anyone involved in this activity would advise a novice on the best type to obtain.

The Swiss have three different types of harness in use, the first is the **Sailen** which is the most popular. It is an 8 cm broad padded leather strap sitting on the shoulder joint. There are two straps across the back and one across the chest.

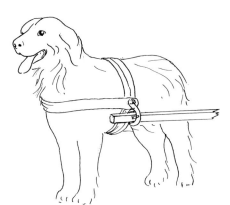

The Sailen.

The second type is the **Kummet** which is a padded ring made of wood, iron or leather. Two ropes are attached to the rings which are fixed to the bar of the cart.

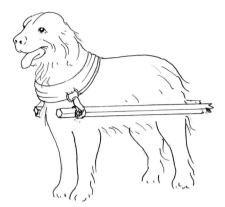

The Kummet.

The **Kragen** or collar is the third type and this is a combination of both the Kummet and the Sailen. The leather widens out at the sides incorporating a strap across the back and the ring from the Kummet, thus relieving any pressure on the windpipe.

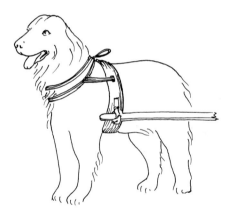

The Kragen.

I had my harness made by the local saddler in special soft leather, which was fitted to prevent any chafing when being worn by the dog, rather like the Kragen mentioned above. The pattern for the one I had made was taken from an actual pad that was placed on a roll of wallpaper and drawn round to provide the pattern needed (see diagram).

As can be seen the leather is one continuous piece that slips over the head of the dog and forms a breast band over the back by a strap joining both sides together under which, on both sides, are D rings with straps attached for the shafts to slot into. At the back of the harness are the traces straps, sewn on top of the girth buckle and straps. My dogs are of average size and the harness measures 36 inches long and 30 inches wide in the centre rising to 10 inches where the strap goes over the back (see diagram), the whole fitting comfortably without being too big or too small.

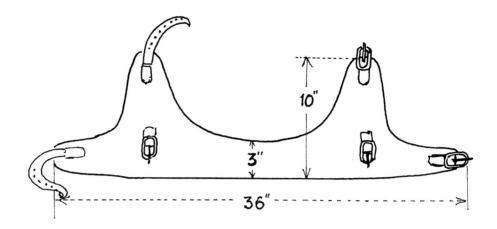

The author's harness.

The youngster needs to get used to wearing it and a few minutes at a time, two or three times a day is usually sufficient, but the important point to get over is that the dog stands still to have it put on (and taken off) without dancing about or what is worse, rolling over onto his back. Therefore the command 'stand stay' has to be taught for this purpose. Another of the first and early steps is to get behind the dog and drive it (so it gets used to someone or thing behind it) before putting it in a cart proper.

Once the dog is accustomed to the harness the next step is to set it into the cart. It is not very intelligent to put an untried Bernese into your best cart for a first attempt as almost anything could happen, and probably would. Some people advocate using a large cardboard box 18 × 24 inches to start with as it does not matter what happens to it as it is easily replaced. Start by making two holes in the front of the box near the bottom, thread a light rope of 5–6 feet through and fasten either end to the D rings of the harness, this gives sufficient distance between the dog and the box. A jacket or other lightish object should be left in the box to provide ballast and prevent the box from bouncing about.

Another method is to obtain a wooden box or plastic baker's tray, attach broom handles for shafts and get some pram wheels off the nearest tip. But remember that four wheels, one at each corner, are a lot more stable and therefore safer than just two in the centre. But whatever method you choose to start off with it makes sense to begin on grass so that noise from behind is not going to spook your dog. Some people use a simple lead attached to the collar for steering purposes, but, perhaps because I am used to driving horses, I prefer two reins (one either side of the collar) so that to change direction pressure can be applied on the correct side, thus helping the dog to turn,

Once having got used to having the harness on it makes sense to get

Traditional cart and milk churns.

the dog used to shafts coming down from above. Do not drop them down all of a sudden, but carefully raise and lower them several times with the dog in 'stand stay' position until he is used to this procedure. The cart has then to be attached to the harness and the girth fastened, then all is ready to go.

Once having harnessed up to move off give the command for this to the dog. It does not matter which words you use, I say 'get-up', some say 'pull', others 'hey' but always use the same words. You will also need

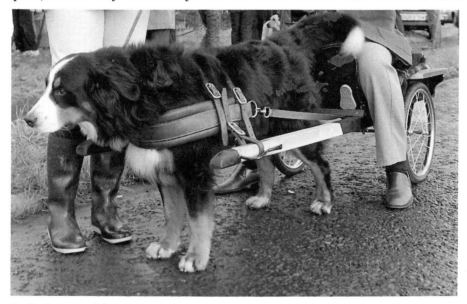

Typical cart and harness.

'whoa' and 'back' in order to stop or reverse. It helps if you have another person in the early stages to try and keep the dog straight and teach it to lean into the harness when pulling by holding back the cart at the rear. Walk normally and talk to the dog, using your voice to encourage him in his task. When he gets more experienced you can take him on gravel and road surfaces remembering to go up hills (if possible) and not just keeping on the flat. Perhaps at this point I should remind carting enthusiasts that an old nineteenth century law relating to dogs in carts is still operative. You will be breaking the law if you take your dog in his cart on the public highway without special permission, such as to take part in a procession for example.

Adult Bernese can pull three times their own weight so can give rides to children or pull loads without too much trouble. I use my dogs when I am fetching wood from the fields to the saw bench for logging in the winter and they seem to enjoy the exercise for they love pulling. Some do and some do not pull but most will providing they are not frightened in any way, and get plenty of experience at each stage so they become used to things slowly. One problem that can occur is that whatever the dog is pulling appears to be chasing him and one wants to avoid at any cost the fear incurred if the cart 'runs-up' onto the dog. The cardboard box will not do this of course but do make sure the traces are held firm to the shafts of any cart and so prevent them doing so.

A dog's movement is restricted by shafts and this is another factor he has to come to terms with when turning to go round corners or obstacle courses. One method used to give experience in this particular facet, if you find your dog is not a natural, is two pieces of wood about 1½ inches thick and 5 feet in length joined together at the back. Holes (equal distances apart on both) are drilled in each so that they can be attached to the harness at any point, thus varying the distance from the dog to the backboard. Practice can be done with this before using the cart proper if your Bernese shows any apprehension.

Carts can be bought or made and come in many shapes and sizes. I have two, one my husband made which is for rough work like wood fetching and one I bought in Holland (which was for children) and fortunately packed flat for transporting home. I then got my joiner to remove the single pole that came with it and replace it with shafts made of ash. Some people have located and purchased the typical Swiss carts with open rungs and others have had haywains, traps and a number of other copies of nineteenth century horsedrawn vehicles made for their dogs, faithfully reproduced in every detail. The carts always cause a great deal of interest whenever they appear in public and make quite a spectacle, especially if they are decorated and the handlers are in Swiss costume for good measure.

OBEDIENCE

The second of the opportunities for working the breed can be found in Obedience, which for its devotees, is a world of its own. Bernese cannot hope to compete on equal terms with breeds such as the Border Collie or German Shepherd Dog, but dogs and owners can get a great deal of satisfaction from taking part, and of course it is usually those dogs who have been properly trained who walk away with all the top prizes at the Garden Party events even if at no other time.

The best method of training for obedience is to join a club, of which there are over 500 registered at the time of writing in this country, or attend one of the dog training evening classes run by most local authorities. If you wish to enter competitions your dog must be listed on the Kennel Club Obedience Register.

There are six Obedience competition classes each with its laid down requirements. Dogs must be entered in the lowest class for which they are eligible plus one other if desired. The first test **Pre-beginners** can only be scheduled at Limited and Sanction shows, and if the dog or handler has won a first prize in any show previously they are barred from entering this one. The second or **Beginners** also has a stipulation that it is only open to an owner, handler or dog that has not won two or more firsts in Beginners or a first in any other class. **Novice** bars dogs that

Miss Debbie Marsh and Drummann the Wayfairer competing at Crufts.

have won twice in any class except Beginners while **A** is open to dogs that have not won three firsts in **A**, **B** or **C**. **B** also has a bar at three firsts but only if in classes **B** or **C**.

In class C entry is allowable to all at an Open show, but has limits on dogs at a Championship show to the effect that to enter this class dogs must have had two wins at Novice, two at Class A and two at Class B levels plus a win at Open Class C before being eligible. This is because Champion obedience shows award qualifying certificates (three of which make up a Champion) to the winning dog and bitch in Class C for entry to Crufts. The winning of this is the top honour of the year and counts for two certificates, thus making up any dog to Champion who is not already at that level.

Certificates, however, are withheld if the winners lose more than 10 marks out of the 300 total. Obedience shows vary from breed shows in some of their regulations, although in both disciplines bitches in season are barred for obvious reasons. If you are used to stuffing food into your dog in the show ring be warned that no food at all is allowed in the obedience one. A slip (choke) chain or smooth collar is stipulated for control and marks may be deducted for unruly behaviour whilst in the ring, of dog or handler.

The tests themselves are graded in difficulty from the basic heel on and off lead, recall, retrieve, sit and down exercises of the lowest classes, which now include a temperament test. Scent discrimination, send away and distance control are added for the higher tests, and in all classes there are no penalties for using the dog's name in conjunction with a command or signal. You need to stay awake though, for if you are not present when the stay and scent exercises are called you will be considered to have withdrawn from the class.

As I said earlier, Bernese are not likely to be in contention for the top awards in the cut throat world of Obedience as other breeds are more suitable for the level of perfection necessary these days in order to win classes. But certain standards can be obtained and if this is where your interest lies, good luck in your attempts.

AGILITY

The other type of working open to Bernese Mountain Dogs is Agility tests. They are designated fun competitions in the Kennel Club Year Book Regulations, designed for enjoyment purposes and so a certain amount of informality is encouraged in their spectator appeal. They were first seen by the general public on TV at Crufts and have caught on to such an extent that they now have a large following dedicated to this type of competition, and a number of Kennel Club registered clubs and societies have sprung up. These can apply for a licence to hold an Agility test and conditions for such a test state that the area must be 40 × 30 yards minimum and contain between 20 and 30 obstacles at least four yards apart. Hurdles, fences, gates, tunnels, ramps, etc can be included in the course but none may involve the use of fire. Dogs involved in

An Agility test.

Agility must be over 12 months and are not allowed to wear any sort of collar whilst in the ring working. Bernese owners can get a taste of Agility at the club working days when a course is provided for practice and competition.

WORKING TRIALS

Before leaving this chapter I must mention Working Trials which are a mixture of Obedience and Agility skills and are perhaps the least known field in competitive dog work. Animals (except Bloodhounds) have to be 18 months old to be eligible and guaranteed not to be of savage disposition.

Working trials like Obedience competitions can be held at Championship and Open level with the addition of Members' Stakes as well. Kennel Club Working Trial Certificates are awarded at the former competition in the two top levels. These are Patrol Dog (PD), sometimes called Police Dog, and Tracking Dog (TD) and are awarded if the dog obtains 70% or more marks, while 80% gains the coveted 'Excellent' which can be added to the title. This win will also get them into the Stud Book. Winners of these certificates are eligible to enter the Kennel Club Annual Working Trials Championships normally held in the third week of October each year.

These Working Trial tests, like those in obedience are again graded in difficulty with the lowest being Companion Dog (CD) and rising up the scale Utility Dog, Working Dog, Tracking Dog to Patrol Dog. The only

A PAT dog on a visit to a centre for the mentally and physically disabled.

qualifications for each test being based on previous wins at that or higher levels. Each stake is divided into different group headings all containing control and agility and all but UD covers nosework, while CD stakes also include Group II on stays and PD a section on 'man work'.

Fly Ball

This latest competition is a team event brought over from America. Each team consists of four dogs and their handlers. One at a time the dogs have to run over a course which includes hurdles, to a box with a weighted spring. When the dog strikes the pad a ball is released which the dog has to catch and retrieve to the handler. The first team to finish is the winner.

This event seems to be catching peoples' interest and looks set to grow very quickly.

Bernese Mountain Dogs are not just 'a pretty face' in the show ring and can also do well in work situations, proving it was not chance that put them in the Kennel Club Working Group but by merit.

Appendix 1
Champions

As, at the time of writing, Bernese have only been eligible for Challenge Certificates for 14 years, researching the list of Champions made up in this time is not nearly so arduous a task as looking at the history of one of the older breeds might be. As I explained in the chapter on showing the acquisition of three Challenge Certificates under separate judges, one of which at least, must be won over the age of 12 months, will give a Bernese the right to preface their name with the letters Ch or Champion. In the gundog breeds for example, or Border Collies, they may only put Sh Ch until they have passed a separate working test to make them up to full Champion.

The history of any breed can be found in succeeding copies of the annually published Kennel Club Stud Book which records all the Championship shows, judges and top four award winners in each breed for the previous year. It also records the results of the first three places in Limit and Open classes in each sex, which positions qualify a dog for entry into both the Stud Book and the following year's Crufts show. In a separate section are listed Junior Warrant holders, Field, Working and Obedience Test C winners names. Also shown are the dog's sire, dam, date of birth, sex, colour, owner and breeder, plus the extended pedigree of three generations. The dog is assigned a Stud Book number, which should be used in preference to his K.C. registration number in any correspondence with the Registration Department in Clarges Street.

The Stud Book was first produced via the Kennel Club in 1874, one year after the Club's inauguration. Mr Frank C S Pearce was the member responsible for producing the information, a task that was made very difficult by virtue of the fact that almost every other dog in those days was called Ben or Sam, to say nothing of the Besses that were abounding. To solve this problem Frank Pearce listed the owner's name alongside that of the dogs, but had to record as 'parents unknown' the pedigrees in very many cases. Once started, of course the job grew somewhat easier until recent times when the sheer weight of registrations keeps a whole department at the Kennel Club more than usually busy, often resulting in a long wait for litter registrations to be processed.

The Stud Book has been published yearly ever since the first one (1874) even during both World Wars, although the latter were very thin, in keeping with the de-escalation of canine activities during these periods, but providing an on-going historical record of all breeds recognised in the U.K.

Bernese Mountain Dogs received their first mention in the 1974 Stud Book as classes were awarded at the National Working Breeds Championship Show the September previously, although the breed did not actually get tickets until Crufts 1977.

The first Bernese to gain a title was the two year old bitch Ch Forgeman Folksong of Tarncred in 1977 who was bred by the Griffiths, but campaigned by Lena Robbins, thus bringing together two of the breeds most successful early pioneers. Two dogs were made up the following year, Folksong's brother (shown by Diana Cochrane) Ch Duntiblae Forgeman Fusilier followed by the very first dog to gain his title, Ch Tarncred Puffin owned and bred by Lena Robbins. Fox von Grunnenmatt took two CC's in 1977 but unfortunately died before he could gain his third and, therefore, his title.

The Stud Book is a good source of information, providing the latter is correct, which was not always the case in the early days. To make doubly sure these days the proofs of each breed are sent out to a member of the breed to check over for mistakes, this job is done for Bernese by John Garrod. Up to the end of 1990, 31 dogs and 38 bitches had gained the coveted Ch before their names in this country. The table of successes starting with the early kennels showed Tarncred – four dogs, five bitches and two foreign Champions; Forgeman – three dogs, three bitches and six foreign Champions; Duntiblae – three dogs, one bitch and one foreign Champion; Meiklestane – two dogs; Millwire – one dog, one bitch and one foreign Champion. More recently Meadowpark have bred three dogs and four bitches; Gillro two dogs and one bitch; and Choristma one dog, two bitches and one foreign Champion.

If you are interested in your dog's pedigree it is quite fun to obtain a 10 generation one from Dog Breeders Associates (address in Appendix 6) and see how far you can go back in your dog's history, but it does take some concentration to get it right, however, Tippex is always available for removal of mistakes these days. If I have awakened your interest in this side of things all to the good and I wish you the best of luck in your quest.

DOG CHAMPIONS

Name	Sire	Dam	D.O.B.	Made up	Owner	Breeder
CH TARNCRED PUFFIN	DUNTIBLAE NALLE	TARNCRED BLACK WATCH	21.3.76	1978	Lena Robbins	Lena Robbins
CH DUNTIBLAE FORGEMAN FUSILIER	DUNTIBLAE NALLE	CH KISUMU BELLE FLEUR OF FORGEMAN	2.3.75	1978	Grahame & Diana Cochrane	Brenda & Don Griffiths
CH MEIKLESTANE DARK ACE	DUNTIBLAE NALLE	TARNCRED TARA	5.6.75	1979	Cynthia Bailey	Wendy (Fletcher) Morphet
CH TARNCRED TARQUIN OF TEMERAIRE	DUNTIBLAE NALLE	TARNCRED BLACK WATCH	21.3.76	1979	Eliz. Wrighton (Walpole-Day)	Lena Robbins
CH MILLWIRE DOUBLE BLANK	DUNTIBLAE DARK FORTUNE	MILLWIRE ACE OF DIAMONDS	22.5.79	1981	Mrs B Lever	Carol Lilliman
CH DUNTIBLAE DARK AVENGER AT FORGEMAN	DUNTIBLAE NALLE	DUNTIBLAE EVA	5.5.74	1982	Don & Brenda Griffiths	Grahame & Diana Cochrane
CH MEIKLESTANE BLACK BENJAMIN	TROLL VON DER LECKENBECKE	TARNCRED TARA	8.1.77	1982	Mr & Mrs McKay	Wendy (Fletcher) Morphet
CH FORGEMAN FOOTPAD	MUSTANG VON NESSELACKER OF GLANZBERG	CH FOLKDANCE AT FORGEMAN	25.4.80	1982	Pam Aze	Don & Brenda Griffiths
CH TARNCRED BULLFINCH	CH TARNCRED PUFFIN	CH FORGEMAN FOLKSONG OF TARNCRED	28.2.80	1983	Alec & June Thew	Lena Robbins

Name	Sire	Dam	D.O.B.	Made up	Owner	Breeder
CH JUMBO VON WALDACKER AT COLIBURN	ARTOS VON WALDACKER	NORA VON BERNETTA	1.6.79	1983	Brian & June Simonds	Von Gasser
CH GILLRO JACK FLASH OF MANADORI	TAKAWALK KALAMOUN	GILLRO SABELLA	18.10.80	1984	Dot Fry	Gill Sharman
CH FORGEMAN FREELANCE OF MEADOW PARK	DINGO DE FROIDEVILLE	CH FOLKDANCE AT FORGEMAN	29.9.82	1984	Bernice Mair	Don & Brenda Griffiths
CH DUNTIBLAE DARK PROTECTOR	CH DUNTIBLAE FORGEMAN FUSILIER	DUNTIBLAE BERNAX BARDOT	17.8.82	1985	Grahame & Diana Cochrane	Grahame & Diana Cochrane
CH CHORISTMA MONCH OF VINDESSA	CH TARNCRED BULLFINCH	CH TARNCRED MUTZI OF CHORISTMA	2.9.83	1985	Ann Waterman	Muriel Majerius
CH MEADOWPARK THE BRIGADIER	CH DUNTIBLAE FORGEMAN FUSILIER	DUNTIBLAE DARK & ENDEARING	6.4.80	1985	John Mair	Bernice Mair
CH TARNCRED TOM TOM	TARNCRED DRUMMER	CH FORGEMAN FOLKSONG OF TARNCRED	18.3.79	1985	June & Alec Thew	Lena Robbins
CH CRENSA TRAFALGAR OF DALSETTER	BERNER BAKKENS FROY OF GLANZBERG	CH TEMERAIRE PENNY BLACK OF CRENSA	21.10.83	1986	Gerry Fallas	John & Betty James
CH GILLRO GENTLE GENIUS	CH TARNCRED TOM TOM	GILLRO GADABOUT	18.12.82	1986	Gill Sharman	Gill Sharman

CH DELHURST DARK EAGLE	MIXBURY MAGNIFICENT MAJOR	ATTILA SNOWQUEEN	30.10.81	1987	Mr & Mrs Ted Groocock	Mr & Mrs P Ackroyd
CH CARLACOT FIDO	CARLACOT CANDYMAN	GLANZBERG'S KIRSCH OF CARLACOT	24.2.85	1987	Julie Vaughan	Julie Vaughan
CH TRANS-CONTINENTAL BOY OF CLENRAW	INCHBERRY GREAT BEAR OF CLENRAW	BONEIDLE QUICKSTEP	18.12.82	1987	Mr R Glendenning	Mrs C S Wilcox
CH ELNSIDE MAYO SPIRIT	SNOWSTORM OF PENNINGHAME	INCHBERRY ANNALEISE	5.11.84	1988	Mrs H B Macaulay	Mrs H B Macaulay
CH SIR STANLEY FROM MEADOWPARK	CH FORGEMAN FREELANCE AT MEADOWPARK	MEADOWPARK CHOREOGRAPHY	16.3.84	1988	Gary & Beryl Rayson	Dr & Mrs L Orme
CH LACELAW STATESMAN	CH JUMBO VON WALDACKER OF COLIBURN	TAKING A CHANCE OF LACELAW	27.3.82	1988	Pam Wallace	Pam Wallace
CH CLASHAIDY NORDIC FIRE	CH TARNCRED BULLFINCH	TARNCRED TATTOO OF CLASHAIDY	30.9.83	1989	Virginia Stenner	Virginia Stenner
CH DUNTILBLAE DARK VIKING	CH CHORISTMA MONCH OF VINDESSA	DUNTIBLAE DARK PLEASURE	27.7.85	1989	Mrs B Manley	Grahame & Diana Cochrane
CH MEADOWPARK LANCELOT	CH FORGEMAN FREELANCE OF MEADOWPARK	DELHURST SWEET SUNSET	30.9.84	1989	Kate MacDuff	Bernice Mair
CH MEADOWPARK SENSATION	CH MEADOWPARK THE BRIGADIER	BURBANK SUMMER SONNET	1.10.85	1989	Miss B K Miller	Bernice Mair

Name	Sire	Dam	D.O.B.	Made up	Owner	Breeder
CH ELNSIDE HUGGY BEAR	SNOWSTORM OF PENNINGHAME	INCHBERRY ANNALEISE	13.11.85	1989	Mrs C L Martin	Mrs H B Macaulay
CH CHORISTMA EINSELMUTZ	GILLRO FLAPJACK AT FORGEMAN	CH CHORISTMA JUNGMUTZI	2.9.87	1990	Mrs M Thurman	Mrs M Majerus
CH KATELYN WAKE OF THE STORM	RASE NOOKIE BEAR	KATELYN GRIN & BEAR IT	4.1.89	1990	Mrs M Yates	Mr & Mrs H Frost

BITCH CHAMPIONS

Name	Sire	Dam	D.O.B.	Made up	Owner	Breeder
CH FORGEMAN FOLKSONG OF TARNCRED	DUNTIBLAE NALLE	CH KISUMU BELLE FLEUR OF FORGEMAN	2.3.75	1977	Lena Robbins	Brenda & Don Griffiths
CH KISUMU BELLE FLEUR OF FORGEMAN	FOX VON GRUNNENMATT	KISUMU APHRODITE	25.4.73	1979	Don & Brenda Griffiths	Irene Creigh
CH KISUMU BONNE ASPERANCE OF MILLWIRE	FOX VON GRUNNENMATT	KISUMU APHRODITE	25.4.73	1979	Carol Lilliman	Irene Creigh
CH FOLKDANCE AT FORGEMAN	CH TARNCRED PUFFIN	CH FORGEMAN FOLKSONG OF TARNCRED	11.10.77	1979	Don & Brenda Griffiths	Lena Robbins
CH MAJANCO GALLINA	SINOVA LARCH	ERICA VON SCHNET-ZENSCHACHEN OF MAJANCO	26.3.75	1980	Gordon Howard	Doris Lendon

CH CARLACOT AMALIA	CH DUNTIBLAE DARK AVENGER	KISUMU DUCHESSE	12.2.77	1981	Julie Vaughan	Julie Vaughan
CH TARNCRED TEAROSE	CH TARNCRED PUFFIN	CH FORGEMAN FOLKSONG AT TARNCRED	11.10.77	1981	Lena Robbins	Lena Robbins
CH TEMERAIRE PENNY BLACK OF CRENSA	CH TARNCRED TARQUIN OF TEMERAIRE	TEMERAIRE TRANQUILITY	17.9.80	1982	John & Betty James	Elizabeth Wrighton
CH TARNCRED TROIKA	TARNCRED DRUMMER	TARNCRED BLACK WATCH	14.7.78	1982	Lena Robbins	Lena Robbins
CH CARLACOT BRACKEN	CH DUNTIBLAE FORGEMAN FUSILIER	CH CARLACOT AMALIA	21.12.79	1983	Julie Vaughan	Julie Vaughan
CH MILLWIRE FOREVER ESPERANCE	CH TARNCRED TOM TOM	MILLWIRE DIAMOND CLUSTER	19.10.81	1983	Carol Lilliman	Carol Lilliman
CH TARNCRED KLEINE AT TIMBERLOG	MUSTANG VON NESSELACKER OF GLANZBERG	CH FORGEMAN FOLKSONG OF TARNCRED	4.3.81	1983	Sandra Gatwood	Lena Robbins
CH DAGILL SOLITAIR OF RASE	BERNAX SIOUX CANTEKOLA	TARNCRED TOPAZ	3.3.82	1984	Paddy Petch	Jill Jefferies
CH CHORISTMA JUNGMUTZI	CH TARNCRED BULLFINCH	CH TARNCRED MUTZI OF CHORISTMA	2.9.83	1984	Muriel Majerius	Muriel Majerius
CH WALCHWILL CLASSY LASSIE	MUSTANG VON NESSELACKER OF GLANZBERG	CH MAJANCO GALLINA	10.3.78	1985	Gordon Howard	Gordon Howard

Name	Sire	Dam	D.O.B.	Made up	Owner	Breeder
CH TEMERAIRE TENDER TYMES	CH TARNCRED TARQUIN OF TEMERAIRE	TEMERAIRE TRANQUILITY	6.11.82	1985	Elizabeth Wrighton	Elizabeth Wrighton
CH MIXBURY MODERN MILLIE OF MEADOWPARK	CH TARNCRED TARQUIN OF TEMERAIRE	DUNTIBLAE DARK EMBER OF MIXBURY	21.4.79	1985	Bernice Mair	Sheila Lee
CH MEADOWPARK CAPTIVATION	JUMBO VON WALDACKER OF COLIBURN	CH MIXBURY MODERN MILLIE AT MEADOWPARK	1.7.81	1986	Carol Hartley	Bernice Mair
CH TARNCRED MUTZI OF CHORISTMA	MUSTANG VON NESSELACKER OF GLANZBERG	CH TARNCRED TROIKA	25.11.81	1986	Muriel Majerius	Lena Robbins
CH FORGEMAN FOOTSTEPS	MUSTANG VON NESSELACKER OF GLANZBERG	CH FOLKDANCE AT FORGEMAN	25.4.80	1986	Mr & Mrs Cooper	Don & Brenda Griffiths
CH GLANZBERG'S HELVETIA	MUSTANG VON NESSELACKER OF GLANZBERG	TOSCALENA OF GLANZBERG	4.11.81	1986	Sonia Gorbould	Sonia Gorbould
CH BRICK KILN MATILDA	JUMBO VON WALDACKER OF COLIBURN	FORGEMAN FANDANGO	13.3.84	1986	Anne Francis	Anne Francis
CH FORGEMAN FANCY FREE AT MIXBURY	DINGO DE FROIDEVILLE	DUNTIBLAE FORGEMAN FORGET ME NOT	6.3.83	1986	Margaret Flynn & Sheila Lee	Brenda Griffiths

CH LOTS O' LOVE FROM MEADOWPARK	CH FORGEMAN FREELANCE OF MEADOWPARK	HEIDI DORRIT OF ALTBERG	5.5.84	1987	Mrs D Johnson	Sara Pharo
CH WAYS & MEANS AT MEADOWPARK	CH FORGEMAN FREELANCE OF MEADOWPARK	MEADOWPARK FRIENDLY PERSUASION	23.6.85	1987	Mr & Mrs Harrison	Bernice Mair
CH MEADOWPARK KISSIN' COUSIN	CH FORGEMAN FREELANCE OF MEADOWPARK	MEADOWPARK EBONY & IVORY	3.9.84	1987	Bernice Mair	Bernice Mair
CH BEEVOR BALLERINA OF STIRLEY HILL	CH FORGEMAN FREELANCE OF MEADOWPARK	MEADOWPARK CHOREOGRAPHY	16.3.84	1988	Mesdames Slater & Waring	Dr & Mrs Orme
CH DUNTIBLAE DARK PLEASURE	CH DUNTIBLAE FORGEMAN FUSILIER	DUNTIBLAE BERNAX BARDOT	17.8.82	1988	Diana Cochrane	Diana Cochrane
CH GILLRO GIPSY MAGIC	CH GILLRO GENTLE GENIUS	GILLRO GRETAL	30.7.85	1988	June Thew	Gill Sharman
CH GLANZBERG'S EIDELWEISS OF MANADORI	MUSTANG VON NESSELACKER OF GLANZBERG	TOSCALENA OF GLANZBERG	10.5.80	1988	Dot Fry	Sonia Gorbould
CH INCHBERRY SPANGLED BANNER	INCHBERRY BIG BAD WOLF	INCHBERRY CHRISTMAS ROSE	21.6.83	1988	Virginia Fick	Dorothy MacVicar-Campbell
CH KYLEBURN NIGHT SONG	CH CRENSA TRAFALGAR OF DALSETTER	KYLEBURN NIGHT SONG	12.8.85	1988	Margaret Eaves	Margaret Eaves

Name	Sire	Dam	D.O.B.	Made up	Owner	Breeder
MEADOWPARK LIKELY LADY OF MARGAND	CH FORGEMAN FREELANCE OF MEADOWPARK	MEADOWPARK DELHURST SWEET SUNSET	30.9.84	1989	Mr & Mrs Skedd	Bernice Mair
CHORISTMA BLISS	GILLRO FLAPJACK AT FORGEMAN	CH CHORISTMA JUNGMUTZI	29.8.87	1989	Mr & Mrs Parker	The late Muriel Majerius
CH TROUBLE-SOME LASS	CH JUMBO VON WALDACKER	MILLWIRE FORTUNE TELLER	7.2.86	1990	Mr & Mrs M Elliott	N Headington
CH COLLANSUES BRIGITTA	GILLRO FLAPJACK AT FORGEMAN	HEIDI OF COLLANSUES	11.5.87	1990	Mrs Sue Botting	Mrs Sue Botting
CH CARLACOT FLAME	CARLACOT CANDYMAN	GLANZBERG KIRSCH OF CARLACOT	24.2.85	1990	Mr & Mrs T Williams	Mr & Mrs P J Vaughan

NB   Certain lady breeders have married or for other reasons changed their names:
Cynthia (Totty) Bailey
Julie C (Devonald) Vaughan
Mrs Godfrey – Miss Oliver
Gaye (Whistanley) Sansom
Liz (Walpole Day) Wrighton

BRITISH BRED FOREIGN CHAMPIONS

Name	Sex	Sire	Dam	D.O.B.	Owner	Breeder
Australia						
CH FORGEMAN FOLK HERO	(B)	GLANZBERG BLUE WIND	CH FOLKDANCE AT FORGEMAN	4.12.80	Mr Malcolm Smith	Don & Brenda Griffiths
CH FORGEMAN FIGARO	(D)	CH DUNTIBLAE FORGEMAN FUSILIER	MILLWIRE BRIGHT & BEAUTIFUL	7.4.79	Mr Malcolm Smith	Don & Brenda Griffiths
CH MILLWIRE CLOCKWORK SOLDIER	(D)	DUNTIBLAE DARK FORTUNE	MILLWIRE ACE OF DIAMONDS	4.4.78	Lyn Brand	Carol Lilliman
England & Australia						
CH CHORISTMA MONCH OF VINDISSA	(D)	CH TARNCRED BULLFINCH	TARNCRED MUTZI OF CHORISTMA	2.9.83	Ann Waterman	Muriel Majerius
CH MARKING TIME	(D)	CH TARNCRED TOM TOM	CLASHAIDY SEA CRYSTAL	19.5.85	Lyn Brand	Mrs Holdsworth
CH ATTILA SNOW PRINCESS	(B)	CH DUNTIBLAE DARK AVENGER	BERNAX APACHE SQUAW AT THE ATTILA	27.3.79	Lyn Brand	Malcolm Smith
New Zealand						
CH FORGEMAN FANCY	(B)	CH DUNTIBLAE DARK AVENGER	CH KISUMO BELLE FLEUR OF FORGEMAN	29.4.76	Mrs D Murdoch (via Irene Creigh)	Don & Brenda Griffiths

Name		Sire	Dam	D.O.B.	Owner	Breeder
CH MAJANCO GHIANTI	(D)	SINOVA LARCH	ERICA VON SCHNET-ZENSCHACHEN	26.3.75	Mrs D Murdoch	Doris Lendon
U.S.A						
CH TARNCRED TZARINA	(B)	CH TARNCRED PUFFIN	CH FORGEMAN FOLKSONG AT TARNCRED	11.10.77	Marty Reisienger	Lena Robbins
CH DUNTIBLAE DARK WATCHMAN	(D)	CH CLACHAIDY NORDIC FIRE	DUNTIBLAE DARK RAHNI	17.9.85	Dr Roger & Betty Pearson	Diana Cochrane
CH MAJANCO LANGUARDO	(D)	FARO VON HURSTFELD OF SINOVA	ERICA VON SCHNET-ZENSCHACHEN	1.4.77	Mrs J Pike	Doris Lendon
Sweden						
CH FORGEMAN FLORA	(B)	CH DUNTIBLAE DARK AVENGER OF FORGEMAN	CH KISUMU BELLE FLEUR OF FORGEMAN	29.4.76	Mrs Knuttson	Don & Brenda Griffiths
CH FORGEMAN FELLINI	(D)	DUNTIBLAE NALLE	CH KISUMU BELLE FLEUR OF FORGEMAN	2.3.75	Monica Sossronow	Don & Brenda Griffiths
Norway						
INT & NOR CH TARNCRED TROOPER	(D)	CH TARNCRED PUFFIN	CH FORGEMAN FOLKSONG AT TARNCRED	11.10.77	Mrs Tekla Hansson	Lena Robbins

Ireland

Name		Sire	Dam	Date		
CH BERNAX DAKOTA CHIEF	(D)	MUSTANG VON NESSELACKER OF GLANZBERG	SINOVA SOLO	21.3.78	Michael Forte	Fiona Carolus
CH ASHBROOK ASTOR BOY	(D)	COCA KOALA OF CHANTELLE	LEON FORT LADY DIANA	30.5.85	A Reeves-Smyth	Fiona Carolus
CH COCA KOALA OF CHANTELLE	(D)	WADEENSEE BAS	BERNAX CHEROKEE FLUTE	3.7.82	Miss S Hardwick	Diana Nicholls
CH FORGEMAN FOOTSTEPS	(B)	MUSTANG VON NESSELACKER OF GLANZBERG	CH FOLKDANCE AT FORGEMAN	25.4.80	Mr & Mrs Cooper	Don & Brenda Griffiths

English & Irish

Name		Sire	Dam	Date		
CH INCHBERRY SPANGLED BANNER	(B)	INCHBERRY BIG BAD WOLF	INCHBERRY CHRISTMAS ROSE	21.6.83	Virginia Fick	Dorothy MacVicar-Campbell

Appendix 2
Important Pedigrees

Name of Dog: Dora v. Breitenhof of Nappa (Deceased)
Date of Birth: 20.5.69
Sex: Bitch
K.C. No. Swiss No. 179629
Stud Book No. (Not given before 1977)
Breeder: Herr Fritz Kobel
Owner: Irene Creigh then Guide Dogs For The Blind

Parents	G.P	G.G.P	G.G.G.P
Galan v. Mattenhof	York v. Fluhwald	Astor du Devens	Anton v. Belfaux
			Asta v.d. Holegg
		Erna v. Myffelhof	Arno v. Meinholzli
			Diana v. Nyffelhof
	Cita v. Balmhof	Ch. Beny v. Dursrutti	Ch Alex v. Angstorf
			Anita v. Dursrutti
		Bella v.d. Petersinsel	Edi v. Enggistein
			Felictas v. Enggistein
Briska v. Grunenmatt	Goliath v. Dursrutti	Alex v. Angstorf	Ossi v. Allenluften
			Christine v. Schwarzwasserbachli
		Anita v. Dursrutti	Drall v.d. Pfrund
			Desia v. Gotthelfsegg
	Madi v. Oberscheidegg	Bruno v. Bauernheim	Zorro v. Muhlstein
			Madi v. Munnenberg
		Anita v. Ballenberg	Godi v.d. Holzweid
			Onda v. Oberbottigen

Name of Dog: Oro de Coin Barre of Kisumu (Deceased)
Date of Birth: 8.12.69
Sex: Dog
K.C. No. Swiss No. 185376
Stud Book No. (Not given before 1977)
Breeder: Z P Mathez
Owner: Mrs Irene Creigh

Parents	G.P	G.G.P	G.G.G.P
Astor v. Gitzirain	Int Ch Alex v. Bauernheim	Max v.d. Schonau	Edy v.d. Gotthelfsegg
			Babette v. Fellenberg
		Madi v. Munnenburg	Eiger v. Munnenburg
			Heidi v. Munnenburg
	Mja v. Kyburg	Balz v. Zeughaushof	Zorro v. Muhlstein
			Basi v.d. Schonau
		Aga v. Pfaffenbrunneli	Nestor v. Chorrichterhof
			Fortuna v. Dursrutti
Linda v. Blaumatthof	Echo v.d. Gotthelfsegg	Cowboy v.d. Gotthelfsegg	Banz v. Munnenberg
			Babeli v.d. Gotthelfsegg
		Finette v. Munnenberg	Alex v. Angstorf
			Dorli v. Munnenberg
	Freya v. Blaumatthof	Athos v. Brandis	Mutz v. Oberbottigen
			Aida v. Waldsaum
		Britta v. Mistelholf	Eiger v.d. Waldheimat
			Asta v.d. Ruglen

Name of Dog: Duntiblae Nalle (Deceased)
Date of Birth: 9.11.72
Sex: Dog
K.C. No. 101480/73
Stud Book No. (Not given before 1977)
Breeder: Eva Berndt
Owner: Mrs D Cochrane

Parents	G.P	G.G.P	G.G.G.P
Swed. Ch Soderkullas Vivo	Int. & Nor. Ch Eros v. Gehrimoos	Beny v. Dursrutti	Alex v. Angstorf
			Anita v. Dursrutti
		Diana v.d. Holzmuhle	Bari v.d. Holzmuhle
			Madi v. Brandis
	Soderkullas Mitzy	Soderkullas Chang	Int. & Nor. Ch Ulo v.d. Nau
			Ch Ulrika v. Alpenhutte
		Soderkullas Arsie	Urban v. Alpenhutte
			Ch Ulrika v. Alpenhutte
Swed. & Nor. Ch Soderkullas Orli	Ch Junker v. Rappenfluh	Carlo v.d. Grandfeybrucke	Bari v. Belfaux
			Erna v. Schneggenberg
		Colette v. Leuenbuhl	Garro v.d. Holzegge
			Enzian v.d. Rappenfluh
	Soderkullas Tatiana	Int. & Nor. Ch Eros v. Gehrimoos	Beny v. Dursrutti
			Diana v.d. Holzmuhle
		Soderkullas Yrsa	Barle v. Staufenblick
			Soderkullas Hennie

APPENDIX 2

Name of Dog: Fox v. Grunenmatt (Deceased)
Date of Birth: 22.3.71
Sex: Dog
K.C. No. Swiss No. 197974
Stud Book No. (Not given before 1977)
Breeder: Herr E Schluchter
Owner: Mrs H Curtis

Parents	G.P	G.G.P	G.G.G.P
Astor v. Chaindon	Ch Carlo v.d. Grandfeybrucke	Bari v. Belfaux	George v.d. Broyehohe
			Carissa v.d. Grandfeybrucke
		Erna v. Schneggenberg	Felix v.d. Oberscheidegg
			Ella v.d. Grandfeybrucke
	Diana v. Ruegsbach	York v. Fluhwald	Astor du Devens
			Erna v. Nyffelhof
		Karin v. Oberscheidegg	Beny v. Dursrutti
			Anita v. Bellenberg
Nadja v. Burgistein	Alex v.d. Oberei	Mars v. Moosseedorf	Junker v.d. Oede
			Cilla v. Ranfluh
		Jutta v. Kneubuhl	Balz v. Zeughaushof
			Gundi v. Kneubuhl
	Pita v. Dursrutti	Dani v. Reid	Dursli v.d. Holzmuhle
			Diana v. Bernerland
		Kandy v. Dursrutti	Beny v. Dursrutti
			Cundi v. Dursrutti

181

Name of Dog: Forgeman Footpad
Date of Birth: 25.4.80
Sex: Dog
K.C. No. E 573324 E10
Stud Book No. 2783 BQ
Breeder: Mr & Mrs Griffiths
Owner: Miss Pamela Aze
        Breed Record Holder

Parents	G.P	G.G.P	G.G.G.P
Mustang v. Nesselacker of Glanzberg	Duc v. Findlingsbrunnen	Finon v. Altich	Goliath v. Dursrutti
			Cilli v. Ruttihof
		Erna v. Findlingsbrunnen	Prinz v. Findlingsbrunnen
			Lisa v. Kirchrain
	Zusi v. Nesselacker	Astor v. Chaindon	Carlo v.d. Grandfeybrucke
			Diana v. Ruegsbach
		Miggi v. Nesselacker	Carlo v.d. Grandfeybrucke
			Anette v. Nesselacker
Ch Folkdance at Forgeman	Ch Tarncred Puffin	Duntiblae Nalle	Soderkullas Vivo
			Soderkullas Orli
		Tarncred Black Watch	Fox v. Grunenmatt
			Black Velvet of Nappa
	Ch Forgeman Folksong of Tarncred	Duntiblae Nalle	Soderkullas Vivo
			Soderkullas Orli
		Ch Kisumu Belle Fleur of Forgeman	Fox v. Grunenmatt
			Kisumu Aphrodite

Appendix 3
Bernese Mountain Dogs Imported into the UK 1969–1990

1   **Oro De Coin Barre. d.**
    Imported by   Mrs I Creigh from Switzerland
    Breeder   Herr P Mathez
    Sire   Astor v. Gitzirain
    Dam   Linda v. Blaumatthof
    Date of Birth   8th December 1969

2   **Dora von Breitenhof. b.**
    Imported by   Mrs Coates from Switzerland
    Breeder   Herr F Kobel
    Sire   Galan v. Mattenhoff
    Dam   Briska v. Grunenmatt
    Date of Birth   20th May 1969

3   **Carin von Hinterfeld. b.**
    Imported by   Mrs I Creigh from Switzerland
    Breeder   Frau Margrith Hanni Erb
    Sire   Galan v. Mattenhof
    Dam   Corina v. Schneggenberg
    Date of Birth   28th August 1970

4   **Fox v. Grunenmatt. d.**
    Imported by   Mrs H Curtis from Switzerland
    Breeder   Herr E Schluchter
    Sire   Astor v. Chaindon
    Dam   Nadja v. Burgistein
    Date of Birth   22nd March 1971

5   **Groll von der Leckenbecke. d.**
    Imported by   Mrs A Grey from Germany
    Breeder   Herr Hugo Seel
    Sire   Arno v. Kiesenthal
    Dam   Billie v. Koblhang
    Date of Birth   11th July 1970

6   **Duntiblae Eva. b.**
      Imported by   Mrs D Cochrane from Sweden
      Breeder   Mr and Mrs M Stromberg
      Sire   Ch Ulmdorfs Angello
      Dam   Corry
      Date of Birth   26th October 1972

7   **Duntiblae Nalle. d.**
      Imported by   Mrs D Cochrane from Sweden
      Breeder   Eva Berndt
      Sire   Ch Soderkullas Vivo
      Dam   Ch Soderkullas Orli
      Date of Birth   9th November 1972

8   **Erika v. Schnetzenschachen of Majanco. b.**
      Imported by   Mrs D Lendon-Ludwig from Switzerland
      Breeder   Herr W Pfister
      Sire   Graf v. Barenried
      Dam   Helga v. Pfaffenbrunneli
      Date of Birth   6th April 1973

9   **Faro v. Hurstfeld of Sinova. d.**
      Imported by   Mr and Mrs Horrex from Switzerland
      Breeder   Herr M Schweizer
      Sire   Arno v. Bucheggberg
      Dam   Gerda v. Mattenhof
      Date of Birth   21st July 1974

10   **Mustang v. Nesselacker of Glanzberg. d.**
      Imported by   Mr and Mrs Gorbould from Switzerland
      Breeder   Herr A Krauchi
      Sire   Duc v. Findlingsbrunnen
      Dam   Zusi v. Nesselacker
      Date of Birth   16th July 1975

11   **Duntiblae Bernergardens Gina. b.**
      Imported by   Mrs D Cochrane from Denmark
      Breeder   Inger and Klaus Hansen
      Sire   Micho
      Dam   Ch Della Montadina Tanya
      Date of Birth   5th February 1976

12   **Bernina of Forgeman. b.**
      Imported by   Mr and Mrs D Griffiths from Denmark
      Breeder   Mrs Lisfen
      Sire   Ch Hollvikens Chan
      Dam   Cilla
      Date of Birth   11th March 1976

13   **Felix v. Unterzelg. d.**
Imported by   Mr and Mrs Simonds from Switzerland
Breeder   Herr F Schmid
Sire   Alex v. Fexenried
Dam   Eiseli v. Hubelihof
Date of Birth   20th April 1977

14   **Cita v. Holz Chilchli of Caprima. b.**
Imported by   Mrs M M Steele from Switzerland
Breeder   Mrs M Wuthrich
Sire   Astor de la Grandeferme
Dam   Fara v. Hasliwald
Date of Birth   10th April 1978

15   **Casar v. Chujerhof of Tarncred. d.**
Imported by   Mrs A Robbins from Switzerland
Breeder   Frau M Fankhauser
Sire   Asso v. Hogerbuur
Dam   Cresta la Morges
Date of Birth   27th February 1978

16   **Onka v. Grunenmatt of Gillro. b.**
Imported by   Mrs G Sharman from Switzerland
Breeder   Herr E Schlucter
Sire   Groll v. Grunenmatt
Dam   Mery v. Grunenmatt
Date of Birth   15th April 1978

17   **Ch Jumbo v. Waldacker at Coliburn. d.**
Imported by   Mr and Mrs B Simonds from Switzerland
Breeder   Frau V Gasser
Sire   Arthos v. Waldacker
Dam   Nora v. Bernetta
Date of Birth   1st June 1979

18   **Coca des Pannissiers. d. (Swiss Ch)**
Imported by   Mr E L Westerhuis from Switzerland
Breeder   Herr C Buri
Sire   Fjort v.d. Froburg
Dam   Fabi du Boiron
Date of Birth   29th December 1977

19   **Jna du Boiron. b. (Swiss Ch)**
Imported by   Mr E L Westerhuis from Switzerland
Breeder   Herr W Kuert
Sire   Jumbo de Bottassiaux
Dam   Fina du Boiron
Date of Birth   12th May 1974

20   Hiska v. Nesselacker of Glanzberg. b.

Imported by	Mr and Mrs J Gorbould from Switzerland
Breeder	Herr A Krauchi
Sire	Pius v. Forst
Dam	Odette v. Nesselacker
Date of Birth	15th May 1979

21   Rena v. Lyssbach at Coliburn. b.

Imported by	Mr and Mrs B Simonds from Germany
Breeder	Herr R Bigler
Sire	Gori v. Eichholzertal
Dam	Flica v. Bernetta (Int Ch)
Date of Birth	17th January 1979

22   Dingo de Froideville. d.

Imported by	Untraced from Switzerland
Breeder	J and J Steffen
Sire	Dingo de la Cidreria
Dam	Andra v. Grederhof
Date of Birth	6th February 1977

23   Netti v. Nesselacker. b.

Imported by	Mr and Mrs J E and A Haynes from Switzerland
Breeder	Herr A Krauchi
Sire	Int Ch Hondo v. Bernetta
Dam	Miggi v. Nesselacker
Date of Birth	9th October 1975

24   Leonfort Mackenzie. d. I.K.C.N.

Imported by	Mr and Mrs R A Stringer from Ireland
Breeder	Messrs M Leonard and M Forte
Sire	Bernax Dakota Chief
Dam	Darlodge April Love
Date of Birth	25th February 1981

25   Bernerbakkens Froy of Glanzberg. d.

Imported by	Mr and Mrs J Gorbould from Norway
Breeder	Mr and Mrs B Skaug
Sire	York v.d. Baarerau
Dam	Leika (Int Ch)
Date of Birth	8th September 1981

26   Belinda v. Lehnwaldli. b. (Swiss Ch)

Imported by	Mr and Mrs C J E Gorbould from Switzerland
Breeder	Mr O Streit
Sire	Prajabo's Kuno
Dam	Anita v. Wolfgalgen
Date of Birth	13th May 1983

27   Imp Priska v.d. Schwarzwasserfluh at Coliburn. b.
Imported by	Mr and Mrs B Simonds from Switzerland
Breeder	Herr G Zbinden
Sire	Sasso La Vaux
Dam	Elka v.d. Schwarzwasserfluh
Date of Birth	8th January 1985

28   Imp Tirass v. Waldacker at Coliburn. d.
Imported by	Mr and Mrs B Simonds from Switzerland
Breeder	Frau V Gasser
Sire	Hansi v. Seewadel
Dam	Ira v. Waldacker
Date of Birth	22nd December 1984

29   Jamie des Potteries. d.
Imported by	Mr and Mrs Peter Watson from Belgium
Breeder	G Galand
Sire	Kay V Gabiar
Dam	Galdi des Potteries
Date of Birth	12th September 1985

30   Jenny des Potteries. b.
Imported by	Mr and Mrs Peter Watson from Belgium
Breeder	G Galand
Sire	Neor v. Tonisbach
Dam	Alla v. Brandis
Date of Birth	6th October 1985

31   Carex v.d. Landscheider Muehle. d.
Imported by	Mr and Mrs J P and P Kroeger from West Germany
Breeder	Messrs Kuehn and Kuehn-Wittkamp
Sire	Grey v. Waldacker
Dam	Myrte vom Bucheggberg
Date of Birth	14th September 1984

32   Am Ch Grunberg Kalais at Liskarn. b.
Imported by	Mr G Bridges from USA
Breeder	Ms D Mulvey
Sire	Am Ch Shepherd's Patch Carl B
Dam	Asta v. Gitzirain
Date of Birth	29th May 1983

33   Bigpaws Guinevere of Caprima. b.
Imported by	Mrs M Steele from Canada
Breeder	Mrs S Quinn
Sire	Can Ch Harlaquin's Thor the Bear
Dam	Can Ch Bigpaws Kate
Date of Birth	13th June 1987

34   Bigpaws Guy of Caprima. d.
Imported by	Mrs M Steele from Canada
Breeder	Mrs S Quinn
Sire	Can Ch Harlaquin's Thor the Bear
Dam	Can Ch Bigpaws Kate
Date of Birth	13th June 1987

35   Tawajah's Leopold. d.
Imported by	Mesdames Stenhouse and Campbell from Belgium
Breeder	Messrs P Baelen and C Berten
Sire	Gallow v. Leubschimos
Dam	Tawajah's Ibis
Date of Birth	5th May 1986

36   Bari v. Waldacker at Coliburn. d.
Imported by	Mr and Mrs B Simonds from Switzerland
Breeder	Ms V Gasser
Sire	Dutch and German Ch Berri v.d. Horlache
Dam	Tina v. Waldacker
Date of Birth	1st July 1987

37   Eiger v. Staalenhof at Coliburn. d.
Imported by	Mr and Mrs B Simonds from Switzerland
Breeder	Mr E Langenegger
Sire	Pius v. Nesselacker
Dam	Dora v. Wolfgalgen
Date of Birth	1st July 1987

38   Elsa v. Staalenhof at Coliburn. b.
Imported by	Mr and Mrs B Simonds from Switzerland
Breeder	Mr E Langenegger
Sire	Pius v. Nesselacker
Dam	Dora v. Wolfgalgen
Date of Birth	1st July 1987

39   Amor-Grey v. Nesselacker of Glanzberg. d.
Imported by	Mr and Mrs J and S Gorbould from Switzerland
Breeder	Mr A Krauchi
Sire	Pius v. Nesselacker
Dam	Zusa v. Nesselacker
Date of Birth	9th January 1988

40   Bova v. Dreispitz at Buganeezee. b.
Imported by	Miss S Hogg from Switzerland
Breeder	W Brogli
Sire	Pius v. Nesselacker
Dam	Ella v. Steinholzli
Date of Birth	18th May 1988

41   Brita v. Dreispitz at Sentaria. b.

Imported by	Miss M Newton from Switzerland
Breeder	W Brogli
Sire	Pius v. Nesselacker
Dam	Ella v. Steinholzli
Date of Birth	18th May 1988

42   Ella v. Vielbringen. b.

Imported by	Mrs H Mansell from Switzerland
Breeder	Mr B Niklaus
Sire	Pat du Perreux
Dam	Kitty v. Breitenhof
Date of Birth	5th April 1988

43   Finette v.d. Haagermuhli of Hildrek. b.

Imported by	Mr and Mrs D Edmunds from Switzerland
Breeder	Ms M Dietschi
Sire	Int Ch Gaston v. Nesselacker
Dam	Ruska v. Weierwald
Date of Birth	13th March 1988

44   Tawajah's Mister Micawber of Abbeycott. d.

Imported by	Mr and Mrs D and K Wilshaw from Belgium
Breeder	Mr and Mrs P and C Baelen-Berten
Sire	Int and Belgian Ch Gigolo van het Bressershof
Dam	Jiente van de Weyenberg
Date of Birth	16th February 1988

45   Basgal v. Trubergluck. d.

Imported by	Mr and Mrs J and R Rich from Switzerland
Breeder	Mrs L Habegger
Sire	Hansi v. Seewadel
Dam	Dolly v. Schlossberg
Date of Birth	23rd June 1986

46   Ginette v. Waldacker at Coliburn. b.

Imported by	Mr and Mrs B Simonds from Switzerland
Breeder	Ms V Gasser
Sire	Mutz v. Waldacker
Dam	Tina v. Waldacker
Date of Birth	26th January 1989

47   Gaby v. Waldacker at Coliburn. b.

Imported by	Mr and Mrs B Simonds from Switzerland
Breeder	Ms V Gasser
Sire	Mutz v. Waldacker
Dam	Tina v. Waldacker
Date of Birth	26th January 1989

48   Chivas v. Wiedewa. d.

Imported by	Mrs Angela Hadow from Holland
Breeder	Mrs A Staaps
Sire	Int Ch Pilatus
Dam	Dutch & Belgian Ch Grasja Uit t'Groes B
Date of Birth	31st May 1990

49   Odette-Poppy v. Vieräogler. b.

Imported by	Mrs Tricia Lewis from Belgium
Breeder	Mrs Horemans
Sire	Int Ch Pilatus
Dam	Marusha v. Vier
Date of Birth	21st June 1990

50   Fero v. Buetigen. d.

Imported by	Mrs Sonia Gorbould from Switzerland
Breeder	Ursula & Peter Linder
Sire	Int Ch Gaston v. Nesselacker
Dam	Uta v. Schofschürli
Date of Birth	31st March 1990

Appendix 4
Hereditary Ailments

Under this heading can be found conditions which vets think are passed on from parents to offspring. These can develop at various periods in the dog's life, some earlier some later.

Very often there is not a great deal of proof but some lines of breeding seem more affected than others, as for example with Tremblers Disease in puppies. Some diseases can be problems to define as hereditary because although they can be inherited they often arise from other causes, such as the way puppies are reared and brought up.

Cataract
This can be inherited and occurs in a number of the working breeds, particularly the GSD, and animals under the age of 12 months are most usually affected. It is responsible for causing the lens in the eye to cloud over and become opaque, thus leading to blindness. The treatment is removal of the lens by surgery.

Ectropian
This is the turning out of the lower eyelid, which inflames the conjunctival membrane. This causes a pus discharge and crusting of the eyelids, often gluing them together. This is an inherited fault though not a particular problem in Bernese, but St Bernards suffer from it extensively. Surgery is sometimes possible and affected animals should not be bred from.

Entropian
This is the opposite to Ectropian and in this case eyelids turn inwards causing the eyelashes to rub on the cornea of the eye. This condition is very painful and leaves the eyes permanently running. Breeds like the Chow and some gundogs are worst affected. It is possible to operate but again breeding and showing are non-starters.

Epilepsy

Epileptic fits ususally take place while the dog is asleep. This is another condition which can be inherited although there are other causes, for example brain tumours and problems due to shortage of oxygen. Epilepsy occurs within the brain and causes the dog to convulse due to abnormal electrical activity in the brain. The fits last from about one to four minutes.

It particularly affects GSDs, Tervuerens, a number of gundog breeds, Poodles and some Terriers. Treatment is by drugs and whilst a fit is in progress the dog should not be touched.

Hernias

Groin hernias, particularly those found in bitches, are inherited and are likely to be passed on if an affected bitch is used for breeding.

Hip dysplasia

In Bernese Mountain Dogs most stock being used for breeding are x-rayed, the pros and cons of which I have already discussed in Chapter 6. The hip is formed with a ball and socket joint and the femur fits into the pelvis. Where there is HD changes occur within the socket, either to the socket itself or to the head of the femur called the acetabulum, so that in the most severe cases dislocation is caused in both hips. The condition is very painful and causes lameness to varying degrees and is an inherited factor in many large breeds.

Trembler disease

This is so called because an affected puppy seems to tremble and somehow undulate when learning to walk at around the age of two weeks old, although it could be later when it is first seen. Its proper name is Hypomyelinogenisis and it was diagnosed in 1983 for the first time. Other puppies in other litters were also affected in due course and in 1986 a meeting was called between veterinary and genetics experts from Cambridge University Veterinary Department and committee members of the Bernese Clubs to discuss the matter.

The cause of Hypomyelinogenisis is a shortage of myelin, a substance which protects the nerves in the spinal cord. This results in delayed impulse to the muscle, which causes the trembling. This can become so rapid as to seem to run into a single movement unable to be detected when the puppy is seen from a distance. The trembling can worsen as the puppy grows older in some cases, while in others it stays constant.

The panel, after discussion, decided that the condition was due to an inherited recessive gene and that the first known carrier in this country, albeit an unwitting one, was Duntiblae Nalle who was born in 1972. They also found that several of todays top Champions are also carriers of the disease and, therefore, the greatest care should be taken when choosing breeding stock to avoid passing on the condition. Dogs that are carriers appear perfectly normal but have affected forbears on both sides of their pedigree.

To produce Trembler puppies both parents have to carry the Trembler gene. The percentage of affected puppies in a litter depends on whether the dog and bitch mated are compatible because if affected themselves up to half the subsequent litter could suffer from Tremblers from birth.

Torsion

I have already covered this condition in Chapter 6 but have mentioned it again in this appendix because it is thought by some vets to be inherited. The tendency to bloat seems to run in certain breeding lines.

Abdominal pain can of course be caused in various ways – from a foreign object, poisoning (whether of food or other variety), colic, intussusception (where a portion of the intestine passes into the lower intestine) or rubarths disease, sometimes called contagious hepatitis, (caused by viral infection in the liver). All require prompt veterinary attention.

Soft palate

This is an inherited condition where the flap of skin, or palate, in the back of the throat seems to constrict. This closes the air passage or trachea and causes breathing difficulties or even asphyxia.

It is brought about by stress of some kind and the soft palate enlarges due to vibrations. The only cure is an operation to reduce the size of the skin flap, but this is not always possible. Stock affected in this way should not be bred from.

Dogs and bitches that suffer from a soft palate condition are more often affected by heatstroke due to a predisposition to oxygen restriction.

OCD

There are several conditions which can contribute to lameness in the Bernese Mountain Dog and over the last decade much research has been done concerning the most common problem, that of Osteochondritis Dessecans (or OCD). This causes lameness in the foreleg, stifle and hock, of which the former is the most usual. Lameness can also be caused by the failure to unite the ball and socket joint bones as in the Coronoid Process (FCP), or the detatchment of a piece of bone in the elbow (UAP). But the problem most often seen is the separation of cartilage from bone during early puppy growth, in other words OCD.

In 1987 Dr Heather Pidduck of the Royal Veterinary College did a survey for the Bernese Mountain Dog Club of Great Britain on the incidence of OCD in a sample of 1200 Bernese in the UK. She found that in those dogs that were affected there was some relationship to lines of descent, particularly in the male dog lines. It was also found that the likelihood of this condition appearing was increased in those dogs that matured too early. The incidence also increased in infected stock who were too closely bred.

It is a difficult condition to diagnose but it seems to occur mostly in dogs around the age of six months and is manifest in lameness from shoulder, foreleg, elbow or hock. Rest will improve things temporarily but the lameness is likely to flare up again when exercise is recommenced. Some muscle wasting may be present, but this is not necessarily the case. The only lasting answer is surgery to remove the cartilage, or floating bone chips, when the dog may then go sound.

It is very easy to blanket all conditions where a puppy is lame as OCD, but it can easily be an injury such as muscle strain. All the heavy breeds of dogs such as Bernese, Rottweilers, St Bernards and others are very liable to damaged shoulders as they carry so much weight.

OCD occurs in both sexes, but particularly the males are affected as they grow heavier and more quickly than the bitches. Obviously stock found to have OCD should not be used for breeding.

Appendix 5
Glossary of Terms

Action	Gait or movement. The way a dog trots.
Affix	The Kennel Name registered with the Kennel Club.
All Rounder	A judge capable of judging many breeds.
Angulation	The angle formed at a joint where bones meet.
Anal Glands	Pear shaped glands at base of tail. Can become painful, if not emptied naturally veterinary attention necessary.
Awards	The placings decided by the judge.
Balance	Pleasing symmetry, relationships of parts to whole.
Barrel	Rounded rib section.
Beefy	Thick, heavy, overweight.
Benching	Compartments used for dogs at shows.
Benched Show	A show where benching is provided.
Best in Show	Overall winner at a dog show.
Best of Breed	Best dog or bitch in a breed at a show.
Bitchy	Feminine looking male dog.
Bite	Meeting of the teeth.
Blanket	Solid red on back and sides between neck and tail.
Blaze	White stripe up centre of foreface (essential to this breed).
Bloom	The sheen on the coat of a dog in perfect condition.
Blown	Loss of coat when moulting.
Bodied up	Mature, well developed animal.
Bolting eye	Protruding eye.
Bone	Relative size of the front leg bones.
Brace	Two dogs of similar appearance.
Breastbone	Bone or floor of chest (Sternum).
Breed standard	Description of ideal specimen.

Brisket	Lower region of ribcage between the forelegs.
Brood bitch	Female used for breeding.
Butterfly nose	Parti coloured nose; pink patches on nose – a fault in this breed.
Canker	Wet or dry condition of ear, needs treating.
Canines	Two upper and lower long pointed teeth.
Carpals	Wrist bones.
Castration	Removal of the testicles.
Cat-foot	Short round foot, like that of a cat.
Challenge Certificate	A certificate granted by the Kennel Club, and awarded by the judge at a Championship show to the best specimen of a breed, provided that it is deemed worthy.
Champion	A dog that has won three Challenge Certificates under different judges.
Character	Combination of type, appearance, disposition, behaviour.
Chiselled	Clean cut, showing bone structure of foreface.
Cloddy	Thickset, heavy. A fault in this breed.
Close coupled	Relatively short between last rib and loin.
Coarse	Lacking refinement.
Cobby	Short in the body, compact.
Conformation	Form, structure, arrangement of parts.
Corkscrew tail	Tail twisted, not straight.
Coupling	The body between ribs and pelvis; the loin.
Cow hocked	The hocks turning inwards towards each other. A fault in this breed.
Crabbing	When moving, the body is at an angle to the line of travel.
Croup	Part of back from front of pelvis to root of tail (Rump).
Cryptorchid	Adult male whose testicles have not descended into the scrotum. A fault.
Dam	Female parent.
Dentition	The number and arrangement of teeth.
Dew Claw	Fifth digit on the inside of legs. Must be removed soon after birth in this breed to avoid possible damage when working.
Dewlap	Loose skin under the throat.
Dish Faced	Concavity from the stop to the nose tip. Most undesirable in this breed.
Dome	Skull rounded at peak.
Down at pastern	Weak pastern set at a pronounced angle from the vertical.
Drive	Powerful thrusting from the hindquarters when moving essential in a good moving dog.

Eclampsia	Shortage of calcium in bitches suckling a litter.
Ectropion	Condition in which the lower eyelid is turned outwards, leading to inflammation and loose eye.
Elbow	Joint between upper arm and forearm.
Entropion	A condition, often painful, in which eyelashes are turned inwards and rub on the cornea. A fault in this breed.
Expression	General appearance of all features of the head as viewed from the front.
False pregnancy	*See* Phantom pregnancy.
Feathering	Long hair on ear tips, legs, tail and stomach.
Field trial	A competition in which dogs are judged on style and ability in finding game.
Flat sided	Ribs too shallow as they approach the sternum.
Flecked	Light ticking of coloured spots on the white parts.
Flews	Pendulous corner of the lower lips.
Forearm	Front leg between elbow and pastern.
Foreface	Front part of the head, muzzle.
Forehand	Front part of the dog, including head, neck, shoulders, upper arm, legs and feet.
Fringes	*See* feathering.
Front	Forepart of the body, as viewed from the front.
Gait	Movement of legs and feet at various speeds.
Gaskin	Second or lower thigh.
Gay tail	Tail carried too high, over the back. Undesirable in a Bernese Mountain Dog.
Gestation	Period of pregnancy. 63 days in dogs.
Goose rump	Croup is too steep or sloping.
Hackles	Hair on neck and back raised when dog is frightened or angry.
Hackney Action	High lifting of the front feet. Incorrect in a Bernese Mountain Dog.
Haemotoma	Blood filled ears which leave thickened flaps.
Hare foot	Long foot with long toes. A fault in this breed.
Haw	Third eyelid in inside of the eye. Red in colour.
Heat	Menstruation in the female. Season, or oestrus.
Height	Measured at the withers.
Herring gutted	*See* slab sided.
Hindquarters	Rear part of dog from the loin.

Hip Dysplasia	Abnormal formation of the hip joint.
Hock	Joint on hind legs between second thigh and rear pastern (metatarsus).
Hypomyelinogenesis	'Trembler' disease in puppies.
Inbreeding	Mating of closely related dogs, i.e. father to daughter, sister to brother.
Incisors	Upper and lower front teeth between the canines.
Junior Warrant	Certificate from Kennel Club on obtaining 25 show points between the ages of 12 to 18 months.
Jowls	Flesh of lips and jaws.
Kinetic Balance	Having balance when moving.
Knuckling over	Faulty structure of wrist joint, allowing it to double forward under weight of dog.
Layback	The angle of the shoulder blade viewed from side.
Leather	The flap of the ear.
Leggy	Too long in the leg for correct balance.
Level back	Line of the back horizontal to the ground.
Level bite	Front teeth (incisors) meet exactly edge to edge.
Line breeding	Mating of related dogs within a family, or with a common ancestor.
Litter	The puppies of one whelping.
Loaded shoulder	Too much muscle on the shoulder pushing the blades outwards.
Loin	That part of the body between the last rib and the hindquarters.
Long cast or Long coupled	Having a long loin.
Maiden	Bitch which has not produced puppies.
Mandible	Lower jaw bone.
Mastitis	Painful condition of lactating bitches teat which hardens causing milk to clot.
Maxilla	Upper jaw bone.
Metatarsals	Bones between hock joint and foot.
Mismarked	Incorrectly marked dog. Usually too little tan, or too much or too little white.
Monorchid	A dog with only one testicle descended into the scrotum.
Moult	Casting or loss of coat.
Moving close	When the hind legs move too closely to each other.

Muzzle	That part of the head forward of the eyes.
N.A.F.	Name applied for to the Kennel Club.
Occiput	Upper point of skull. In this breed should not be too prominent.
Oestrus	*See* Heat.
Osteochondritis Dessecorns	Or 'OCD' faulty bone growth of front legs causing flaking.
Out at elbow	Elbows turned away from the rib. A fault.
Out at shoulders	Shoulder blades loosely attached, shoulders jutting out.
Out of coat	Lacking in coat due to moult.
Outcrossing	Mating of unrelated stock within the breed.
Overshot	Front teeth of the upper jaw overlap, and do not touch the front teeth of the lower jaw when the mouth is closed. A fault.
Pacing	Moving of front and back legs of same side at one time.
Pads	Soles of the feet.
Paddling	Front feet thrown out sideways in an uncontrolled manner.
Parvovirus	Condition in young puppies causing dehydration, usually fatal.
Pastern	That part between foot and wrist.
Patella	Kneecap.
Pedigree	Written record of a dog's ancestry.
Phantom pregnancy	Following a season, a bitch exhibits the signs of being in whelp, although she has not been mated.
Pincer bite	*See* level bite.
Plaiting	Manner of moving in which legs cross. Also called weaving.
Pounding	Short stride of front legs with hesitant hard step. A fault.
Progressive Retinal Atrophy	Condition of eye which progressively causes destruction of retina or eye sensitive tissue.
Put Down	Prepare a dog for a show, usually regarding a terrier breed. Alternatively, a dog not placed in competition. Euthanasia.
Pure Bred	A dog whose sire and dam belong to the same breed, and are themselves of unmixed descent.
Pyometra	Pus in the uterus, can be fatal if not operated on to remove womb in time.
Quality	Refinement, elegance. Overall perfection.
Queen Anne front	Out at elbow, pasterns close, and feet turned out.

Racy	Giving impression of speed, as in the Irish Setter.
Rangy	Dog of long slender build, long in leg.
Reachy	With long neck.
Register	To record with the Kennel Club a dog's breeding. Essential if dog is to be shown or bred from.
Roach Back	Convex curvature of the back towards the loin. Undesirable in a Bernese Mountain Dog.
Roman Nose	Nose whose bridge is comparatively high, forming slight convex line from forehead to tip of nose. Undesirable in a Bernese Mountain Dog.
Runt	Weak, small puppy in a litter.
Scapula	Shoulder blade.
Scimitar tail	Tail carried in gentle curve.
Scissor bite	Upper teeth closely overlapping lower teeth. This is the correct bite for a Bernese Mountain Dog.
Season	*See* Heat.
Second thigh	That part of the hindquarter from the stifle to the hock. *See also* Gaskin.
Service	The act of mating, when a bitch is served by a stud dog.
Set on	Placement of tail on body, and ears on skull.
Set up	Posed in a standing position for the show ring. Also called stacking.
Short coupled	Short in the loin.
Shoulder height	Height measured from withers to ground.
Sickle hocked	a) Hocks turned outward viewed from behind; b) Inability to extend hock joint on backward drive of hind leg.
Single tracking	Footprints falling in a single line of travel.
Sire	Male parent.
Skully	Thick and coarse through skull.
Slab sided	Flat sides with insufficient spring of ribs.
Snipy	Narrow pointed foreface lacking strength. Undesirable.
Soundness	Normal state of well being. Freedom from physical faults, particularly applied to movement.
Spay, Spaying	Surgical removal of uterus and ovaries.
Spring of rib	Degree of curvature of rib cage.
Stacking	*See* Set up.
Standard	*See* Breed standard.
Static balance	Having balance when standing still.
Sternum	Breastbone.

Stifle	Upper joint of hind leg. Knee.
Stop	Indentation between the eyes where nose bone and skull meet.
Straight in Pastern	Little or no bend between pastern and hock. Not correct for a Bernese Mountain Dog.
Straight in Shoulder	Insufficient lay back of shoulder.
Straight in Stifle	The bend at the stifle is insufficient.
Stud dog	Male dog used for breeding.
Substance	Solidity, correct muscularity and condition.
Swayback	Concave curvature of the back line between withers and hip bones.
Symmetry	Overall balance.
T.A.F.	Transfer of ownership applied for with Kennel Club.
Temperament	Qualities and traits which produce character.
Throatiness	Excess of loose skin in the throat area. Undesirable in a Bernese Mountain Dog.
Ticking	Small spots of coloured hair on a white ground.
Topline	Dog's outline from withers to tail set.
Tuck up	Concave underline of body curving upwards from end of rib to waist.
Type	Characteristic qualities distinguishing a breed.
Undershot	Front lower teeth projecting beyond the upper teeth when the mouth is closed. A fault in this breed.
Upper arm	Humerus, or bone of foreleg between shoulder blade and elbow.
Upright shoulder	Insufficient angulation of shoulder blades.
Weaving	*See* Plaiting.
Weedy	Lacking substance, light bone structure.
Well laid	Optimum shoulder angulation.
Well sprung ribs	Ribs springing out from spine giving correct shape.
Whelp	Unweaned puppy.
Whelping	Act of giving birth to puppies.
Withers	Highest point of body immediately behind the neck.
Wry mouth	Lower jaw does not line up with upper jaw.
Zygomatic arch	Arch of bone forming lower border of eye socket extending to base of ear.

Appendix 6
Useful Addresses

Canine Publications

Dogs Monthly
Unit 1, Bowen Industrial Estate
Aber Bargoed
Mid-Glamorgan   CF8 9ET
Telephone: 0443 821839

Dog World
9 Tufton Street
Ashford
Kent   TN23 1QN
Telephone: 0233 621877

Kennel Gazette
Kennel Club
1 Clarges Street
London   W1Y 8AB
Telephone: 071 493 6651

Our Dogs
5 Oxford Road
Station Approach
Manchester   M60 1SX
Telephone: 061 236 2660

Veterinary connections
Animal Health Trust Small
   Animal Centre
Linwades Park
Kennet
Nr. Newmarket
Suffolk
Telephone: 0638 661111

British Small Animal Veterinary
   Association
5 St. George's Terrace
Cheltenham
Gloucestershire
Telephone: 0242 584354

Peoples Dispensary for Sick
   Animals
P.D.S.A. House
South Street
Dorking
Surrey   RH4 2LB
Telephone: 0306 888291

Pet Health Council
4th Floor
Waller House
418–422 The Strand
London   WC2 0PL
Telephone: 071 836 2843

Royal College of Veterinary
   Surgeons
32 Belgrave Square
London   SW1X 8PP
Telephone: 071 235 4971

Export and Import
Ministry of Agriculture Fisheries
   and Food
Hook Rise South
Tolworth
Surbiton
Surrey
Telephone: 081 330 4411

Dog Nutrition
Pedigree Petfoods Education
   Centre
Waltham on the Wolds
Leicester   LE14 4RS
Telephone: 0664 410000

Petfoods Manufacturers
   Association
6 Catherine Street
London   WC2B 5JJ
Telephone: 071 836 2460

Spillers Foods Limited
New Malden House
1 Blagdon Road
New Malden
Surrey   KT3 4TB
Telephone: 081 949 6100

Canine Education
Bellmead Kennels
   (Training for Kennelmaids)
Old Windsor
Berkshire   SL4 2JN
Telephone: 0784 32929

Canine Studies Institute
London Road
Bracknell
Berkshire   RG12 6QR
Telephone: 0784 431599

Canine Counselling
49 Beaumont Road
Purley
Surrey   CR2 2EJ
Telephone: 081 668 8011

Welfare Organisations
Blue Cross
1 High Street
Victoria
London   SW1V 1QQ
Telephone: 071 834 5556

Guide Dogs for the Blind
Alexander House
Park Street
Windsor
Berkshire
Telephone: 07535 55711

Hearing Dogs for the Deaf
2 Chinnor Hill
Chinnor
Oxfordshire   OX9 4BA
Telephone: 0884 53898

National Canine Defence League
1 Pratt Mews
London   NW1 0AD
Telephone: 081 388 0137

Royal Society for the Prevention
   of Cruelty to Animals
RSPCA HQ
Causeway
Horsham
West Susses   RH12 1HG
Telephone: 0403 64181

Insurance
Dog Breeders Insurance Co Ltd
9 Stephens Court
St Stephens Road
Bournemouth BH5 6LG
Hampshire
Telephone: 0202 295771

Pet Plan Ltd
Pet Plan House
10–13 Heathfield Terrace
Chiswick
London   W4 4JE
Telephone: 081 995 1414

General
Dog Breeders Associates
   (Breeders Register & Kennel
   Printing)
1 Abbey Road
Bourne End
Buckinghamshire   SL8 4NZ
Telephone: 06285 20943/29000

Pro Dogs
Rocky Bank
4 New Road
Ditton
Kent   ME20 6AD
Telephone: 0732 848499

Clubs and Societies
Bernese Mountain Dog Club of
   Great Britain
Secretary & Rescue Secretary
Mrs Angela Hadon
Cotswold Hillview Farmhouse
Tiltups End
Horsley
Nr Stroud
Gloucestershire   GL6 0QE
Telephone: 0453 383 4588

The Kennel Club
1 Clarges Street
London   W1Y 8AB
Telephone: 071 493 6651

Southern Bernese Mountain Dog
   Club
Secretary
Mr P Worrow
16 Ridgemount Avenue
Coulsdon
Surrey
Telephone: 07375 54471

Bernese Mountain Dog Club of
   Scotland
Secretary
Mrs M Skedd
104 Deanswood Park
Livingston
W. Lothian
Telephone: 0506 410490

Northern Bernese Mountain Dog
   Club
Secretary
Mr David Franks
3 Canterbury Road
Ofrerton
Stockport
Cheshire   SK1 4DR
Telephone: 045 383 4588

Bibliography

Schweizer Sennenhunde – *Hans Raïser.*
Die Schweizer Sennenhunde-Rassen – *Hans Raïser.*
Schweizer Sennenhunde in Wort und Bild – *Dr H J Mehis.*
Dogs – *Ivan Swedup.*
Hutchinsons Dog Encyclopaedia, Part 4
Working Dogs of the World – *Clifford Hubbard.*
The Bernese Mountain Dog – *Diana Cochrane.*
Doglopaedia – *J M Evans and Kay White.*
Dog Shows and Show Dogs – *Catherine Sutton.*
Reader's Digest Book of Dogs
A Dog of Your Own – *Salamander.*
The Complete Bernese Mountain Dog – *Jude Simonds.*
A Concise Guide to Dog Showing – *Paddy Petch.*
The Kennel Clubs Illustrated Breed Standards

Index

INDEX